To my wife, Isabel, my cosmic lover, healer, fellow psychonaut, playmate, and supportive pillar—the person who gave me the confidence to meaningfully engage in the work of the Psychedelic Mindmeld.

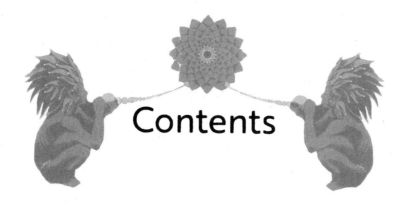

Contents

Truth and Sacred Space

When we reveal ourselves to our partner and find that this brings healing rather than harm, we make an important discovery—that intimate relationship can provide a sanctuary from the world of façades, a sacred space where we can be ourselves, as we are. . . . this kind of unmasking—speaking our truth, sharing our inner struggles, and revealing our raw edges—is sacred activity, which allows two souls to meet and touch more deeply.

JOHN WELWOOD, *LOVE AND AWAKENING:*
DISCOVERING THE SACRED PATH
OF INTIMATE RELATIONSHIP

Foreword

Martin W. Ball, Ph.D.

It was with great pleasure that I received the invitation from Wade Richardson to write a foreword for this unique, provocative, and inspiring book. For one, it's a fascinating and well-researched read. For another, it's the only book I've seen that takes my own work to heart and incorporates a variety of subjects that are otherwise found only in my own writings, such as fractal energetic yoga, nondual energetic therapy, the Divine Imagination, and embodied nonduality. Given how much Wade includes of my work in this book, how could I not agree to lend some words of support?

I've read a lot of books about psychedelics. After my first psychedelic experiences with psilocybin mushrooms at eighteen, I sought out everything I could find about the subject and found myself gravitating toward more anthropological works than wildly popular, but more speculative, authors. As a graduate student, I went on to earn my M.A. and Ph.D. in religious studies, but even there, my education about the use of psychedelics was mostly self-directed, as the topic of the role of psychedelics and entheogens was never brought to the fore in any of my classes. On my own, I looked for works about the use of psilocybin mushrooms, peyote, ayahuasca, *Salvia divinorum*, and other entheogenic sacraments and medicines that were grounded in actual practice and not just speculating about the mystery and *otherness*.

Fast-forward to several years after completing graduate school, and I started hosting *The Entheogenic Evolution Podcast*, which I've been running for over fifteen years now, As host of the podcast, I've had reason to read a lot more books about psychedelics, as authors bring me their works in the hopes of becoming an interview subject. I have so many books currently sitting in waiting, both on my desk as paperbacks and in my inbox as PDF files, that I struggle to find time to read them all.

There are many good books about psychedelics out there, and the number grows larger every day as more and more people around the world are getting swept up and inspired by the so-called *psychedelic renaissance*. Scientific studies focusing on the health and therapeutic applications of psychedelic medicines have blossomed. Countless local communities now have regional "psychedelic societies." Conferences and gatherings about psychedelics multiply year by year. Podcasts on the topic, which numbered only around three to four when I first started my podcast, now number into the thousands, if not more. Psychedelic-assisted therapy is quickly becoming mainstream. Individuals and organizations are claiming their religious rights by establishing entheogenic churches. Retreat centers abound in countries where they are not hampered by draconian antidrug laws. In short, there are a lot more people from all spectrums of society and demographics involved in the broader psychedelic movement who might then turn to becoming an author and sharing either their personal experiences with psychedelics, their research, or information about their favorite psychedelic plant or substance.

The goal for many authors and publishers is to produce books that appeal to the widest audience possible. At the results level, this means that many of the books published about psychedelics are excellent reads for people who might not have a lot of prior knowledge or experience with psychedelics. It's a comment that I've made to many of the authors I've had as guests on my podcast. It's not meant as a detraction, in any sense, as educating the mis- and uninformed is an important and significant role that authors and educators can play. For the seasoned psychedelics user, it can feel a bit tame, however, and some readers might find themselves asking: Where are the works for people who are looking to go deeper that can provide meaningful guidance, insight, and practice?

Which brings us to *The Psychedelic Mindmeld* by Wade. At this point of my career in the world of psychedelics, it's rare that a book finds its way to me that leaves me genuinely excited and feeling like, "Now here's a book for people with a mature understanding of psychedelics!" In other words, *The Psychedelic Mindmeld* isn't written for a general audience or as a means to introduce the novice or the uninformed about what's possible with psychedelics. To stay with the *Star Trek* theme alluded to in the book, *The Psychedelic Mindmeld* is for those who are looking "to go boldly," not necessarily where "no one" has gone before but certainly where not many have gone before.

Significantly, *The Psychedelic Mindmeld* isn't just a collection of personal anecdotes that might accumulate into little more than, "Look at all the weird shit I've experienced, and ponder this enigma!" (though personal experiences and anecdotes appear repeatedly throughout the work to give specific examples of what the author is discussing), but is primarily a guidebook, filled with instructions, practices, warnings, insights, and analyses. As such, it is a practical manual for how to accomplish the "mindmeld." While various aspects of philosophy, psychology, and metaphysics help frame analyses of mindmeld experiences, the overall focus is primarily phenomenological in nature, meaning that Wade goes to great lengths to describe and map the range of experiences that are included within the larger framework of the mindmeld, along with practical instruction for how it all works. While ontological questions do arise, answering them is not the focus of the book, as the experience is the thing.

The result is that this is undeniably a work for advanced practitioners. This isn't a guidebook about how to create sacred ritual or how to engage in psychedelic therapy (though therapeutic potentials are discussed in detail), nor is it a book of philosophy (though again, philosophy, primarily in the form of nonduality, is discussed throughout). This is a guidebook for those who want to explore what's possible beyond the artificial boundaries of the limited egoic self and fully immerse themselves in what's to be found when all boundaries are crossed or dissolved, with full nondual absorption at the pinnacle of human experience where the unitary nature of reality is directly experienced without the egoic filter of beliefs, concepts, or separation.

In presenting all this and offering grounded, practical guidance, Wade does a radically thorough job of exploring the mindmeld from a wide variety of perspectives and topics of concern and interest. One need only take a cursory look at the table of contents to see that Wade hasn't left anything out, has considered all the angles, and has upturned all relevant stones, and, in the words of Maude when mentioning her doctor to the Dude, "He's good . . . and thorough."

Which is precisely what a work on this level of magnitude and sophistication needs. In presenting this information and series of practices, techniques, and experiences to the reader, Wade is taking a bold risk as much of what he presents does not conform to conventional psychedelic wisdom and is leaps and bounds beyond the sanitized approach to working with psychedelics that is now being promoted within therapeutic environments, where therapists largely serve the role of trip sitters. As with Burning Man, there are no observers here: participants only!

As a work on nonduality, Wade is looking at the phenomenon of transcending and dissolving boundaries between subject and object, and in this context, this includes not only the full nondual experience of universal being, but also "melding" with a fellow journeyer, with archetypes, with inner presentations, and, phenomenologically speaking, with visionary beings, realms, and consciousness. Rather than asking "What's real here?," Wade is focused more on the practical questions of "What's possible here?," "How do we do it safely and responsibly?," and "What do we have to gain from such experiences?" As the title suggests, a mindmeld, by definition, involves more than one subject and more than one relatively discrete "mind" melding with another relatively discrete "mind." But how many "minds" are there really, if such boundaries can be crossed, melded, blended, exchanged, interacted, and synched? The nondual perspective answers this question unequivocally: there's actually only one. Wade's informative book explores all the ways that this reality can be explored through psychedelic work where the energetic boundaries between self and other start to blur, or disappear entirely, into states of unparalleled intimacy. In a culture that often seems unable to distinguish between energetic intimacy and sexuality, this is an important contribution and provides much-needed mature insight.

None of this is for the novice, or the simply curious. As Wade states many times in his book, these experiences can be so challenging that they often leave him wondering why he bothers with such intense and overwhelming psychedelic experiences. And while it has benefits, it is not for therapy, per se, though therapeutic benefits, and interactions, can take place, albeit far outside the limited realm of what is generally considered psychedelic therapy. This is work and practice for the bold and for those who are daring and courageous, not for the timid or faint of heart.

As someone who has also been bold and revolutionary in his approach to working with psychedelics and grounding their use within nonduality, it is personally a pleasure for me to see how Wade has taken many of my own discoveries and ideas and run with them, bringing them into new contexts and new situations and following his own lead, using significant portions of my work as guideposts along the way. Back when I was an active facilitator, the comment from a client along the lines of "Was that just some kind of Vulcan mindmeld?" was uttered more than once, so Wade's appellation is certainly fitting. Wade has done an excellent job here of mapping out, explaining, and detailing these profound states of ultimate intimacy and how to work with them, navigate them, and intentionally use them in a way that is respectful of all involved and done with integrity.

For those who are ready to go boldly, here's your guidebook. Use it well. Expect the unexpected. Carefully take in all that's presented in these pages, and take your time to digest it. From this foundation, those who are ready can launch into their own experience of the Psychedelic Mindmeld.

Enjoy, and live long and prosper.

MARTIN W. BALL, PH.D. is the author of over 20 books on entheogens and transformative experience, including *Entheogenic Liberation: Unraveling the Enigma of Nonduality with 5-MeO-DMT Energetic Therapy*. He is the host of *The Entheogenic Evolution Podcast* and organizer of the annual Exploring Psychedelics Conference, held at Southern Oregon University where he teaches as an adjunct professor of religion. He has presented at MAPS, the Science and Nonduality Conference, the Spirit Plant Medicine Conference, Burning Man, Breaking Convention, and EntheoMedicine, among others, and is regularly interviewed on multiple media platforms.

Acknowledgments

I thank my wife, Isabel, my family, and the friends who stepped forward with the know-how to comfort and validate me when I needed it most in support of my ongoing recovery from injuries I sustained years ago. Their support made it possible to write this book.

Many have dared to dive into unknown territory and engage in the mindmeld with me. They opened themselves up to new levels of vulnerability and new levels of intimacy. Without these brave souls, this book would not have taken form. Watching some participants later mindmeld with others has been exciting and rewarding.

There are many whose knowledge added breadth and depth to this book, and they are found in the bibliography. Of special mention is Martin Ball. His work and insights validated many of my experiences, helping me penetrate deeper into my consciousness than ever before. He also introduced me to 5-MeO-DMT, for which I will forever be grateful.

I also want to thank all who took the time to read drafts of the book and provide their valuable feedback to this project: DH, HK, IF, JD, LC, SG, and ST.

I thank all of the professional team at Inner Traditions for their great support in making this project come to fruition and Jon Graham for seeing the potential in my proposal.

Most importantly, I thank Grace for allowing the profound and mystical experiences discussed throughout this book to come forth. While the ego plays a conscious role in deciding to participate, it is Grace and its mystery bringing forth the ineffable and greater connection to the Divine and the many physical and discarnate beings in the universe. Thank you to the Great Divine for Creation.

Prologue

My wife, Isabel, and I take the mushrooms and lie down side by side, holding hands. We meditate in stillness. There is no intent or destination for our trip beyond letting go of our egos and seeing what will happen.

Rainbow colors flash through the mind's eye in fractal form. Egos dissolve. I'm in a small, ancient, wooden teahouse in Japan, drinking tea. It's busy with patrons. I wear a kimono. I'm seated next to Isabel. She too is dressed in a kimono, flowing with flowery patterns in yellow, reds, and oranges. We are in ancient Japan together! We look at each other with the fully embodied acknowledgment that we are lucidly sharing this experience in an alternate space-time. Exciting!

The imagery in the world we're immersed in is full of fractals with jeweled patterns. The walls have the color and texture of wood, but they shimmer with emerald green and hints of the rainbow spectrum. The air is dank and heavy. We finish our tea and the experience evaporates.

This was our introduction to journeying to another locale together in the Psychedelic Mindmeld. We were both dumbfounded by our telepathic connection and shared vision. We had never been to Japan nor had any intent to travel there.

What else are we capable of exploring together telepathically? This book explores what is possible and recommends techniques for telepathic engagement using psychedelics.

A Call to Explore the Depths of Consciousness

Where does consciousness begin and end? Science has not answered this question. But experientially we can explore the infinitude of consciousness. We can map out what science has been incapable of measuring or making tangible. This book is an invitation for you to jointly work telepathically with another person to explore the mystery of your minds and bodies and their fantastical qualities and capacities while using psychedelics. This invitation extends to exploring new ways of healing the mind and body. If you are ready to accept this invitation, this book describes a co-creative and revolutionary approach to working with psychedelics in partnership, making explicit the possibility of what has been popularized as the Vulcan mindmeld in the science fiction of *Star Trek*: melding the consciousness of two minds. Working with psychedelics can elicit multidimensional cosmic experiences. These experiences can be biological, somatic, emotional, psychological, relational, historical, ancestral, perinatal, biographical, futuristic, prophetic, spiritual, transpersonal, and transcendent. All these experiences can be shared with another person in consciousness in the mindmeld.

My hopes in writing this book are threefold. First, I want to introduce people to a new way of interacting and interfacing with another human being, demonstrating experientially how we, as a species, are all connected in one resonant divine field encapsulating duality and nonduality. These shared events have implications for us: we can wake up to our nondual nature and recognize we are all one in unity consciousness. In these events, we realize that what we do to others, both positively and negatively, we do to ourselves. More profoundly, what we do to ourselves in this universal field, we do to others. With such insight, we can integrate these experiences into our lives, leading us to treat each other with greater empathy, compassion, and respect. Internalizing our nondual nature through experience helps to deconstruct the judge working overtime in our rational, egoic minds. We can then more clearly see the nonsensical nature of violence, racism, bigotry, sexism, and other forms of discrimination and prejudice toward those who are ultimately just a reflection of ourselves. Experiencing the ultimate truth of nonduality provides a cornerstone upon which we can build a more meaningful life, embodying self-love and working in loving service for others. We can find ourselves more attuned to nature and all of its manifestations.

Second, I want to share what is humanly possible. Since the dawn of time, there have always been small numbers of people who have summoned the courage to journey into the unknown, unexpected, and unpredictable depths and heights—the territory—of consciousness. These explorers dive into human motivations, hopes, fears, traumas, healing, wisdom, creativity, and alternate realities and dimensions, some of which may be portals into our afterlife. They return and share the maps of their adventures. But these journeys usually are made alone. In the mindmeld, you journey with another person to explore and expand this territory together. Here, new and higher heights of intimacy are waiting to be discovered. This intimacy includes looking into the center of the other person and seeing and feeling their shadows and struggles, and concurrently, all of their divine beauty, wonder, and potential. And while this journey can be arduous and painful, this intimacy can dovetail with opening physical and psychic healing.

I stumbled along for years without knowing what was possible with psychedelics, such as telepathic connection or working with one's own physical and psychic energy beyond conscious volition. By sharing what I have experienced, it is my hope that others, who are already doing this work in isolation, will feel validated in their efforts, thus avoiding the trauma of not understanding what is happening to them. Hopefully, they will be inspired and have the courage to go further in expanding the maps of their human potential with greater focus, avoiding some of the pitfalls of trial and error. Ideally, reading this book can also be a psychoactive experience for readers: by learning what is possible, people will be able to imagine, potentiate, and accelerate the realizations possible in the mindmeld. Knowing what is possible affects our paradigm of belief, shifting our frames of reference, and creates room for expansion of consciousness. The techniques outlined in this book can help accelerate the expansion of your potential.

Third, I want to ensure that such an energetic and psychically expansive practice is approached mindfully and safely. As you will find in the coming chapters, to embrace expanded awareness is to accept the darkness and the light within yourself and the other. It is also important not to get overly caught up in the story of the experience. Instead, I recommend holding stories lightly and fluidly, similarly to a dream, open to interpretation from a multitude of perspectives, no one more vital or more "real" than any other, and all being ripe with meaning to shape daily life.

Welcome to the magical mystery tour of the Psychedelic Mindmeld. Here, you and your chosen fellow psychonaut can explore as cosmic citizens the infinite realization to be found in the Divine Imagination of the universe.

1

What Is the Psychedelic Mindmeld?

The Psychedelic Mindmeld is two people coming together using psychedelics in deep meditation to meet each other in the spaciousness of universal or cosmic consciousness. Fusing a psychic telepathic link between two minds manifests a co-creative and shared experience. Here the dyad experiences its "interbeingness."

Throughout this book I use the word "psychedelic," coined by Humphrey Osmond, to describe the chemical tools (e.g., DMT, LSD, mescaline, psilocybin, etc.) employed to initiate the mindmeld. I chose psychedelic because it means "mind-manifesting," which so well captures what happens in the mindmeld: two minds manifesting a shared conscious experience.* Psychedelic also incorporates the mind-manifestation of the conscious intelligence of the psychedelic plants themselves as part of the shared process of engagement in the mindmeld.† This broader definition includes both us and the plants as parts of the unified manifestation of Nature.‡

---

*Other words commonly used to refer to psychedelics include entheogens, hallucinogens, psychodysleptics, psychotomimetics, and psychotropics.
†See Stephen Buhner's *Plant Intelligence and the Imaginal Realm: Beyond the Doors of Perception into the Dreaming of Earth* (2014) for an in-depth exploration of plant intelligence. See Eliot Cowan's *Plant Spirit Medicine: A Journey into the Healing Wisdom of Plants* (2014) to begin exploring how to connect with plant intelligence.
‡I use "plants" as an umbrella term that includes fungi and its derivatives (e.g., ergot and its derivative LSD).

While psychedelics are used for various purposes, I view them primarily as tools for exploring and expanding our consciousness. While consciousness is not well understood, we can consider human consciousness as sentience or as one's awareness of the contents and quality—the affect—of internal and external existence. It is the appearance of the external world in waking states. It is also the appearance of inner worlds, whether in dream states, psychedelic states, or meditative states. This is a very simple description of how we as humans relate to consciousness, but it serves as a starting point for diving deeper as we continue. A basic understanding of human consciousness helps describe the territory we enter in the mindmeld.

To deeply explore human consciousness is to penetrate through the layers of mind and explore an individual's relationship to their multidimensional being. Here we are not dealing with pharmacological states, the biological effect of a drug on the body, but, more particularly, employing psychedelics as tools with the specific intent of enabling greater access to the latent capacities of the infinite mind as mediated by our physical brain. My rough map of inner territories charted by myself and others consists of metaphorical signposts or waypoints to aid navigation. When journeying with psychedelics, or other techniques or tools of exploring consciousness, the process of encountering the signposts is not necessarily linear. Still, there is often a felt sense of progress or of penetrating through layers, both in individual sessions and over time in serial sessions. However, what we are penetrating is still largely a mystery. As such, I add a caveat to this rough map of consciousness: *Hic sunt leones.* "Here are lions" was used on ancient maps to signify that the cartographer did not have sufficient knowledge of what lay beyond the boundary, denoting the possibility of wild beasts lurking and other unforeseen dangers. This caution is pertinent when exploring the unknown depths of consciousness.

We have yet to definitively determine where consciousness originates and resides: Is the human relationship to consciousness endogenous to the human brain, or is it exogenous? Does consciousness originate outside the human body as a phenomenon interpenetrating all things in the universe like a massive ocean of infinite consciousness but mediated by the human brain on an individual level? We do not even know where human memory is encoded, even if we have indications that various brain parts are more responsible for memory than others.

Below I offer an experiential understanding of how we can relate to our experience of consciousness and concept of self. It is a rough map of several possible theories of consciousness. The map I present is intended to facilitate an understanding of the mindmeld. It helps identify how to enter the mindmeld and describes what can arise in the experience when we get there. At the same time, we want to hold our maps and models loosely, not wanting them to constrict our perspective and limit our capacity to access, observe, and respond to anything that may lie beyond our conceptual framework. We want to remain open-minded, not caught rigidly in limited opinions.

We begin where, on the surface of our lived experience, we relate to the world through the use of our conscious, waking, rational/intellectual mind, which processes and analyzes data from the external world through our exteroception using the physical senses, including sight, touch, smell, taste, and hearing. We also have proprioception rooted in our sense of balance, agility, and coordination, relating each of our body parts to each other and the external world. Another form of physical awareness is interoception, the subtle somatic feelings (e.g., hunger, thirst, temperature, and feelings connected to emotions). Here, with practice, we can focus our awareness of sensation to the size of a needle point anywhere on our body, or to feeling the movement of individual organs. We can also diffuse our awareness to the trillions of atoms in our body, which can manifest as a feeling of a three-dimensional map of energy floating in space beyond the weight of the body. We also have chronoception or an awareness of the passing of time. Our capacity for cognition (the mental action of acquiring knowledge and understanding through thought, experience, and our senses), and where we focus our awareness, is mediated by the ego. The ego's faculty of executive functioning helps us navigate the day-to-day world we live in. (A proposal for the function of the ego is described in chapter 7 under the heading "The Ego.") While most of our responses to stimuli in our environment are emotional, reflexive, reactionary, and unconscious, we are also able through perception, recognition, insight, and discrimination to judge the value and even the aesthetic beauty of what arises in our sensory experience. Our capacity to make subjective judgments enables us to decide how to engage and respond to our experience, which is sometimes called "free will." While our perceptions can be faulty because of the limitations of the brain (e.g., the illusions of motion aftereffects, color constancy, depth perception, and auditory illusions), they do not stop us from (rightly or wrongly) interpreting incoming data. Within the conscious self then, there is a measure of self-control and knowing capable of acting, responding, making decisions, and adapting to inner impulses, feelings, desires, and ambitions.

A layer deeper into the mind is the unconscious, or subconscious, referred to by Buddhists as the substrate mind or storehouse consciousness. Occultists refer to the mental plane, the place of thoughtforms. The unconscious refers to the active thought processes in the mind occurring beyond conscious awareness, including the storehouse of all experiences that have consciously and unconsciously entered one's awareness since conception. Unconscious content is not readily available to introspection, yet, in many ways, it is our navigational black box. We have a vague sense of what is in this box from our dreams and *holotropic** states of consciousness in the forms of stories, symbols, and patterns. The mysterious nature and origin of our thoughts is presumed to be found inside the black box of our unconscious. It is from the unconscious and its connection to the nervous system that our emotions and

---

*Stanislav Grof (Grof & Grof, 2010) coined the neologism "holotropic," which means moving toward wholeness. Throughout this book, I have used this term because it best fits the discussion of psychedelic-induced states of consciousness, thus opting out of using terms like "altered" or "nonordinary," as these have clinical implications or include broader phenomena than discussed.

intuition arise, directly giving rise to our thoughts and influencing our motivations and conscious decisions. The unconscious can also hijack our sense of self-control, manifesting as knee-jerk emotional reactions or overreactions. If the nervous system is overloaded, then irrational, hysterical reactions are even more pronounced, making it challenging to focus and concentrate. The unconscious is also connected to our brain/body functions of the survival instincts or drives related to the protection and maintenance of the body. These instincts are entwined with our innate autonomic nervous system, also called neuroception, that detects danger. When faced with external threat, this innate safety system leads us to spontaneously react in modes of fight (for dominance), flight (to escape), freeze (submission), faint (shut down), or fawn (inducement and/or compliance). Unfortunately, these reactions are not always appropriate for a given situation, especially if the nervous system is in a hypervigilant state due to trauma or ongoing exposure to danger, whether real or perceived (Walker, 2013).

Carl Jung (1969) theorized that we have a "shadow" in our unconscious: the disowned, undesirable, or rejected parts of personality that the ego-self ignores, subordinates, or annihilates to maintain an idealized self-image. When impulses erupt from the shadowy areas inside us, they give rise to unpleasant emotions like fear, greed, jealousy, hatred, loneliness, hopelessness, helplessness, and inferiority. Even so, many have surmised it is from the unconscious mind that human imagination, aesthetic realization, and creativity arise. It may be the originator of will and ambition. The unconscious is also our supercomputer. It continually works beyond conscious thought to solve problems presented to it by our conscious mind. The unconscious holds the memory of the perinatal, of our development in the womb and the trauma of being born into the world (Maté & Maté, 2022; Tucker, 2005). Psychiatrist Stanislav Grof (1976; 2008; 2009) goes further and argues that by entering the perinatal domain in the unconscious, we enter the doorway to transpersonal levels of consciousness, including archetypal cycles of birth, aging, dying, death, and rebirth. By becoming lucid in dreams (including out-of-body experiences), and in other holotropic states, we can bring greater awareness to the unconscious and can gain insight. The unconscious is thus a double-edged sword: the root of delusion and revelation and the root of the destructive and creative impulses.

To penetrate a layer further in the mind is to enter the superconsciousness, the transpersonal, the transrational, the supernatural, the astral plane, the nonlocal mind, the collective unconscious* of our species, the Universal Cloud, the *Anima Mundi* ("Soul of the World"), and archetypal, daemonic, or deific realms. Here we find the experience of the soul, archetype, and myth—a connection to the timeless and primordial, which gave birth to all form in the universe. In the realms of superconsciousness we can encounter discarnate beings (sometimes referred to as nonordinary, nonphysical, or daemonic beings). This list includes aliens, ex-galactics,† elementals, entities, plant teachers (e.g., Mescalito from peyote; Great Mother Goddess Pachamama from ayahuasca), spirits, spirit guides, spirit animals, therianthropic beings (partly animal and partly human), souls (inclusive of deceased persons like ancestors),‡ devas, deities (e.g., Mahakala, Shiva,

---

*Jung (2011b) refers to the collective unconsciousness as containing the whole spiritual heritage of mankind's evolution, born anew in the brain structure of every individual as an unceasing ocean of primordial images, figures, and symbols drifting in and out of consciousness in waking states, dreams, and abnormal states.

†An ex-galactic is a soul who has traveled from another galaxy to live in this galaxy, usually in a physical human body on Earth.

‡Here *soul* refers to the part of an individual capable of traveling out of the body (e.g., in shamanic journeys to other worlds) or surviving the death of the body. In other cultures, this "soul" is also referred to as dream-soul, death-soul, ghost-soul, image-soul, shadow-soul, the astral body, daimonic body, or subtle body. For ease of definition, human *spirit* can be said to be an entangled part of soul. It plays the unifying, ascending, and transcending role of soul or the animus/yang force of soul versus the anima/yin, or imaginative, unconscious, immanent, multiple, dark, chaotic aspects of soul (Harpur, 2003). Many cultures account for two souls in the individual. The second soul is the ego-consciousness in connection to the id, often referred to as the psyche, animating our life force, including innate drives and emotion. It lives and dies with the physical body. In the psychedelic journey, when we relegate our ego we become more in touch with our "dream-soul," which is still connected to the notion of ego insofar as it still has its own individual identity in duality. It is possible, however, to lose this identity altogether in nondual states of consciousness, which is discussed in chapter 11.

Tara, or Vajrapani), jinn, angels, demons, monsters, "Grand Masters" (e.g., Buddha, the Cosmic Christ, or Metatron), and more. Access to this level of reality opens us to the possibility that we are immortal souls journeying around the universe from lifetime to lifetime in different bodies and forms to have experiences, learn and grow at a soul level to deepen our wisdom, and participate in the evolution of consciousness.

A layer further into mind reveals what Buddhists call Clear Light Mind, *Dharmakaya* (Clear Light of Absolute Reality), ground luminosity, nature of mind, or Big Mind, or universal mind. Hindus refer to the Self, *Satcitananda*, *Shiva*, *Brahman*, and *Vishnu*. Sufi mystics call it the Hidden Essence. Theosophists refer to the Buddhic Plane. In Western traditions this layer of mind is often referred to as primordial awareness, cosmic consciousness, universal consciousness, the Self, or God-consciousness. It is also sometimes referred to as devotion of ecstasy by Christians. Shamans may identify with finding oneness in the Great Mother or Creator. To enter this state of "absolute" consciousness is to enter nondual states of awareness. There are many competing definitions for these concepts. And there are subtle variations in the realizations themselves. But for our purposes it is a state of consciousness that drops the vagaries of the judgmental egoic mind, where the chatter in one's mind stops, and the experience is of pure divine perfection and completeness in the interconnectedness of the All. It is infinite; it is radiant; it is immanent; it is conscious, aware and alive. These experiences elicit philosophical ideas of monism, panpsychism, and pantheism.* The origin of primordial love is found at this center as the divine flow of energy holding the universe together as one infinite living phenomenon.

Through these layers of mind, we bring an awareness to the human psyche. The psyche is the internal mental and psychological motive force within us connected to the sum of all conscious and

---

*Monism: reality is one unitary organic whole with no independent parts. Panpsychism: everything material, however small, has an element of individual consciousness/sentience. Pantheism: the whole universe is a manifestation of God.

unconscious contents, including the collective unconscious and non-dual awareness.

There are many ways to explore consciousness and penetrate the layers of mind. Many have been practiced for millennia. The techniques can generally be divided into two categories: (1) down-regulation and (2) up-regulation. Examples of down-regulation include meditation, engaging the imagination in visionary exercises (e.g., vision quests, past-life regression, lucid dreaming, and astral travel), breathing techniques, sweat lodges, and isolation. Up-regulating techniques include induced pain (e.g., deep piercings at Sun Dance or Sufi ceremonies), fasting, forms of ecstatic dance, and more. The lines between categories can also be blurred; for example, the use of trance drumming or the use of mantras. Even meditation styles vary from those with high levels of concentration with a single focus to more free-floating witnessing and observing of all arising phenomena. Spontaneous out-of-body events can also occur (e.g., through high fever, near-death, childbirth, sexual orgasm, and extreme fatigue, or while just walking down the street).

Psychedelics are another tool to penetrate consciousness and the layers of the mind. For our purposes, we are discussing working with "breakthrough" dosages. This involves a person taking a high enough dosage of a psychedelic to help push themselves through the first two layers of mind to the mystical and allow them to connect energetically and psychically with another person.

When entering the mindmeld, there is no fixed destination. The technique may take you into the unconscious, superconscious, or clear light mind. In these states it is possible to experience what is often referred to as gnosis in the West or levels of *samadhi* or *jnana* in the East. Knowledge is immediate in experience where the known, the knower, and the knowledge are one. Naked reality is experienced and known, as is the interconnectedness of all things, free from the constraints of space and time.

It is in these states that the "real" magic happens. The mindmeld is a joint undertaking into unknown territory where the unpredictable is guaranteed once egoic control is released. To enter this space is dangerous and exciting, precipitous and rewarding. In holotropic states of consciousness, like gnosis/samadhi, other human abilities can arise. In the West, these abilities are referred to as extrasensory perception, exceptional human experience, psi, or psychic or magical powers. In some Eastern traditions, these abilities are called *siddhis*. Examples include telepathy (images or emotions shared between minds), clairvoyance (perception of distant events or images related to physical states of affairs), clairaudience (psychic perception of voices, like spirits of the dead), precognition (perception of distant events or images through time), psychokinesis (influence of distant systems via mental intention), out-of-body journeying to other times and places, planets, or dimensions, and shape-shifting, among other abilities.

Through conscious intent and the relaxing of the ego, the mindmeld can arise. Mindmelding is a form of telepathic exchange of physical energetic and psychic contents. There can be layers of empathic or intuitive telepathic sharing of emotions. Here, the joint exploration of emotional processes can induce psychic expansiveness, enhance cognitive fluidity, and creatively lead to attitudinal changes and greater internal harmony. This co-creative exercise of communion can lead to physical and mental healing and regeneration. But the mindmeld can go even further to a complete sharing of consciousness between people, where shared visions and exploration into superconsciousness is possible. At its furthest profundity, when the borderlands of superconsciousness are breached in the mindmeld, both participants can find themselves in nondual states of consciousness where there is no separation: duality is dropped. There is no distinction between subject (the active living "I") and object (the "other" in the field of awareness)—both participants are absorbed in unity consciousness. All of these possibilities are detailed in chapters 10 and 11.

While science struggles to prove these various psi abilities are "real" empirically, what matters to us as explorers of consciousness is the experience itself. The mindmeld can stretch the experience of ourselves in connection with others, broadening our views of human capacity and potential, and possibly contribute to the evolution of consciousness itself.

2

Warning: The Psychedelic Mindmeld Is for the Initiated

Entering the mindmeld is not for the faint of heart. It is an experience so far beyond the bounds of day-to-day reality that it is difficult to describe or even imagine what it is. In this context, it is something to try for those who are at least familiar with and initiated into the geography of consciousness accessed through high-dose psychedelic use. The approach I am proposing is generally not for the uninitiated. While I have been working with psychedelics for over fifteen years, each time I use one, I still feel great trepidation—even outside of coupling in the mindmeld. The reason for the apprehension is, I never know what to expect. While being in the zone of the experience is familiar, the territory to be explored is often new, vast, and unpredictable and is often overwhelming. I rarely have a session where I don't question why I even bother taking psychedelics and whether I want to take them again.

For those who have done high-dose psychedelic sessions, you know exploring consciousness in this way can profoundly change your life. When engaging in the mindmeld you are exploring new territory. By exploring new territory, held assumptions and beliefs can be shattered.

These sometimes uncomfortable shifts are explored in this book. For example, you may experience the melting away of solid physical and psychic boundaries between yourself and another, together slipping away from the real to the apparently "unreal" and mystical. This may lead to long-held certainties of some belief systems, especially those based on a materialistic and rational scientific worldview, becoming tenuous and confused. Confusion can cause stress and anxiety. So, while exploring new territory can be expansive and wondrous as two people approach and enter states of nondual consciousness, it can also be terrifying. To experience absolute divine wonder and love in unity consciousness and then return to the mundane world can also be discombobulating.

In this context, I consider the approach of the Psychedelic Mindmeld as work, not recreation. I am brought back to these experiences because of my fascination for the unknown, to seek personal growth and healing, to share in love and compassion, to experience the light within, and to come to terms with darkness.

Joseph Campbell (2008) powerfully describes the work required for personal transformation:

The agony of breaking through personal limitations is the agony of spiritual growth. Art, literature, myth and cult, philosophy, and ascetic disciplines are instruments to help the individual past his limiting horizons into spheres of ever-expanding realization. As he crosses threshold after threshold, conquering dragon after dragon, the stature of the divinity that he summons to his highest wish increases, until it subsumes the cosmos. Finally, the mind breaks the bounding sphere of the cosmos to a realization transcending all experiences of form—all symbolizations, all divinities: a realization of the ineluctable void (p. 163).

It is vital to ask yourself why you want to explore this work. Are you ready to open your mind completely to another, making it transparent to the point where you do not know what is and isn't going to be shared? Are you ready to go to hell and back with another person? To heaven? Are you prepared to open up to an intimacy more extraordinary than anything else you have ever experienced?

If you are in a romantic relationship, there is a further consideration. If one person wants to do this work without the other or the support of the other, know that the experiences can possibly cause a sense of separation or conflict. The reason for this is it may become difficult for each person to relate to the other as one expands in their experience of consciousness and their beliefs (and possibly values) and the other does not. The same is more generally true where I have seen struggles in various relationships just from one person trying psychedelics and the other not wanting to. But the mindmeld can add another layer of separation, especially if people are working with someone other than their romantic partner, which can introduce jealousy. Thoughtful communication, and defined boundaries, however, can bridge these differences. Participants have told me they have moved on to feel closer to their romantic partner and seen improvements in their sexual relationships after sessions with me. They have expanded their felt sense of loving awareness and let go of energetic patterns not serving them.

So, there is a lot to consider. Let's first explore prerequisites for the Psychedelic Mindmeld, and then finish the chapter discussing the differences between the experienced mindmelder and the beginner.

PREREQUISITES

Discussing prerequisites is complicated. There is no school to prepare anybody for what I am proposing. Nor are there any definitive prerequisites. While skills can be developed and honed, the most profound things to arise in sessions come from beyond the cognitive, rational, intellectual, and robot mind. Instead, what often appears comes from a place of mystery some may label intuition, grace, the higher self, spirit, soul, the big Self, the Great Divine, or even God. Some aspects of experience seem related to the collective unconscious or the shared field of consciousness that we as humans can consciously connect to.

As mentioned above, telepathic ability may be referred to as a *siddhi*, or as psi. Many practitioners would argue this ability is a gift and not easily explained in terms of its origin, even if such ability can be developed and honed through practice. Others see telepathy as a natural milepost in one's personal spiritual development, as an inherent capacity of being human. While you will have to figure out how qualified you are to explore my proposed approach, you do not require a background in telepathy. In my introductory story, where Isabel and I journeyed in shared consciousness to Japan, it was only her second time using psychedelics. She had no history of working with psychedelics or with psi. And from my research, this type of spontaneous psi phenomenon is not unusual, especially when working with psychedelics.

What follows is a personal example of my first introduction to paired work as a precursor to co-creative mindmelding, where I had no obvious prerequisites. I was ingesting ayahuasca for the third time after trying it twice in the two years prior. I had no prior exposure to or previous work with metaphysical processes (e.g., human energy work, yoga, any form of meditation, or psi, magick, etc.) or any other mindful exposure to working with psychedelics.

A Shipibo-trained shaman facilitated the ceremony. Ten of us lay or sat in a living room cleared of furniture. The ceremony started after sunset, and there was just enough ambient light to see the outlines of the walls.

Despite having already participated in two ayahuasca ceremonies, I was highly skeptical of psychedelically induced states of consciousness. While I had read about shamanism, I was still convinced the accounts I read were based on the wild imaginings of those within the spectrum of mental health issues such as psychosis. At best, I believed people could create all sorts of imaginative visions in their mind's eye by closing their eyes and creatively playing with their thoughts, which had no relevance to "reality." For this reason, I refused to close my eyes during the ceremony. Rightly or wrongly, I wanted a more tangible experience to play out in front of me beyond my inner world. So, I sat there with legs stretched out and my back against the wall, staring into the darkness.

As the ayahuasca took effect, a fractal garden of colorful flowers started to grow from the far side of the room toward me. The garden reached my feet and enveloped them. I didn't feel any negative effect, so I continued to sit entirely still and stayed attentive to the disappearance of my legs. The garden then grew up my torso until it reached my neck. At this point, a nervousness raced through me as my head felt like it was floating in space unconnected to my body. Now the garden had an unstoppable momentum that I surrendered to.

Suddenly I entered the proverbial white tunnel of light so often reported in near-death experiences. I was rushing through the space of the white light, feeling connected to all things, absorbed in being the All. Just as quickly as it started, I abruptly found myself on the other side of a portal, somewhere else in the universe and approaching a planet. Soon my visual awareness dropped into a long valley with living, organic square pyramids on either side of me stretching the valley's length. Each of the pyramids was larger than any of the pyramids on Earth. Red and orange vegetation covered their four sides, breathing in and out with their breath that was entering and leaving their apex.

I floated down the valley toward a massive golden and crystal palace. I entered the court and found myself seated around a table of ten indigo-colored light beings. None could be distinguished from the other by looks; each was oblong with no defining features.

I felt at home. The light beings made it clear I was welcome through a telepathic connection, a form of communication completely foreign to me. When I eventually left, these beings somehow turned on latent intuitive healing capacities in me through some form of information download.

I returned to my body through the roof of the house where the ceremony was still in progress. When my awareness dropped back into my body, I found it had not moved since I left. As I looked out into the room, I realized my attention had shifted, and I could see the energy matrix of the room, which was similar to the green lines of streaming data in the movie *The Matrix*. What was more intriguing is I quickly realized my thoughts were connected to and capable of shifting the energy matrix.

The shaman was singing over a man struggling with lower back issues. I decided to focus my energy, drawing in the energy immediately surrounding me, and send it to the shaman to help in her work. A bright beam of white energy began to shoot from my heart to her. The more I focused, the stronger it got. Suddenly, two indigo light-bearers arrived at my back and melded into each of my shoulders, and the beam became much more potent and brighter. Then—BANG!—my consciousness again left my body, moving down the stream of energy, through the shaman's body, and into the man she was working on. My awareness was now in the man's lower spine, and I could see fissures in his spine and tissues. My conscious presence became engaged in trying to heal the damage. I was not there for long, and I was overwhelmed with the strangeness of the situation as my rational mind tried to grapple with what was happening, which immediately cast me back into my body.

In the morning, I shared what had happened with the shaman. She was surprised but assured me such experiences were real. I struggled to make sense of what had happened. What helped validate my experience was that the man with the injured back told the group that during the session he felt a force internally massaging his lower back and providing him with some relief.

I had no prerequisites, no training, for what happened in this ceremony, yet I was engaged in sharing loving energy and healing. This event made clear to me that engaging in the mysteries of energetic healing required letting go of my ego and trusting a wisdom beyond my mind. I have since wondered whether my energy could have contributed further to his recovery had I not struggled with an egoic resistance related to fear and bewilderment while my awareness was in his spine.

As I have mentioned, nothing had prepared me for what happened. At the time, I did not even know such things were possible. As the years pass, I have learned that we all have an inner healer inside us—an inner shaman. This being said, the mindmeld should be approached with great respect and caution. Below, I offer some basic guidelines for the mindmeld based on my insights over the years to help assess if you are ready to do this work. Categories for consideration are: (1) experience with psychedelics; (2) openness to personal growth; (3) experience with meditation; (4) good medical health; and (5) mental preparedness. In chapter 8, I also provide suggestions for maximizing the safety of participants.

Experience with Psychedelics

Have you ever been psychedelicized? For the Psychedelic Mindmeld this is a crucial question. Having experience with psychedelics is a helpful and grounding prerequisite for doing this work. Working with psychedelics is neither easy nor predictable. Experience brings calm when faced with the strangeness of the content and the ebbs, flows, and discharges of energy in the psychedelically induced mindscape.

Practical resources for working with psychedelics reach as far back as the 1950s. While these early resources were usually published in books and research papers, there has been an explosion of publications, chat groups, online courses, and YouTube video presentations in the past decade. The majority of available resources on psychedelics are introductory or intermediate. Such resources discuss the importance of set and setting, which this book also does. There is also a groundswell of research on therapeutic uses. But the dominant paradigm focuses on intrapsychic work (internal exploratory and therapeutic work), not interpsychic or telepathic work.

Intrapsychic work is still essential in our case. A person should be familiar with how strange and demanding the inner landscape can become while using psychedelics. Working with psychedelics can evoke sensory illusions and projections, delusional interpretations of the world, and shifts in space-time. One should be familiar with penetrating one's unconscious and with the psychological ordeals that may arise. There may be difficult memories, perhaps of past traumas, inclusive of perinatal challenges (e.g., exposure to infections, toxins, or other noxious influences while in the womb). There may be challenging life (or past life) reviews. Repressed and uncomfortable emotions can surface, with the associated discomfort of moving blocked energy, which can cause nausea or vomiting, restricted breathing, evacuating of bowels, or screaming and yelling. Such emotions can include grief, sadness, depression, disappointment, anxiety, embarrassment, fear, helplessness, aggression, anger, hatred, guilt, shame, annoyance, contempt, envy, disgust, and irritation. People can be confronted with visions of death, dismemberment, and apocalypse. Beautiful and ecstatic states can also manifest. Conversely, familiarity with rapturous states, such as transcendental peace, serenity, and cosmic unity, is helpful. So is exposure to deeply felt bliss, empathy, compassion, love, happiness, elation, excitement, and joy.

There is the possibility of having out-of-body experiences, journeying to fantastical lands, which can include other places on our planet or other planets altogether. It is also possible to enter different dimensions and parallel universes in the multiverse. Many have also encountered discarnate beings, mentioned earlier, and have made claims of channeling them. Having familiarity and comfort with the above make it easier to do telepathic work, as it reduces the risk of being overwhelmed by the unknown.

Long-term deep serial work with psychedelics usually creates a story arc of progressive growth and energetic purification for individuals. The length and depth of this process tends to be influenced by the degree of emotional difficulties the person is faced with and the amount of underlying trauma needing to be resolved (Grof, 2008). Although this process is often not linear, the progression tends to start with addressing historical biographical and ancestral psychological challenges, often related to high emotional content, difficult memories, and unresolved conflicts and trauma. As psychological issues are increasingly resolved, users often find themselves dealing more with perinatal issues. These can include traumatic issues faced within the womb in gestation through to the birthing process. Physical issues can involve struggles around entrapment or exposure to noxious influences. Deeper issues can involve expanding to the primordial cycle of life and death or more profound existential questions about the purpose of life, which may entail fears of insanity. Why am I here? Why do I not feel complete? Why do I never feel completely satisfied? Why is there so much suffering? As perinatal issues are increasingly worked through or resolved, people tend to move more into transpersonal states, which can include accessing the superconscious or collective unconsciousness and experiencing the collective wonders and miseries at these levels (Grof, 1976; 2008; 2009; 2019a).

Through all these levels of development, there is a repeated theme of ego-death or annihilation of the self. Ego-death can manifest as real feelings of immediate impending physical death, as the destruction of all frames of personal reference to identity and the world, and as the catastrophic end of the entire universe. Specific eschatological content of the thought processes and vision can accompany the experience, including dying individuals, decaying corpses, coffins, cemeteries, hearses, funeral corteges, nuclear explosions, and raining fire. Symptomatically, the experience can manifest as intense, pervasive feelings of anxiety, suffocation, agonizing physical pain, tremors, violent shaking, blacking out, vomiting, confusion and disorientation, and yelling and screaming in terror, just to list a few examples. But on the other side of ego-death is healing, liberation from negative emotional charges, and positive transformation (Grof, 1976; 2008; 2009; 2019a).

It is helpful to have had exposure to these experiences as it contributes to clarifying what material is surfacing and which is yours versus the other person's, and also to distinguishing what may be emerging from the collective unconscious. Familiarity with the general psychedelic mindscape is crucial because it fosters greater equanimity and openness to deeper exploration. As you will see in later chapters, broad exposure is important, but more essential is accepting, through the lens of nonduality, everything that arises as being you, as you are interconnected to All.

Part of the risk in doing joint work is one person having a challenging or "negative" experience and projecting it or blaming it on the other person, not accepting that it is arising internally or possibly from the shared field of the collective unconscious. And if a demanding experience, such as one with uncomfortable emotions or sensations, arises from the other person directly, and one is empathetically experiencing them, one should be able to observe what is transpiring and not get negatively caught in it. It is vital to see these moments as transitory and fleeting, passing through the field of awareness with no sense of permanence. At best, one should be able to offer validation, solace, and comfort to the struggling other person, either telepathically, verbally, or with body gestures. To hold space for the other person is not to judge their experience or try to fix something but to let them work through their process. As such, what makes mindmeld work more advanced is the need to observe and allow the most bizarre of experiences to flow through one's awareness while not getting attached or caught up in negative projections or reactions. These subjects are discussed in more detail throughout this book.

Experience with the particular psychedelic used is also helpful. While there can be lots of overlap in experiences with many psychedelics, each has its unique qualities. Equally important is being familiar with dosages. In our case, participants need to be familiar with higher doses, where they know their ego will be relegated from its dominant position of controlling one's experience.

Openness to Personal Growth

To open oneself to the Psychedelic Mindmeld is to open oneself to personal growth. Growth requires curiosity, a desire to learn, and openness to being changed and experiencing a greater self-unfoldment. One has to be ready to transcend one's limits. In the mindmeld, this means an agreement to be acted upon by the other. It is a process of radical honesty, or, that is, being honest with oneself and being open and honest with the other. It is also a commitment to constructive joint struggle. The process is not for entertainment but is work.

Being genuinely open to personal growth requires courage to face one's fears. Baring the core of oneself, including both one's beauty and one's warts, can be frightening. But with loving acceptance, the process can engender liberation. It can lead to greater opening and surrender and, ultimately, greater self-actualization. Newfound authenticity can arise in personal expression.

Experience with Meditation

To help with one's capacity to observe and allow interenergetic and inter-psychic experiences to develop, flow, and pass, it is ideal to have experience with meditation. Meditation is a learned skill that can directly enhance one's abilities in this work. Meditation allows for gradual penetration into the layers of the mind, making it easier to stay grounded. But there are dozens of different styles of meditation. For example, one can meditate with eyes open or shut, while sitting still, moving, sitting down, or lying down. Meditation can focus on observing bodily sensations, breathing, observing thoughts, manifesting specific thought patterns (e.g., repeating mantras), creatively creating mental imagery, and invoking emotional states (see chapter 9, under the heading "Meditative Technique: Opening the Heart"). Inward journeys using meditation techniques can include invoking spirits and deities, healing self and others, past/future life regression, states of dreaming (e.g., invoking lucid dreaming), and out-of-body journeying.

So, what works best for the mindmeld? As long as the mind is directed by forced concentration in meditation (such as focusing on a single point), or mantra meditation, the ego is engaged. Because mindmeld work is about releasing the ego's firm grasp, it is best to use a meditation style facilitating this, such as free-flowing meditation with complete physical stillness. An example is being the witness to one's experience, observing one's mind attentively but loosely.

Meditation styles focused on slowing the busy chatter of the mind, the incessant internal dialogue commenting on everything, which is commonly referred to as the "monkey mind" in Eastern meditative traditions, can lead to profound states of silence and even nondual states of consciousness. Calming the mind is the direction of meditation we are striving toward, so any meditation experience of this type is helpful. Settling the mind in these ways will contribute to calming the ego into a more restful place and will allow mystical experiences to more easily manifest. It is here that the power of psychedelics steps forward. When one is reaching the limits of meditation for penetrating the mind, psychedelics are a tool to shunt the ego more forcefully out of the way, and they let something deeper in consciousness rise to the field of awareness. Meditation techniques to help facilitate the mindmeld while using psychedelics are detailed in chapters 9 and 12.

Good Medical Health

People should be in good medical health to work with psychedelics. There are no contraindications for participating in the mindmeld beyond the standard precautions for psychedelics.

What is shared below is common wisdom regarding the general use of psychedelics. I am not a doctor, so what I am suggesting is not medically prescriptive. Because there is a real risk in using psychedelics, this is another reason to have previous experience with them, to ensure one is physically and mentally strong enough to work with the mindmeld.

To begin with, people should be in reasonable physical shape, with no health issues relating to their heart. This is because traumatic material can surface in the session, lending to intense physical strain and release. High physical intensity can overload a compromised cardiovascular system. Severe cardiovascular disorders to be concerned about are high blood pressure/malignant hypertension, decompensated heart failure, severe arteriosclerosis, thrombosis with a danger of embolism, aneurysm, a history of heart attacks, brain hemorrhage, myocarditis, atrial fibrillation, or other similar problems (Grof, 2008, p. 129).

Another concern is convulsive disorders like grand mal epilepsy. There is a lack of scientific evidence around the safe use of psychedelics for people with convulsive disorders. If someone were to have a grand mal seizure during a session without a sober sitter present, it would likely be challenging for the other participant to provide adequate medical attention for the person having the seizure, particularly because both people are in "altered" states of consciousness. A seizure event could also potentially traumatize one or both participants.

There is an element of common sense to be invoked for other physical issues, such as physical injuries, recent medical operations, or contagious diseases. Because the bodywork in the mindmeld can be both intense and unpredictable, people should not be in recovery from bone fractures, dislocated shoulders or knees, herniated disks, incompletely healed surgical wounds, or other similar afflictions. Past detachment of the retina, or glaucoma, associated with elevated intraocular pressure, are conditions not amenable to deep physical energetic work (Grof & Grof, 2010, p. 57). Due to prolonged physical contact in the mindmeld, contagious disease is obviously contraindicated for the work.

It is not recommended to engage in the mindmeld while pregnant. There is a lack of scientific research into how psychedelics affect the fetus in pregnancy. This is reason enough to avoid doing this work while pregnant. Further, the work can already be very intense. Adding another participant into the mix of sharing consciousness, including physical and psychic energetic contents, creates too much risk for participants, particularly the unborn.

Several pharmaceuticals are contraindicated for use with psychedelics, such as antidepressants or selective serotonin reuptake inhibitors (SSRIs), St. John's Wort, heart medications, antibiotics, antihistamines, and others (Metzner, 2015, p. 148). This is not an exhaustive list, so checking with your doctor is recommended before using psychedelics. There is a real risk of serotonin toxicity when using certain drugs in combination with psychedelics, which can cause extreme hyperthermia, severe autonomic dysfunction, or extreme mycoclonus (convulsions or seizure-like activity).

If you have any concerns about your health because of the above-mentioned issues, you should check with your doctor before using psychedelics.

Mental Preparedness

There are two layers to mental preparedness: (1) one's overall constitution, which I describe below, and (2) a person's state of mind on the day of the experience (described in chapter 7 on set).

The mentally stable person who chooses to enter holotropic states voluntarily can face the unexpected consequences of being insufficiently adaptive to exploring the unknown. But while the person may face mortal terror, they can return from the experience and make meaning of it, possibly engendering inspiration, adaptation, and reconstruction of their inner world.

The mentally stable are capable of deep trust. They can face fear. They're capable of loving connection and being present for the other. In short, they are grounded and self-confident, allowing for vulnerability and openness.

On the other hand, those struggling with long-term mental instability should generally avoid this work. It is likely they have been running away from something in their own psyche, which has been growing in the unconscious from neglect to a size that can devour them and cause horrific psychotic hallucinations. In this context, people should avoid working with psychedelics if they are prone to psychosis, bipolar disorder, or other similar psychological challenges unless being treated by a trained psychiatrist.

Martin Ball (2017) identifies another type of person who should avoid this type of work—those "who tend to displace responsibility from themselves and blame others or situations for their victimhood show[ing] a lack of ability to take personal responsibility and a tendency to project onto others" (p. 23). The particular risk when engaging in the mindmeld is facing difficult emotions one is unwilling to take ownership for. If the blame for one's state of consciousness is projected onto the other, it can be destructive to both the process and the relationship between those engaged in the experience. Issues of projection are discussed further in chapter 13.

While I believe we are all susceptible to mental instability for different reasons (e.g., struggles with a sudden injury, disease, trauma, loss, grief, etc.), it is helpful to have a personal sense of adaptability and resilience before trying the mindmeld. The work is trying physically, mentally, and energetically.

THE EXPERIENCED MINDMELDER VERSUS THE BEGINNER

After someone gains a lot of experience doing mindmelding work, they may be tempted to label themselves a practitioner. Practitioner labels are tricky because they instantly create a sense of uniqueness and separateness and generally produce a sense of expertise the ego can easily co-opt into: "I am better than you." While there is nothing inherently wrong with labels, this book and the techniques it outlines are meant to focus on the opposite: breaking down the barriers of separation and experiencing how we are all connected in unity consciousness. Regardless of our worldly accomplishments, or struggles, we are all fundamentally equal. At the same time, we are unique expressions of the Divine.

The mindmeld is, first and foremost, a co-creative engagement and sharing of physical and psychic energetic contents. Both people are full participants and are working collaboratively. Regardless of past experience doing mindmeld work, the role of who is taking the lead in a session can easily and quickly reverse. But having said all of the above, experience counts for something.

Experience brings familiarity and comfort with the unusual geography of holotropic states of consciousness, which can increase the capacity for surrender into deeper states of consciousness and ultimately enhance the mindmeld. The more experience one has, the more one can guide a beginner. As someone who has done this work for years, I have worked with people who did not have any of the abovementioned prerequisites. Many such people have shared that they feel guided and supported in sessions.

But at what point is someone with mindmelding experience qualified to work with someone else who has no experience mindmelding and doesn't have many of the prerequisites? In addition to the capabilities already described, what distinguishes someone as "experienced" is their ability to effectively work with their own physical and psychic energy in a grounded way when using psychedelics, and then with others. While discussed last, this is a critical qualification. Much will be discussed in later chapters about sharing physical and psychic energy, but at this point it is useful to briefly cover some things that an individual should be familiar and comfortable with regarding working with their own physical and psychic energy and as an extension to others.

Psychic Contents

Most psychedelic trips, most of the time, are dualistic. There is a subject and an object in awareness. In other words, you, the experiencer (the subject), have an experience (the object) you relate to as being separate from you in your awareness. To keep this simple for now, all the things arising internally for you in experience are psychic contents, all with their own energetic signatures. Psychic contents include everything from your external affairs relating to people, pets, and doing the dishes to how you internally process connecting to discarnate beings in psychedelic journeys.

Psychedelic trips are renowned for connecting to discarnate beings, as mentioned earlier. These connections are similar to what can occur in the dream world and, for some, in the waking world. Many strange and unpredictable beings and happenings can arise in psychedelic experiences; one should have both experienced occasions with the strange and unpredictable nature of these experiences and an underlying acceptance and equanimity with them.

The same is true of the psychic contents of the unconscious. Because psychedelics are a powerful tool for accessing and amplifying the unconscious, they can act as a therapeutic tool to work with past traumas. It is important to identify, relate, accept, and surrender to trauma-induced experiences as they arise in psychedelic trips. If you cannot deal with your traumas, how do you expect to relate to and deal with the traumas of others as they arise directly in your field of awareness, both psychically and physically? It is also helpful to be able to distinguish between your psychic and physical contents and those of another. While these subtleties of "self" and "other" become more distinguishable with experience, having a solid sense of your "self" provides grounding in the mindmeld.

Having had nondual experiences is valuable when working with psychic content because it helps put into perspective that everything manifesting in experience is ultimately you. In other words, all the psychic contents displayed in your field of awareness as subjects appearing separate from you, be it aliens, the people around you, their trauma, your trauma, or the physical objects around you, are all you. Nondual experiences speak to the proverbial "unity consciousness" where you are the Divine, God, the Everything, the All. Likewise, when not in a nondual state of consciousness, you can step back and rationalize that you are one finger of the infinite divine hand of God. As we get into these subjects further, you will see how valuable having nondual experiences can be. They can create a broader perspective in which to relate to what is manifesting and increase one's comfort in sharing all the possible physical and psychic contents from another person.

Physical Energetic Contents

Being aware of your physical energy is also critical. This sounds simple enough: it is being aware of bodily sensations and of your body's movement, action, and location. However, when working with psychedelics, it can quickly become more complicated.

While mentioned only in brief here, an experienced mindmelder needs to be familiar with what has been more recently termed "fractal energetic yoga" in the psychedelic community (Ball, 2009, p. 88), or kundalini energy/yoga by Eastern traditions. Fractal energetic yoga is the free movement of the body that can occur after one has processed one's ego-based resistance to penetrating deeper into the layers of consciousness. The action is smooth and fluid. It can be both symmetrical and asymmetrical. The movements can reflect yoga-like positions or manifest as slow-moving dance, like qigong. These actions occur when the ego is relegated or transcended.

As discussed later, fractal energetic yoga can be disorienting to the uninitiated. It can feel like the body is possessed by something outside of itself, yet upon deeper observation, this is generally not the case. The movement comes from within as an internal way for the psyche and body to work together intuitively to move stuck and distorted energy. Not being familiar with fractal energetic yoga can lead to false narratives about the experience, which could lead to unnecessary confusion, drama, and trauma.

Working with a beginner requires a lot of briefing and debriefing to clarify these points and others outlined in this book. Having someone anchored in experience helps create a grounded sense of normalcy in the face of strangeness. In this context, having one person navigate the strangeness and difficulties calmly can offer serenity to the other person to help them more deeply explore their inner world.

3
Caveats

I am human. This statement may seem strange, but I want to emphasize that I have gone through profound life struggles and suffering, like everyone else, with my own flavor and intensity. Many of the stories in this book are fantastical and hard to believe. The experiences do not make me special, and I am not enlightened. I am simply human, one who is exploring our inherent capacities, seeking to grow, individuate, expand my sense of self, and experience loving connection, within myself, with others, and with the Divine. I also put effort into maintaining good physical and mental health to arrive at the highest level of homeostasis I can.

I have had the benefit of white male privilege, positioned comfortably in the middle class, grounded in the responsibilities of a career in senior management roles. Even so, I grew up in a home with an emotionally unavailable and abandoning father. While this trauma pales compared to many others, it still left a mark. The patriarchy of control was geared toward fundamentalist protestant religion, which I rejected. My father persecuted me for my choice. Love was discussed as an extension of the teachings of Jesus and the Church but not meaningfully practiced by my father, who was incapable of intimate connection. While I can look back and see he had my interest for "eternal salvation" at heart and provided for my living necessities, I lived a life estranged from him. My mother was much more supportive of me and had more liberal views. Her loving presence allowed me to become whatever I wanted without judgment. I became successful as measured by standard societal materialistic indicators, despite childhood struggles. My ceremonial use of psychedelics in my thirties contributed to addressing existential questions and angst and led me away from destructive habits like using alcohol.

Then, I suffered a major, life-changing injury in a severe traffic accident. I lost friends, my career in senior management roles in health and education, and the capacity to do many of the activities I enjoyed, including several sports, socializing in larger groups, attending public events, and international travel. My ego suffered a radical assault. My employer and the insurance company victimized me, which is commonplace for people with chronic health conditions in our performance- and profit-driven society. I cried daily for a year, half because of the sequelae of my injury and half because of egoic grief of loss. It wasn't until the end of the third year that the labiality stopped.

While I had been working with psychedelics for ten years and had experienced the dissolution of my ego on numerous occasions, I was not prepared for the horrors of the injury I suffered. All the masks were ripped off. The ego was fully exposed to an onslaught of grasping, shame, loss of self-esteem, and grief. I was stripped of social status but, more critically, deprived of the capacity to work and socially engage. I projected my struggles onto others with resentment and anger. Along the way, I often contemplated suicide to escape my pain. It has since been a long path of recovery. Psychedelics have helped, but only to a point. They are not a silver bullet, which is part of my point in sharing this story. But my journey in suffering and healing has provided a broader perspective, contributing to many of the ideas in this book in support of the mindmeld work.

I wanted to briefly share my personal story because this book is written partly to help us move toward personal growth, and I have found that many teachings on human development, be it religious, spiritual, or psychological, can create an image of the author as a "special" individual. But when digging deep enough, these illusions are usually quickly dispelled. The guru, teacher, leader, or psychologist turns out to be very human. Many are exposed for abuse (sexual, physical, or emotional), corruption, self-aggrandizement, lacking consistent loving awareness and attention (ironically, the opposite of what is proclaimed), or all of the above. In fact, several esoteric authors who are accepted teachers in their religion, and whom I have referenced in this book, have been exposed for alleged immoral or unethical behaviors or misconduct. Others have been exposed for their failures in human relationships, including family and friends. Many are more wholesome, but they all have their human failings, despite what they proclaim. I have repeatedly seen the human propensity to say or write one thing and do another. Nevertheless, these human failings do not trump the profound insights made by the people I reference.

This book takes an optimistic view of human development, high-lighting that we are all in it together, acknowledging our human short-comings, our shadows, and our traumas, but also our strengths to heal, learn, and become better people. I have learned personal development is not a linear process. Just when we think we have figured something out, the universe throws another hurdle at us. It is up to us to see our way to learning, finding meaning in our lives, and growing from our challenges.

Many traditions describe "liberation" as being liberated from the exclusive identification of the limited conscious, ego-driven self. There is no doubt the use of high-dose psychedelics can contribute to libera-tion, as they can help activate states of ego-dissolution. The Psychedelic Mindmeld holds this possibility as well. Once you have shared con-sciousness with another person, it is impossible to exclusively view the world through the disconnected individual experience constantly medi-ated by the ego. The further you explore shared and nondual states of consciousness, the more you awaken to your cosmic identity. Self-awareness expands, as do the domains of infinite realization.

This book provides many ideas and techniques. Even so, my intent is not to be overly prescriptive. For those with a background with psychedelics, much may be repetitive, but you may still find insights outside your experience or knowledge. The practices in this book should be seen as part of a more extensive repertoire of practices for self-growth. Chapter 15 presents thoughts on how best to integrate psychedelic experiences, and perhaps life experiences, into a more holistic approach to living.

As you will see throughout this book, my beliefs lean toward monism/pantheism, which comes to me through my experiences. As such, I often use the word "Divine" to refer to the universal intelligence and energy flowing through everything, and I capitalize it when using it in this way.

A final and more general caveat regards the challenge of language. Different wisdom traditions, philosophies, and academic approaches use identical words differently. I have tried to be clear in my definitions, show where there is overlap, and hope I do not add to the confusion. Some of my word choices and statements may also come across as hyperbole. For the uninitiated, I apologize. For the initiated, I trust my choices will resonate. We have to remember our experiences are subjective. It is often difficult to distinguish between fantasy and "reality." When science is shifting our understanding of human perception from first sensing an object and placing meaning on it, to first having meaning then placing it on objects in our experience, we are left with even more doubt about the nature of our lived experience (Peterson, 2022). My point here is that my interpretation (and yours) of my psychedelic experiences may be constructed before I, or you, even consciously have them. As such, presenting my experiences, or those of others, through language is tricky on multiple levels. What I offer in this book is primarily a technique to share consciousness; the rest is a view through my human mind, which is inherently limited. Realizing these limitations means recognizing we are at play in the field of "God" and infinite realization, a field strewn with mystery.

4

Ways of Engaging Consciousness Using Psychedelics

It is helpful to have the lay of the land when working with psychedelics. Below is a list of seven different ways to engage with psychedelics: (1) recreation; (2) creativity and problem-solving; (3) sex and sexuality; (4) healing; (5) exploration and "psychonautics"; (6) spirituality; and (7) nondual energetic therapy. All ways hold validity where valence ultimately lies in the intent and experience of the user. The first three ways involve extroversion, where participants project their awareness outside themselves into the world, even if their experiences are regulated by the internal self. The second four ways generally involve introversion, commonly through physical stillness and by focusing the mind inward at an intrapsychic level.

The distinction between extroversion and introversion matters because the mindmeld is generally an introverted way to work with psychedelics, but it can sometimes be extroverted. Also, what happens *after* the mindmeld during the second half of a session can incorporate aspects of the more extroverted ways of working with psychedelics (see suggestions in chapter 8 under the heading "Planning the Second Half of the Session").

While I have listed seven ways of engaging with psychedelics, all of them can overlap, depending on the user's intent and on how their experience unfolds. For example, someone may be using mushrooms *recreationally* and walking down the street on their way home from a party, when suddenly they experience an explosion of bliss and feel connected to everything in the universe—*a spiritual experience*. Having a broad understanding of the potential uses for psychedelics provides us with insight into what a mindmeld session can incorporate.

RECREATION

Recreational use is a common objective for using psychedelics. This type of use is casual, usually done in lower doses, and often done at parties, clubs, concerts, or raves, or it can include walks in nature or going to an art gallery or movie. It is not unusual for people to mix psychedelics with other substances, such as alcohol, ecstasy, or cannabis.

Recreational use can be fun and celebratory. There are many stories of people going to concerts where they experience *communitas*, or a relationship with community and humanity so profound it is like a shared rite of passage. The interpersonal connections in *communitas* can be so intense as to elicit collective joy and bliss, another form of telepathic sharing. Viewing art or walking in nature can reveal a depth of aesthetic appreciation previously hidden from the user.

However, recreational use is generally the least mindful of the uses. Using psychedelics recreationally is to use them like blunt tools, potentiating danger to the user. One challenge is that psychedelics open people up psychically. As such, it is easy to become overstimulated in highly stimulating environments that are loud, busy, and crowded, such as clubs, festivals, parties, or amusement parks. This type of overstimulation can lead to "bad trips," prompting unprepared users to unexpectedly confront the shadow side of their psyche, where untreated wounds from the past can burst forth and create longer-term adverse psychological effects. Such negative experiences can result in the person never wanting to do psychedelics again. Abstinence, unfortunately, means they will never get the chance to access the profundity of working with psychedelics in more productive, introverted, and meditative ways.

Being in uncontrolled environments also creates risks for the impaired user. It is easier to be in an accident, like falling and getting hurt. If a person has to go to a hospital or has a confrontation with a stranger or the police, the result can become a waking nightmare. Similarly to alcohol use, psychedelic use while driving a vehicle can also lead to accidents causing serious injury or death to oneself or others.

There is also a lack of scientific research on contraindications for using psychedelics with other substances. As such, the risk of mixing psychedelics with other substances is broadly not understood, which creates additional risk.

To enjoy the benefits of recreational use, one should be familiar with the particular psychedelic and its dosage in private and safe settings before experimenting with it in more volatile environments.

CREATIVITY AND PROBLEM-SOLVING

Psychedelics can be used to plumb the depths of human creativity and problem-solving—theoretically through the vast repositories of knowledge in the collective unconscious. Artists, architects, philosophers, writers, scientists, computer programmers, managers, and many others are increasingly using psychedelics to access the recesses of the mind and direct consciousness in novel ways to enhance innovation and cognitive performance. The intent is to break down conceptual barriers, dissolve culturally programmed limitations, and invoke new ways of thinking and creating (Grof, 2008, p. 267).

The use of psychedelics for enhancing performance was already being studied in the 1960s. One such study by James Fadiman (2011, p. 131) in 1966 found study participants' use of 100 micrograms of lysergic acid diethylamide (LSD) led to:

1. Lowering of defenses, reduction of inhibitions and anxiety (increasing ability to more freely explore novel ideas)
2. Ability to see a problem in the broadest terms
3. Enhanced fluency of ideation
4. Heightened capacity for visual imagery and fantasy
5. Increased ability to concentrate
6. Heightened empathy with other people
7. Greater accessibility of data from the unconscious
8. Enhanced sense of knowing when the right solution appears

But for anyone who has worked with psychedelics, hitting the sweet spot of a focused and open mind is not easy. Dosage matters, as does set and setting, as does experience working with psychedelics. In spite of the positive effects listed above, it is also possible to move in the opposite direction when working with psychedelics, toward diminished capacity for logical thought and concentration or a lessened ability to express aesthetic experiences (Fadiman, 2011, p. 122).

SEX AND SEXUALITY

Some people use psychedelics to enhance sex and sexuality. Physical sensations are often magnified during psychedelic trips, so it is not surprising that physical intimacy and pleasure can be radically amplified. Orgasm can reach an explosive ecstasy never imagined possible. For women who can experience multiple orgasms, ecstasy can feel like it transcends space-time into eternity.

I have had what is best described as cosmic sex with my wife, Isabel. The most fabulous peak experience was having an orgasm where I became pure energy and lost all connection to material reality; my consciousness entered unity consciousness, where there was no other, and all was one. We will cover more on nondual states of consciousness below, but the point here is using psychedelics in sexual activity can lead to ecstatic states beyond expectation or comprehension. A caveat, however, is that the inevitable return to "regular" sex can sometimes be a difficult adjustment after such peak experiences.

The dissolution of egoic boundaries by psychedelics also contributes to the overall intimacy in a sexual experience, so much so that it can lead to a mindmeld. But a word of caution: this method of connecting should only be done with an existing sexual partner. Because it is easy for people to feel sexually violated in the intimate space created by psychedelics, no one should ever engage sexually in the mindmeld without consent in advance of a session. Even if people consent before the session, there is a significant risk one person may change their mind partway through. Just as alcohol can impede a person's capacity to hear "no" and stop sexual advances, the same can happen with psychedelics.

A final note on sexuality is the possible surprise of changing gender roles and experiencing being the opposite sex, possibly feeling as though one is in a different body, or accessing a past life in a different gender role. While some people may fear such a possibility, it is an opportunity to explore the fluidity of gender and the strengths and challenges of the opposite sex and ultimately expand one's awareness of other realities.

HEALING

Using psychedelic plants for healing dates back to time immemorial. Shamans of all ages have worked with psychoactive plants to heal physical and mental illnesses in members of their communities.

In the modern context, the therapeutic use of psychedelics has been gaining momentum worldwide. Working therapeutically with psychedelics invites the conscious experiencing of our primal pain to process and resolve it more deeply. Here, we are not running away into escape and oblivion by using "drugs." Instead, we are diving straight into our unconscious and immersing ourselves in our suffering, facing what it is tempting to run away from. To work through trauma in this way is to reconnect more deeply with ourselves and foster greater self-awareness. Through greater self-awareness, we can find within ourselves wholeness, trust, love, compassion, and a sense of possibility. These rewards are rarely immediate or permanent, but patience and commitment to therapeutic work can lead us in our growth (Maté, 2021, p. xiv; Maté & Maté, 2022).

Scientific studies on the therapeutic use of psychedelics are showing promise for treating addiction, depression, post-traumatic stress disorder (PTSD), general tension, some forms of physical pain, sexual disorders, obsessive-compulsive disorder (OCD), cluster headaches, anxiety, sleep disturbance, and fear of death (Carhart-Harris et al., 2016a; 2016b; Fadiman, 2011; Griffiths et al., 2006; 2016; Goldsmith, 2011; Grof, 1976; 2008; 2009; 2019a; McCulloch et al., 2022; Miller, 2017; Read, 2021; Santos et al., 2016; Santos & Marques, 2021; Silverstone, 2022). Based on his research, Fadiman (2011, p. 283) points to other examples of positive results for people seeking to therapeutically improve activities in the following areas:

- Personal habits (e.g., healthier eating and drinking)
- Work and interpersonal relations (e.g., improved work patterns and productivity; better connection to people at work)
- Cultural and creative activities (e.g., heightened awareness of music, philosophy, spirituality)
- Activities involving family members (e.g., emotional connection, marital satisfaction, sexual satisfaction)
- Subjective activities (e.g., material values, introspective activities, fears, dreams)
- Physical functioning and health

Dr. Gabor Maté (2021) reports that psychedelic plants, such as ayahuasca, can also cure physical ailments such as the autoimmune diseases rheumatoid arthritis and multiple sclerosis.

Various research studies have investigated the use of hypnosis while working with psychedelics to improve therapeutic outcomes of psychedelic therapy—and are showing success (Lemercier & Terhune, 2018; Levine & Ludwig, 1965).

As will be seen in chapters 10 and 11, the mindmeld has the potential to potentiate therapeutic benefits through the release and discharge of stored or blocked physical and psychic energies. Similarly, I have seen people I have worked with find healing in several of the challenges listed above and move toward healthier personal habits.

EXPLORATION AND "PSYCHONAUTICS"

Psychedelics can be used to explore consciousness. In some ways, the mindmeld is part of this exploration but as a mapping of shared consciousness.

Psychonauts use holotropic states of consciousness to explore the human condition and potential, gain deeper insights into our inner nature, and have spiritual experiences. Not all psychonauts use psychedelics. Psychedelics are a tool. Many people explore consciousness using other tools such as breathing techniques, lucid dreaming, meditation, hypnosis, past and future life journeys, shamanic journeying, and more. (Near-death experiences, while not purposefully induced, also produce similar psychonautical experiences.) Those who use psychedelics typically work with high or "breakthrough" doses of a particular psychedelic or a mix of them, usually accompanied by an introverted or meditative technique.

As discussed throughout this book, once one is in a holotropic state of consciousness, all sorts of things can occur. People may work through layers of their unconscious material, perhaps reconciling various emotions or traumas, or having a life review, such as witnessing and reliving different past moments. The internal dialogue can also dissolve, creating greater depth, newness, and freshness in the present moment, where it is possible to be more in touch with one's essential self without words or labels. From here, one may connect to psi abilities, like telepathy or

clairvoyance. People may experience synesthesia: experiencing one physical sense as another, such as hearing music as shapes or tasting colors.
It is also possible to go much further and experience being an animal,
a plant, a microorganism, DNA, a crystal, subatomic particles, or the
elements of earth, water, fire, air, or to enter or become the inside of a
machine or computer. At more profound levels, these experiences can
morph into events of evolution—of animal or botanical kingdoms or
even our planet's development or the expansion of the whole universe
(Grof, 1976; 2009). Just as spontaneously, one can enter portals (e.g.,
the tunnel of light) to other worlds, including lower and upper shamanic realms, machine worlds, or other planets and dimensions. Such
exploration can reveal the multiverse, which is filled with discarnate
beings of great variety. To the psychonaut, these beings are paradoxical:
good and evil, benign and frightening, guiding and warning, protective
and maddening (Harpur, 2003). They can be any of these things and
more and can shift polarity seamlessly.

Campbell (2008) describes this pendulum shift within us as part of
the primordial nature of the universe:

> from the standpoint of the cosmogonic cycle, a regular alternation
> of fair and foul is characteristic of the spectacle of time. Just as in
> the history of the universe, so also in that of nations: emanation
> leads to dissolution, youth to age, birth to death, form-creative vital-
> ity to the dead weight of inertia. Life surges, precipitating forms,
> and then ebbs, leaving jetsam behind. The golden age, the reign of
> the world emperor, alternates, in the pulse of every moment of life,
> with the waste land, the reign of the tyrant. The god who is the
> creator becomes the destroyer in the end (p. 302).

Polarity is the nature of duality and affects us all the time, turning back and forth, often on a dime. Awareness and acceptance of this
unstoppable force are potent tools for the psychonaut, especially in the
mindmeld.

When cruising the multiverse, people can also experience "downloads" of esoteric information. Such downloads can include healing abilities, past or future life information, prophetic visions, or archetypal messages or insights. Some examples of archetypal experiences are the hero's journey, the Great Mother, the Terrible Mother, the great flood, the resurrection of godly or spiritual figures, or apocalyptic visions.

Psychonauts can also enter nondual states of consciousness, experiencing the oneness of all reality. For the true psychonaut, there are no boundaries to the exploration, so slipping in and out of the dual and nondual experience is par for the course.

SPIRITUALITY

Since the dawn of humanity, humans have used psychedelics as tools to access the sacred and profane. According to Schultes et al. (1998), almost two hundred plants with distinct psychoactive properties are growing worldwide (p. 30). With broad global access to psychedelics, no doubt cultures wanting to seek personal experiences of the Divine that lead to higher states of insight, knowledge, and illumination could do so.

In a religious or spiritual context, a more modern name for psychedelics is "entheogens." Entheogen is a word derived from Greek referring to realizing or connecting to the god within.

Religious and spiritual use is usually done in groups following a ceremonial modality and embedded in a local tradition. Rituals, songs, chants, prayer, and devotion are usually culturally driven and form the ceremonial context for ingesting the entheogen of choice. Rituals can include prescribed diets and abstinence from sex.

In traditional cultures, there is generally no distinction between spiritual use and "therapeutic" use. Both are intertwined, and connecting to spirit using psychedelic plants is a way to seek healing. Even the plants used in ceremonies are considered to have consciousness, with inherent healing qualities for physical ailments.

Some modern religions incorporate the use of entheogens. In the case of the Native American Church, peyote is the entheogen of choice. For the modern Santo Daime religion of Brazil, it is ayahuasca. For the Rastafarians of Jamaica, it is cannabis. In these instances of religious worship, a syncretic mix of shamanic and Christian beliefs and rituals produces states of healing and self-transformation. These numinous experiences invoke awe and terror, eliciting respect, wonder, and worship (Ball, 2017, p. 23). Examples of more traditional spiritual use of psychedelic plants include the Mazatecs' use of psilocybin mushrooms, the Amahuaca and Jivaro's use of ayahuasca, and the Bwitists' use of iboga.

Just as psychonautical use can lead to encounters with discarnate beings, so too can religious and spiritual use, which illustrates the overlap of experience among the intended purposes of using psychedelics. People with religious or spiritual intent often interpret a connection with other beings or worlds through the lens of a cultural history or dogma that more rigidly defines the significance of the encounter. According to Blackmore, encounters with other beings or worlds, regardless of the use of psychedelics or not, tend to fit with people's cultural upbringing and education. "For example, Christians more often report seeing Jesus, angels and a door or gateway to heaven, while Hindus are more likely to meet the king of the dead and his messengers, the Yamdoots" (Blackmore, 2012, p. 405). But as Grof (1976; 2009; 2019b) points out, it is also possible to reach into the collective unconscious and across cultural boundaries into phenomena that users are unfamiliar with, although this is less likely.

There is also a dark side to the spiritual use of psychedelics. While using psychedelics is not necessary to perform dark arts or black magic, some black witches, sorcerers, or *brujos* use them. Their focus is on increasing power, often for their narcissistic self-aggrandizement. They use their psychic abilities malevolently to attack or manipulate people usually out of rivalry, revenge, resentment, jealousy, envy, greed, or lust. For example, sorcery can be used to try to gain wealth from others or manipulate people into love (Beyer, 2010; Luke, 2019).

Another dark side to the spiritual use of psychedelics in both traditional and more modern spiritual settings is sexual abuse and sexual misconduct. In recent years there have been multiple media reports on sexual abuse and sexual misconduct in ceremonial settings. Such abuse emphasizes the need for diligence and caution when working with others and using psychedelics, especially because they make users more vulnerable, not unlike alcohol and other drugs. And sadly, finding a fully safe container for spiritual use is not easy. Even the therapeutic use of working with psychedelics has started to see issues with therapists acting out sexually with test subjects or clients. As horrific as this is, it should not be surprising, as sexual abuse has been uncovered in most religious organizations. Obvious examples include the Catholic Church and various Hindu/Yoga and Buddhist organizations.

The foregoing descriptions of spiritual use of psychedelics demonstrate how the intent behind using psychedelics as tools influences the psychic mechanics of outcomes, both positively and negatively, depending on practitioner intent. In the same way, we can work with positive or negative intent in life more generally, but because psychedelics are psychic amplifiers, it is essential to be grounded in your intent for using psychedelics, which is discussed further in chapter 7 under the heading "Setting Intention."

NONDUAL ENERGETIC THERAPY

Martin Ball has pioneered the use of 5-MeO-DMT (5-methoxy-N, N-dimethyltryptamine) for what he describes as nondual energetic therapy. According to Ball (2017), nondual therapy leads to "lasting liberation and personal transformation that frees the individual from the restraining and persistent confines of the energetic structures of the ego" (p. 26). For Ball, the pinnacle of psychedelic use is the total absorption into nonduality. In this context Ball refers to 5-MeO-DMT as the "God molecule." Nondual realization exposes the numinous and all other forms of psychedelic use as lower-order levels of experience in which the ego is still active and present. Regarding religious or spiritual use, nondual absorption reveals nothing to worship or obey because there is only one universal self in which everything exists. The appearance of spirits, entities, and deities is simply a manifestation of the universal self—in other words, they are all "YOU" (p. 23).

Ball (2017) describes how all people, caught in duality, carry pent-up and unreleased energy due to the editing and censoring functions of the ego. These blocked energies prevent us from experiencing and expressing ourselves genuinely and authentically—and accepting the authenticity of others without being triggered. Through careful, continuous work of self-observation and energetic expression and by regularly working with 5-MeO-DMT and other psychedelics, it is possible to unwind the energetic patterns associated with ego-driven suffering in pain, judgment, fear, anxiety, frustration, dissatisfaction, and more. If successful, one can break through the artificial construct of the individual self, the persona, and find an infinite unitary state of love, awareness, personal honesty, and authentic being.

In practice, nondual energetic therapeutic use involves taking three to four higher or breakthrough doses of 5-MeO-DMT in a session. After taking a dose, usually by smoking (but insufflation and plugging anally are also options), the person lies on their back and surrenders to the experience, allowing movement of the energy induced by the 5-MeO-DMT and relegation of the ego to flow and clear energetic blockages in the human vehicle. Multiple sessions over months and years can release energetic blockages and help free up a more authentic, healthier individual.

Similarly to the Psychedelic Mindmeld, nondual energetic therapeutic use can be done in pairs. The format is for each person to lie on their back in corpse pose, or śavāsana, with arms by their side and legs shoulder-width apart, facing each other in symmetry with the soles of their feet, about one foot away from each other. Both participants dose the 5-MeO-DMT simultaneously and lie on their backs. The onset is extremely fast when smoking or using insufflation, occurring in seconds. If and when the fractal energetic yoga (see chapter 10) happens, there is an energetic entrainment. One person will spontaneously move up over the other person and begin clearing energetic blockages from them in the form of deep intuitive massage. Energetically clearing others using 5-MeO-DMT is advanced work, and I suggest it is mandatory to first read Martin Ball's work *Entheogenic Liberation: Unraveling the Enigma of Nonduality with 5-MeO-DMT Energetic Therapy* (2017).

Ball's work is groundbreaking and revolutionary. Much of what Ball has explored in nondual therapy also shows up in the mindmeld. What I am presenting in this book is, in some ways, an adjunct to what Ball has explored.

What differentiates this book from his is that I don't consider the mindmeld primarily as a therapeutic approach to working with psychedelics, although the mindmeld can have therapeutic outcomes. Further, much of the experience in the mindmeld is dualistic, where there is generally a definite subject and object in awareness. While the mindmeld can result in layers of nondual experience, it is not the primary destination but one of many destinations. As such, this book explores layers of experience and compares such experiences to each other, whereas Ball makes some absolute conclusions about the nature of reality from the perspective of radical nonduality. A further differentiation is that Ball outlines a narrow set of qualifications to be a nondual energetic practitioner, while the mindmeld is more open-sourced as a co-creative exploration of consciousness.

A valuable insight Ball (2017; 2022) highlights is that working with 5-MeO-DMT can energetically open people up for more expansive experiences during later use with other psychedelics. This greater expansiveness is certainly my experience and the experience of most people I have worked with. I encourage participants to go through a 5-MeO-DMT session a few days or weeks in advance of a mindmelding session when that session will involve working with other psychedelics like magic mushrooms, LSD, or ayahuasca. 5-MeO-DMT not only opens people up energetically immediately when using it, but it appears to have long-term and lasting effects on many people. As such, previous use of 5-MeO-DMT can help relegate a person's ego in later experiences with other psychedelics and help them more easily enter the mindmeld.

5

A Revolutionary Approach to Working with Psychedelics

Why do I say the mindmeld is revolutionary? Revolution refers to a radical change to the status quo. The mindmeld offers a radical new approach for two people to co-creatively engage with psychedelics to actively and jointly explore consciousness. This approach encourages people to work together purposefully and cooperatively to break down the perceived barriers and limits of self and other at energetic and psychic levels. Here, psychedelics are tools that we use in a structured way to foster telepathic joining and symbiosis. In so doing, two people can begin to dissolve the nature of duality and the distinction between subject and object where the intrapsychic experience of one individual is increasingly shared with the other at an interpsychic level. "I" becomes "We." And "We" becomes a nondual "I." It then becomes possible for the mind to break free from the limiting chains of the mundane into the unbounded sphere of the cosmos and a greater shared realization.

There are two central shared and revolutionary opportunities in the Psychedelic Mindmeld experience: (1) interenergetic shared physical experiences and (2) interpsychic shared visionary experiences. In other words, it is possible to share the energetic patterning of the other person at a physiological level, including physical and emotional sensing, processing, and releasing. Further, it is also possible for two people to meditate together with their eyes closed and telepathically share the same visions and interact with each other in the visionary space, sometimes to the point where there is no separation between one another and nondual experiences can arise. This is to enter the real world of magic—a place not of tricks but of mind-bending intuitive and creative potential. Both of these experiences can overlap with each other. These experiences are described in detail in chapters 10 and 11.

Seeking to have such experiences is revolutionary because they are largely unheard of, which means the vast majority of people on the planet do not even know they can begin to explore these layers of shared consciousness. Most people do not realize the extremely complex nature and capacity of their body, brain, and consciousness more generally and that they can explore the universe *together* by closing their eyes and inducing shared consciousness. For those few who may be aware of such possibilities, even fewer have tried it. Yogis of the Eastern wisdom traditions claim to reach telepathic states. Usually this requires many years of meditative practice and, often, particular exercises and diets. These practices are steeped in traditional beliefs and involve hierarchical systems where only the advanced initiates are supposed to reach these and other states of *high* consciousness. Yet, psychedelics can get people to the same states with little or no meditation practice. Fundamentally, we are changing the chemical balance in the brain to enhance access to these states, whether using meditation, psychedelics, or a variety of other methods to induce holotropic states of consciousness.

While I respect the Eastern traditions and what they work toward embodying through meditation—a focused mind, peace, loving compassion, and higher levels of realization, for example—what I am describing in this book is revolutionary because the mindmeld strips away some of the mystery and glorification often ascribed to gurus for their psychic abilities. We can all access these telepathic and nondual states of consciousness without years of meditation. Working with psychedelics as tools to reach these states is not a "shortcut," as often proclaimed by the naïve or those enslaved by the dogmas of tradition, but a valid, often demanding, and immediate way to access our divinely inherent capacities—our internal freeware. No religion, cults, or gurus are needed. The inner guru and inner healer are in you. What meditation experience can do is help one center oneself in the psychedelic experience and more readily penetrate deeper into the mind, as will be discussed in chapters 9 and 12.

What is just as revolutionary is the suggestion people *should* attempt to work together in this way with psychedelics. Using psychedelics to purposely enhance "psi" abilities is largely unheard of, despite it often being anecdotally reported or limited to a relatively small number of research studies over decades (Aiken, 2016; Krippner & Watts, 2006; Luke, 2019; McKenna, 1992; Puharich, 1973; Tart, 1993). Fadiman (2011) and Grof (1976; 2008; 2019a), for example, have reported that telepathy can commonly arise in psychedelic journeys, but there is resistance to acknowledging and studying it. Johnstad (2020) and Luke (2019) highlight the underutilization of psychedelics for exploring psi phenomena, including telepathy, and the dearth of research in the area. In other words, the mindmeld approach upsets the given paradigm or the dominant and assumed legitimate values, beliefs, and assumptions of how humans can, should, and do interact with each other while using psychedelics. As described above, the dominant paradigm of people taking psychedelics is generally to do so only in reference to one's own experience at an intrapsychic level. The mindmeld is an interpsychic engagement and exchange. The following paragraphs more clearly illustrate this point.

A good example of intrapsychic use is the developing model of therapeutic healing with psychedelics. In this regard, there is usually a paid guide, likely a health professional, and their client/patient. While this field is evolving as legalization takes shape for the therapeutic use of psychedelics, the expected norm is the client/patient paying thousands of dollars to take a psychedelic in a regulated and safe environment with a health professional supervising and observing them. The health professional's work would incorporate briefing and debriefing the client/patient, presumably while using therapeutic tools. But what is key to highlight for our purposes is that the client is doing the psychedelic therapeutic work essentially in isolation, generally using a form of meditation, often blindfolded, to observe their internal experience. The process occurs *without* the health professional simultaneously using a psychedelic or generally interfering in the client/patient experience while they are most heavily engaged with the psychedelic. Any form of physical touch is meant to be highly regulated to avoid external distraction but also to avoid issues of sexual abuse or to trigger memories of past sexual/physical abuse.* Any physical or therapeutic touch is discussed ahead of time with the client.†

In religious or spiritual use, there is usually a paid leader or shaman. Participants are encouraged to meditate and focus on their internal experience, although there are rare exceptions. Typically in traditional plant-based shamanic ceremonies (e.g., ayahuasca, peyote, iboga), people sit or lie down and begin meditating once they have ingested the psychedelic. Usually, participants are instructed not to touch anybody else during the ceremony. It is only the shaman(s) or lead practitioner(s) who are allowed to move around the group and offer healing or consoling "touch" to participants.

---

*An exception to pushing physical boundaries in the therapeutic setting is fusion therapy, developed by Joyce Martin and Pauline McCririck in the 1960s. Fusion therapy is for patients who suffered childhood abandonment and emotional deprivation in their infancy. In therapy, clients take medium dosages of LSD. Then, the therapist lies parallel to them and holds them in a close embrace, like a loving parent would do with their child. While this therapeutic approach never caught on for ethical reasons, Grof (2019b) reports that fusion therapy was an effective way to deal with trauma related to anaclitic deprivation or trauma by omission (p. 11).

†Research shows therapeutic touch (e.g., hand-holding or resting a hand on the arm or head) is beneficial in creating a safe and trusting environment, especially if the client has struggled with past attachment issues or abandonment. If therapeutic touch is not offered at a critical moment, it can result in distress and retraumatization (Grof, 2009; 2019a; Mithoefer, 2017).

There are obvious reasons for this approach to touch; the chief among them is safety. Often, people in these ceremonies have just met each other. Apprehension is high. Trust is low. Entering a holotropic state of consciousness is already a harrowing ordeal. Unexpected touch could be traumatizing for some individuals, possibly giving rise to sexual abuse or triggering memories of past sexual/physical abuse.

Shamans also have a deeper concern about physical contact among participants during a ceremony: the possibility of making a psychic connection that no one is ready for. Shamans already have much to do in regulating all participants' individual experiences into the unknown. While incidental telepathic connections can occur, they are not encouraged because of their complexity.

Two dynamics separate the mindmeld approach from those described above: (1) people are encouraged to engage interpsychically, which includes physical touch and (2) it is a co-creative process of joint engagement, attunement, and communion. In the first case, participants explore new territory, including sharing physiological and interpsychic states, considered forbidden territory in therapeutic modalities and most traditions. In the second case, people are meeting each other as equals, which is also highly unusual: normally, there is a power dynamic of a paid expert—the therapist, leader, or shaman—leading the way. This unequal footing sets up a complex hierarchy. Hierarchy introduces the risk of dominance, expertise inflation, inappropriate submission, objectification, and manipulation. In and of itself, hierarchy is a normal approach to spiritual teaching and learning and all therapeutic models. Hierarchy has its place in ceremonies, a therapist's office, and the world more generally. It is, then, revolutionary to work toward dismantling this hierarchy using the co-creative approach of equals sharing in a transformative process. Both people are "in it" together and in this space directly supporting each other. Mutual support is empowering to both participants. Here, a therapeutic, healing alliance of peers is formed without cost in a world of high-priced therapists and psychedelic ceremonies. Such an approach does not undermine or invalidate the value of these other approaches, which all have something to offer, but simply adds another valid approach to human connection and healing.

Ceremonial settings rarely allocate much one-on-one time to individuals. In the mindmeld as a coupled dyad, there can be a deeply felt sense of authenticity and reciprocity in the experience, where challenges are witnessed, shared, and confronted, as are joys and other emotional states. In the fusion, we can experience the humanity in the other and find an acceptance of it in ourselves, including our beauty, greatness, and darkness. There is a mutual practice of giving and receiving. Each person can be profoundly validated by actually being felt and heard by the other, in mind and body, something not possible in standard therapy. Attunement and mirroring in the process can give rise to permission to feel what you feel. Even more, when two energetic beings work together as equals in this co-creative process, there is potential for a greater potency than with either person alone. The narcissistic trap of self-absorption in one's trauma and suffering can, in part, be released by being in healing together, each contributing to a greater wholeness than just themselves. This is not to distinguish the Psychedelic Mindmeld as better than the other approaches described above, only that the co-creative approach is radically different from accepted norms, particularly in its potential mutuality.

To go a step further, the mindmeld can also engender loving relationship, which again takes a revolutionary leap away from the traditional and institutional approaches described above. People yearn for loving connection as one of our deepest-felt needs. Scott Peck defines love as "the will to extend one's self for the purpose of nurturing one's own or another's spiritual growth" (in hooks, 2018, p. 4). The mindmeld can give rise to a loving connection between two participants who are on a joint spiritual journey of exploring their own and the other's body, mind, and spirit—contributing to the personal growth of both participants. The love I am suggesting is not a sexual or romantic love, or any fleeting "feeling" of love, but an intimate loving connection. Love is the expression of oneness in the mindmeld. Both participants engage in the co-creative process with shared intention and action. The process demands care, affection, recognition, respect, commitment, trust, and open communication, all ingredients of a loving relationship (hooks, 2018). I'm not implying participants need to or should become lifelong friends after this type of experience, but one has to be prepared to explore the nature of intimacy in new and profound ways. How participants develop friendships after the experience(s) is up to them, recognizing, in the long run, a loving relationship also requires constancy, reciprocity, and commitment.

It's crucial to highlight that revolution is not without risks. Here we must confront the awesomeness of psychedelics' positive and negative potential. In the mindmeld, two minds are joining to explore the mysterious unconscious contents of two separate individuals—*together*. This is a big deal. Before moving on, I will briefly describe the challenge of revolutionary dynamics because they introduce areas for both caution and possibility.

By its nature, revolution introduces radical change. Radical change can lead in both negative and positive directions. Radical change forces us into unexplored territory. In stepping into the unexplored, we voluntarily open ourselves up to the chaos of the unknown. Chaos can elicit profound fears. Chaos can shake the foundations of who we think we are—our underlying constructs of self. In chaos, there is often a complete loss of self-control and feelings of being so overwhelmed that the only desire is escape. Chaos may reveal hidden shadow sides of our unconscious or old traumas, which may be frightening and onerous to confront and process, never mind accept. Dark archetypal energies or beings, or other negative experiences, may manifest when entering the unconscious's unexplored territory. If our psychological foundations of personal identity are dislodged or shattered, we may experience negative traumatic effects. Personal truths we don't feel ready for may be revealed. Trauma may lead to conscious contraction or restriction (e.g., in reaction to the dismantling of the ego or exposure to fear of the undesired), resulting in psychological dysfunction. But our destroyed sense of self can also lead to rebuilding.

To find our way through the chaos, through trauma, we can expand and transform ourselves. We can find new levels of courage. Entering exceptional nonnormative circumstances can culminate in the rewriting of our entire internal story, guiding affective evaluation and behavioral programming—including the rewiring of neuronal connections. Revolution can, therefore, be a double-edged sword—one of disintegration as well as integration and renewal. To dare to take this revolutionary path is to transcend fear and its associated torment, embrace courage and faith, and open ourselves to experiencing new revelations (Peterson, 1999).

So, let us be revolutionaries and work toward shifting the working model of our reality for the benefit of not only ourselves but all.

6
Finding the Right Partner

Finding the right partner is critical to preparing for the Psychedelic Mindmeld. You want to know what the other person's prerequisites are, and you want to share yours with them. Refer to the list I provided in chapter 2 and ask lots of questions. Remember, the prerequisites I have listed are only guidelines. There are no hard and fast rules. There is no "perfect" setup for starting this work. Use your discretion, discrimination, and intuition.

You will want to know the other person's experience and motivations. How much experience does the person have working with psychedelics, and what have their experiences been like? For example, anybody who has worked often with psychedelics will have had some challenges. Someone who has had only positive and blissful experiences, or only difficult experiences, should not be considered well rounded in the work. What other techniques have they used to enter holotropic states? What kind of a meditation background do they have? Do they have a regular meditation practice, or have they only been to one meditation retreat? In chapters 9 and 12, I describe meditative techniques to help initiate and sustain the flow of the mindmeld; at a minimum, you ideally want to work with someone who can sit completely still for at least an hour while meditating without using psychedelics.

It is important to ask what motivates your potential partner to do psychedelics. Why do they want to try the mindmeld? Are they engaged in a process of genuine personal growth? Or are their motives recreational, part of enhancing a cult of personality narrative, focused on seeking to control others, part of a personal "mission" (e.g., savior complex), or some other ego-driven priority? How have holotropic experiences impacted their worldview? How have holotropic experiences changed their life? For example, is there greater expansiveness, meaning, openness, and love in their life from doing the work? Or is there a perception of self-aggrandizement, delusion, possibly paranoia, or excessive judgment and criticism? Is there a well balanced sense of growth and connection to others in responsibility and play, or is there an exhibition of exclusivity and superiority?

What is the status of their physical and mental health? Answering this question may be more difficult than others. Nobody is perfect, and we all have struggles. We all have layers of trauma to work through and heal from. Healing is part of the reason for doing this work. In this context, ask yourself if the other person is someone who cares about and is motivated to be physically and mentally healthy. Do they work on fostering healthy habits for their body and mind? Or are they caught up in unhealthy addictions and not taking care of themselves, either physically or mentally? Are they working with constructive and healthy ways to emotionally regulate and self-reflect, or are they lost in unhealthy patterns of self-neglect and unconscious of their emotional regulation choices? For example, a cultural norm for emotional regulation is drinking alcohol or smoking commercial tobacco. Because of the toxic nature of these drugs (and others like tranquilizers and amphetamines), I recommend not engaging in the mindmeld with anybody who drinks or smokes regularly.* Furthermore, addiction to these substances usually reflects

---

*Dr. Andrew Huberman, a Stanford neuroscientist, discusses the latest neuroscientific findings that drinking even low to moderate amounts of alcohol over time has multiple profound negative impacts on the brain and body, inclusive of physical and mental health: "What Alcohol Does to Your Body, Brain & Health," *Huberman Lab Podcast* #86. Huberman also discusses the negative effects of tobacco: "Nicotine's Effects on the Brain & Body & How to Quit Smoking or Vaping," *Huberman Lab Podcast* #90.

profound trauma and hidden dark energies. It may be challenging for you to navigate such trauma in the mindmeld if it manifests. It is best if they don't drink or smoke at all, given the toxicity of these substances and how they can undermine a deeper exploration of consciousness. People taking SSRIs should also be avoided, as these drugs are generally contraindicated for use with psychedelics and are a signpost for acute depression and, possibly, personality disorders.

You also want to understand who the other person is in terms of personality and values. Are they well grounded, emotionally literate, and socially mature? For example, do they have a calm and patient presence where they listen and validate you? Or are they irrational, paranoid, excessively neurotic, frenetic, easily agitated and triggered, or easily distracted and struggling to listen? Or maybe they are risk-takers who may expose you to unnecessary hazards. Are they caring, compassionate, and empathetic, or manipulative, domineering, condescending, and narcissistic? Are they someone who will engage you in a co-creative partnership to cooperatively design the session? Or are they self-indulgent and everything has to be done their way? Do they have balanced and lasting relationships built on trust, respect, and open, honest, and constructive communication? Or are they caught in dysfunctional relationships of projection, attachment, delusion, and excessive conflict? Do they show signs of being responsible and reliable; for example, they have a family, are gainfully employed, and participate in the community? If challenges arise during the session, will they be there with a calming and accepting presence to help you? This may not always be possible if the other person is absorbed in an ecstatic state, but you want to know they will do everything they can to offer aid if required. Suppose conflicts or misunderstandings arise during the session, including, for example, unexpected feelings of abandonment or betrayal or a sense of inappropriate touch. Will the other person be able to meaningfully and humbly talk, work through, and repair any interpersonal rupture afterward? Is there openness to forgiveness? Are they open to following up after the session for ongoing debriefing?

Answers to these questions are fundamental. But what is most critical in choosing a partner is being able to trust them. Someone who can be trusted is dependable and truthful and will act with integrity to protect you. Trust provides a sense of safety when you are vulnerable, which is critical for letting go of psychological defenses and opening up in the mindmeld. Trust is the most crucial prerequisite for an effective and positive outcome in the mindmeld. In this context, potential participants may consider doing this work with spouses, partners, family members, or close friends to explore and develop interpersonal connection more deeply with people they already inherently trust.

Working with the wrong partner can result in horrifically adverse and traumatizing events. Worst-case scenarios could include sexual or physical assault. Verbal assault, emotional manipulation, or abuse could occur. Psychic assault through hypnogenic telepathic interaction (purposely inducing a mental state in another) is also possible, in which a person could try to control or manipulate your thoughts, either in or outside the mindmeld. Another negative outcome could be inappropriate or false sexual assault or abuse allegations meted out in spite. If things get problematic for the other person during the session, they could leave the premises and abandon you. If things go poorly, the other person may gossip about you and undermine your reputation in the community. While hopefully none of these things will happen, know there is a risk. Some risks can be mitigated by working out safety protocols and establishing clear sexual and physical boundaries before the session, which is discussed further in chapter 8.

You should also reflect on the questions above to help make sure you are the right person to engage with others in this work.

I have reflected on these questions and can see some of myself in both sides of what I have asked. Such contradiction or hypocrisy is innately part of being human and living in the flux of polarity in duality. I encourage you to be open and honest, which I have tried to do in sharing my stories. As fantastical as my stories are—and I know others have had similar experiences—it is helpful to keep things in context. I have had moments of internal self-aggrandizing, times of thinking I have a divine mission. I have never assaulted anybody in any way, but there has been sexual tension requiring restraint. Concurrently, I have matured in understanding my ego and projections over the years. Perhaps there is a "grand" mission of healing and evolution of consciousness for our species as a whole, and perhaps there isn't. As a theme in this book, I encourage participants to carry their stories and meanings loosely.

For now, in terms of looking for a partner, remember that we are all in the process of growing up and maturing. We need to meet each other where we are with acceptance and encouragement. As in all other areas of life, there will be bumps in the road. There will be misunderstandings, disagreements, and differences. The question is: How ready are we to show up maturely to address issues as they come to the fore, repair them, and continue in relationship? The mindmeld has the potential for self-growth and growth in relationship. Let's look to maximize such potential.

While finding an appropriate mindmelding partner is not the same as finding the right life-long partner, do not underestimate finding a good fit. Be patient. Don't be afraid to ask personal and sensitive questions. If a person is not open to answering intimate questions, they are not likely to be vulnerable and openly meet you in the profound intimacy of the mindmeld.

7
Understanding Your Set

Understanding and preparing for both set and setting are integral to any psychedelic experience, especially the Psychedelic Mindmeld. Set refers to one's mindset or psychic state, including the understanding and intention behind using psychedelics, while setting typically refers to the physical and social environment and the logistics for a psychedelic session. Each is discussed in turn in this and the next chapter.

A person's mindset ("set") or mental state, including mood or emotional orientation, attitudes toward themselves and others present in a session, idiosyncratic perceptions, motivations, intentions, and expectations, plays a major role in their psychedelic journey. Another dimension to set is a person's biography. Biography is defined by a person's current life situation, including socioeconomic status, gender, race, culture, and life history, including the perinatal period, infancy, and early childhood experiences. All of these dimensions can come forward to directly and profoundly influence what transpires in a psychedelic session (Grof, 1976; 2009). These biographical dimensions of set generally manifest unconsciously in psychedelic sessions and, as such, are out of our control. Because of this, the discussion of set will focus on those things we need to be aware of and can influence going into the mindmeld. How biographical dimensions can affect set and what can manifest in the mindmeld will be discussed further in chapters 10, 11, and 13.

Because ego plays a profound role in "set" that includes mediating the overall experience—especially attitudes, perceptions, motivations, and ultimately surrender into the mindmeld—it is discussed first. This is followed by a discussion on the preparatory work of setting intention, which is related to attitudes, perceptions, motivations, and expectations. I then discuss a few points about ritual and finish with considerations for one's mental state, including emotional orientation on the day of the session, and how often one should do this work. Each of these points should be considered during a briefing before the session.

THE EGO

It is necessary to discuss the concept of the ego because it is such a profound part of who we are and because of how we must navigate the ego to drop into the Psychedelic Mindmeld and maintain it. The ego is pervasive: it directly impacts our relationship with ourselves, at both physiological and psychic energetic levels, how we relate to the material world outside ourselves, and how we relate to others, including how we express ourselves. The ego helps us mediate the mindmeld, but paradoxically it also must be navigated so its executive role is moderated from its usual place at the top of the pecking order where it constantly seeks to direct an individual's conscious awareness. While psychedelics are a powerful tool for relegating the ego's dominant position from the citadel of our conscious awareness, the ego still has to cooperate in surrendering its executive role for the mindmeld to work. Ironically, understanding the nature of the ego helps provide the ego comfort to mentally relax its sense of control, ease its concomitant pathology to want to know all the answers, and surrender into the mindmeld.

So, what is the ego? At a minimum, we can construe the ego to be the part of consciousness discerning the individual self in duality. The ego distinguishes between subject and object, between "me" and "other." If human consciousness is one's awareness of the contents and quality, the affect, of internal and external existence, then the ego is the mediator of individual consciousness. This means the ego can choose where to focus the point of awareness where subject and object are in view. Being the mediator of consciousness is a big deal. It places the ego in the executive role of mediating our lived experience. In this role, the ego plays two fundamental functions: (1) it navigates our inner and outer world while interfacing between the two and (2) through time and space, it discerns and defines selfhood and personality. I will discuss each of these functions in turn, and then discuss a further element of the ego, which is that it does not need to relate to the body to have a sense of self. With a greater understanding of the ego, I will discuss in chapter 9 techniques to relegate the ego's executive role to facilitate entry into the mindmeld.

Ego as the Navigator of Our Inner and Outer Worlds

The ego does not exist in a vacuum. As the mediator of our lived experience the ego is inextricably linked to the unconscious instincts and drives of our inner world—our bodily needs, wants, emotional impulses, passions, and desires (i.e., motivations, inclinations, attachments, cravings, and aversions)—what Sigmund Freud (2019) refers to as the "id." The most prominent of these drives is human will and the drive for self-preservation, which arises from the life force propelling the evolution of life in nature.* From human will, volition and agency emanate. Volition leads us in action, inclusive of behavior, to produce an effect, and agency in turn, affects the ownership of our actions. The ego mediates our experience of volition and agency. It can also

---

*Closely associated with this drive are the drives of creativity and sexuality and, in polarity, aggression and the death drive, or the primordial drive returning organic life back into the inanimate state (Freud, 2019).

co-opt our inherent mental capacities—including our attention, perception, cognition, thought, reason, intellect, memory, interoception, and chronoception—and our ability to move, act, and communicate. For Freud (2019), this means the ego controls the approaches to motility—the discharge of our energy or excitations into the external world. It is the part of you constantly commenting on your experience, dialoguing in your mind. To go further, when the ego co-opts the capacities listed above, including its interface with the deeper drives of the id, it casts a felt sense of ownership and control, or domain, over these capacities, regardless of how false this pretense is. For the ego, the façade is that it is in control of unconscious drives, when it is not and is instead only able to mediate the unconscious drives. The challenge is that the ego exploits the concept that it is needed to exist and achieve by bringing forth a multitude of irrational emotional reasons to justify its existence and sidestepping the fact that emotion and irrationality are not synonymous (Monroe, 1985, p. 256). Even when overwhelmed by the unconscious drives of the id, such as sexual aggression, or by strong emotions erupting from the unconscious, such as anger, anxiety, depression, or grief, the ego will use a wide variety of defense mechanisms to create the illusion of control. The ego's long list of psychological defense mechanisms include compensation, denial, dissociation, displacement, fantasy, identification, intellectualization, introjection, inversion, projection, rationalization, reaction formation, regression, repression, somatization, splitting, sublimation, and substitution (Freud, A., 2018; Freud, S., 2019).

Our inner mental world is directly connected to our physical self, inclusive of our brain and nervous system, and its connection to the faculties of our physical senses, which we use to interface with the external world through exteroception. Our relationship to the outer world makes the ego's job much more complex. The challenge of being living organic animals is that we are very vulnerable. The list of human vulnerabilities is long: disease, attack, injury, starvation, dehydration, asphyxia, toxins, exposure to extreme fluctuations in temperature, and ultimately death. As the navigator of the material realm, the ego then has the tremendous onus of protecting us from the external environment. It is no surprise then that Metzinger (2010) describes the ego as a tool evolved for controlling and predicting our behavior and understanding the behavior of others and the world around us (p. 207). Monroe (1985) describes the ego as sprouting from the survival imprint (p. 256). As such, it is also not a surprise that the ego's dominant role is to act as our protector, keeping us safe from harm— both physical and psychological. It is hardwired to seek security and safety. If the emotions of nervousness and anxiety are connected to the instinct or drive to safeguard our future self, the ego is the vigilant protector mediating these emotions. The ego directs our actions to avoid threats and suffering while aiding in meeting our emotionally driven desires, such as pleasure, satisfaction, and ultimately wholeness, as they surface from our unconscious.

In the face of vulnerability and exposure to trauma, the ego quickly contracts defensively into complexes of insecurity and inferiority, often distorting reality. The contraction causes the ego to build increasingly guarded defensive walls of dominance and control or capitulate to self-destructive modes and helplessness, which themselves can be forms of dysfunctional defense mechanisms of retreat. The protective and defensive roles of the ego can be helpful as we navigate our daily lives. The challenge is that the thicker the ego's armored walls, the greater the difficulty in relegating it to access our inner intuitive capacities and enter the mindmeld. And, yet, to break down the barriers of these protective walls, we ironically have to call upon the ego to act by surrendering its armor.

Most of our responses to stimuli in our internal and external environment are unconscious, reflexive, and reactionary. The ego selects which stimuli to analyze and judge. Using our intellect and memory, the ego can decide how to engage and respond to our moment-to-moment experience with a notion of "free will." If we are to engage in the mindmeld, the ego must see the value of engagement and agree to participate. To become a participant there must be a measure of self-control to respond, to make decisions, and to adapt to biological necessities, inner impulses, feelings, desires, and ambitions as we relate and interact with the external world, including our partner in the mindmeld. The ego, co-opting the other capacities of the mind, can discriminate between what it perceives as safe and unsafe, make risk-based calculations, distinguish between what brings pleasure versus suffering, and prompt us to weigh options and make choices when navigating our experiences. Its reality is informed by memory and recall, which can also look forward in anticipation of future events, although they are shaped by the context of the experienced past. The ego then can form intent and follow through with action, both necessary steps for engaging in the mindmeld.

Ego, Self-Image, and the Constellation of Personality

The ego also plays the role of creating a self-image and thus contributing to personality. Here the ego identifies and is preoccupied with form—thoughtforms, emotional forms, and physical forms. The ego is preoccupied with form because it lives in duality, as manifested through subject and object, and is caught in the perception of duality being absolute. To the ego, there is always a "me" and "another." The ego co-opts the mind's capacities of abstraction, memory, reflection, thought, and language. Then, through lived experience and inner dialogue, it constructs a self-image distinguishing itself from others. The ego, paired with the intellect, memory, and capacity for attention and perception, tracks the valence of the objects of experience, identifies patterns and relationships, tries to predict outcomes (albeit usually inaccurately), and makes meaning of our experiences. The ego also mediates emotions and arousal and their connection to desires as they manifest from the unconscious, choosing what to act on, how and when to act, and what to avoid. Through this living process of ongoing learning, the ego creates constructs at an individual and internal level but also socially at a societal level. Together, these constructs define who we are as individuals.*

In combination, language and memory allow us to create a narrative or story of ourselves over time, which is different from the self-awareness we experience in each arising moment. This narrative enables us to *know* we have experience based on our reflections; this knowing enables the creation, development, and retention of knowledge and wisdom. As such, our inner dialogue creates a story from which we can make meaning of our life experiences. The ego compulsively engages in these exercises to construct a character self, an identity, and a personality: a "me," an "I." In its drive for security and safety (penchants of control), it grasps at wanting a self-identity. The ego wants to feel "special" and unique.† It doesn't matter what the identification is with, as long as there is something to identify with and stand out. For example, the ego can identify with possessions or its opposite thoughtform of anticonsumerism; it can become overly attached to pleasure but also wallow in suffering if the victimhood of suffering creates identity and gains the attention of others. Thus, the ego creates a self-model, a persona made

---

*Sigmund Freud (2019) also describes a further aspect of ego—the *superego*—that develops alongside the ego and is socialized or programmed to accept certain ethical and moral laws, values, beliefs, and expectations through family, societal, and cultural norms. The superego then acts as a moralizing driver or judge (the "inner critic") within an individual, creating conflict between the instinctual drives, desires, and impulses of the id, and then having to be mediated by the (super-)ego, which can lead to the use of a mix of the defense mechanisms listed above, depending on the context. At its worst, the superego can manifest deep layers of self-hate, self-disgust, and self-abandonment directly influenced by external expectations (Walker, 2013). One could also argue the superego is simply an extension of the ego and is not really a separate construct as proposed by Freud, as the ego works to mediate one's internal experience within a socialized context. There is not enough room in this volume to discuss the many idiosyncrasies of the relationships among the id, ego, and superego, and therefore I make some broader generalizations and simplifications regarding the treatment of the ego.

†This is a complex paradox for the ego: on the one hand, it is truly special and unique as a finger on the infinite hand of the "Divine" or "God"; on the other hand, in its lived reality of duality its perceived uniqueness prevents the ego from connecting to its true abiding presence in the nondual, where it is an emanation of the "All," as discussed further in chapter 11.

of the artificial masks we create to navigate the world and interact with it. The self-model is a form of autobiography that the ego consciously owns (or sometimes denies) and uses to reflect on its lived historical experience, while trying to imagine, predict, and create its future self. From the perspective above, the ego is all-pervasive in moderating our individual experience.

A significant challenge for the ego in its search for identity is that it never abides in lasting satisfaction. There is never a lasting feeling of being enough or complete, which may be partly related to the existential challenge of living in duality and being separate from divine wholeness or oneness. This underlying, insatiable wanting often leads to compulsive and addictive behaviors, complaints, resentment, greed, and envy. Persistent is a sense of separation. In this context, the ego's drive to feel complete results in a self-image and its concomitant personality always being fluid, constantly moving and changing because this drive can never be permanently met. In its search to be complete, the ego keeps "trying on" different personality traits, like different sets of clothes. Here it is best to think of the personality's makeup as fractals, which means we can potentially find all available human personality traits/patterns inside of ourselves over time—an infinite closet of personality options, influenced by our biography, the id, the collective unconscious, and our relationship to others. The personality is then like a mosaic or a society of subpersonalities jostling together, sometimes aware of each other and at other times not (Kolk, 2015, p. 280).

Conflict can stir among the subpersonalities because of the polarization in the dyads of personality traits, such as calmness versus anxiety, self-control versus anger, sadness versus happiness, honesty versus dishonesty, or loving care versus hatred—each trying to make its claims. Trauma can exacerbate the conflict within us, as it can cause the self-system to break down, where a sense of coherence in the self-system is lost. Schwartz and Sweezy (2020) try to make sense of this apparent internal conflict through the model of Internal Family Systems (IFS). In IFS, there are four main internal parts or characters within each of us. These parts have different, sometimes conflicting but ultimately altruistic, goals and motivations. The four main parts are: (1) managers, (2) exiles, (3) firefighters, and (4) the Self. Each part can be considered as an individual personality with varying levels of maturity, excitability, wisdom, and pain. *Managers* play preemptive, protective, and controlling roles in preventing harm by others or avoiding being overwhelmed by painful or traumatic feelings, often acting out of fear. Examples of managers are neurotic thoughts leading to overthinking, self-criticism, perfectionism, people-pleasing, and caretaking. *Exiles* are parts in pain, shame, fear, or trauma, usually from childhood. Managers and firefighters try to exile these parts from consciousness to prevent this pain from coming to the surface. *Firefighters* are parts who emerge when exiles break out and demand attention. These parts work to distract a person's attention from the hurt or shame experienced by the exile by leading them to engage in impulsive behaviors like substance use, overeating, violence, or having inappropriate sex. They can also distract from the pain by causing a person to focus excessively on more subtle unhealthy activities, such as overworking or excessive socializing. For our purpose, these first three parts are direct manifestations of the ego in its effort to mediate an individual's inner and outer worlds, trying to maintain a sense of short-term stability or preventing worse problems—although in many cases the "protective" behaviors often result in worse outcomes in the long term.

Underneath this collection of parts is the *Self*, a person's true self or spiritual center. The Self has qualities of curiosity, creativity, connectedness, confidence, courage, clarity, compassion, and calmness. These qualities can help heal the other parts and mediate internal leadership skills in how best to moderate the interactions of the different parts, ensuring they are taken care of and keeping them from sabotaging each other.

This concept of subpersonalities helps us understand the contradictory impulses within ourselves. They also help explain some of the polarization and oscillation of experience from positive to negative and back again when using psychedelics and engaging in the mindmeld. With greater consciousness of the parts, we become more aware of how we construct our narratives. With greater awareness of the mechanics of our narratives, we can work to change our stories and, therefore, our reality.

Distinguishing our semiautonomous subpersonalities is valuable because, when sharing psychic contents telepathically, one needs to remember we individually hold all possible personality traits, the mosaic of all the parts. This includes the parts we like and those we don't, those binding us within ourselves and those causing us to go to war within ourselves, those that are thriving and joyous and those that are traumatized and contracted. Thus, whatever arises in the other person when in the mindmeld is in you and vice versa. Recognition of this fact helps foster acceptance and compassion for all of the subpersonalities in you and the other person, both in daily life and in the mindmeld. We are human, and our heritage is the artful kaleidoscope of all possible personality traits and their interactions with each other, collectively and antagonistically.

Awareness of these dynamics helps us see the co-emergent nature of the selves within us. We experience a mix of natural clarity and simultaneous confusion. Confusion emerges from the unconscious, the ego, and parental and societal conditioning. John Welwood (1997) describes this internal tug-of-war as follows:

> Even though we may want to be more fully alive and present, we remain influenced by unconscious factors—old attachments, identities, fears, and projections—that distort our experience and diminish our capacities. Nonetheless, no matter how lost or shut down we are, the sun of awareness is always shining brightly behind the clouds of our confused beliefs. Even in our darkest moments the light of clarity and wakefulness is near at hand (p. 97).

This awareness of the fluidity of light and dark within ourselves can help us cultivate patience and fortitude in the face of internal struggle within the mindmeld or while doing individual psychedelic work. We can better position ourselves to witness the difficulty surfacing, knowing it is impermanent and transitory. Clarity can be just on the other side of the challenge, much like flipping a coin over to see its opposite side. It is helpful to know that the subpersonality trait or emotion being experienced in the now moment has its opposite lying in your unconscious, waiting to be revealed at another time. All of the subpersonalities as polarities have their origin from the same suchness of divine creation; from this perspective, we can try to accept the play of polarity as something bigger than ourselves, letting each side inform the other, allowing ourselves to surrender to the dance of contradiction in our own inner experience and in the mindmeld.

By its external projections, we can gauge how well the ego navigates this inner world of subpersonalities. A healthy ego, for example, can exercise self-control and can self-regulate, keeping a person safe, engaged, and effective in the lived world. It can discern justified anxiety versus false alarms rising from the unconscious and make good decisions. A healthy ego lends itself to cooperation, collaboration, and intimacy. It integrates diverse and challenging experiences and maintains relative consistency of patterned behavior. But Anodea Judith (2004) points out that the ego divides and unites, for it sequesters the less favorable instinctual energies to the shadow realm. While the ego is oriented toward love and purpose in its yearning for wholeness, its shadow is made of those elements capable of interfering with this. The ego is, therefore, capable of denying unwanted or emotionally uncomfortable drives or impulses coming from the id or aspects of lived experience, repressing them in the unconscious, or using various other defense mechanisms, as listed above, to deal with anything that confronts the ego's perceived supremacy. The ego can even engage in protective actions destructive to the organism, such as addictive behaviors to temporarily mute psychological pain at the expense of the body's overall health or in relationship to others. At an energetic level, dysfunctional protective action can disrupt the efficient flow of energy through the body and undermine the basic functioning of bodily systems, which is discussed further in chapter 10. Again, however, whether the ego is healthy and functional or struggling with disintegration, whatever it creates is ultimately a construct: an artificial, fluid, and impermanent creation. When working mindfully with psychedelics, we can dissolve the construct and penetrate deeper into our consciousness and the mindmeld.

There is another element of the ego to distinguish, particularly given the ethereal nature of the mindmeld. Experiments have shown that a relationship to the body is not a requirement of the ego's existence and its connection to selfhood. Lucid dreaming or out-of-body experiences, for example, are conscious experiences that bear no direct relationship to one's physical body nor involve the physical senses directly. Meditators report that there is no need to connect to emotion, acts of will, or the dialogue of thought to still have a sense of "self" (Metzinger, 2010, p. 101). Even so, Metzinger (2010) hypothesizes that the ego is merely a complex physical event—an activation pattern in your central nervous system, responding to subjective experience dictated by biological inputs (p. 208).

Of course, there is an ongoing debate about whether or not the body is a necessary vehicle to experience holotropic states of consciousness. Is it a necessary embodiment for ego? Can these experiences occur in the complete absence of the human body—in the nonmaterial realm, the collective unconscious, the realm of disembodied spirits and souls? Regardless of this debate, for our purposes, the body is a fundamental part of being human and is the vehicle needed for us to engage in the mindmeld. And we are required to understand that the body is an energetic being that the ego is capable of co-opting, regardless of where the ego actually resides (i.e., in the brain, in the collective unconscious, in the Mind of God, in all of these simultaneously, or somewhere else).

For our purposes, then, the ego is the mediator of our relationship to our daily internal and external lived reality. It is an energetic composite of multiple faculties within the body and mind. The ego co-opts the faculties in the human mind and body to create an artifice of selfhood and personality, all influenced by the ever-moving and ego-mediated focus of awareness on experiences arising within the mind and usually, but not necessarily, in connection to the body and the external material realm. The constant force of the ego then directly influences all the energetic systems in the body, positively and negatively, through its interface with the energetic structures of interoception, affect, perception, emotion, thought, and behaviour in the world through expressions, such as physical movement, and speech. The ego is connected to the material realm and conditioned by it, as it acts as a conscious form to navigate our material existence. The ego's preoccupation with the material realm and personality blocks us from our deeper intuitive and spiritual self. As you will see in chapter 9, an understanding of the ego is helpful because the ego needs to be substantially relegated to penetrate the deeper layers of the mind and thus enter the Psychedelic Mindmeld and explore the superconscious and clear light mind.

SETTING INTENTION

Setting an intention is a fundamental part of working with psychedelics and of set. Intention refers to what we are attentive to, driven by volition and agency, usually with an aim or purpose. Intention is usually coupled with a degree of resolve or determination to meet or manifest an aim or purpose. All achievement comes about through intention. Having an intention helps us persevere in the face of the obstacles inevitably presenting themselves, as we actively participate in a process to manifest our purpose, regardless of how simple or complex.

Intention is regularly at play throughout our lives as it directs our focus of awareness. Thoughts surface from the unconscious as both emotionally driven desires and fears. Creative impulses similarly bubble to the surface of conscious awareness and through imagination. Thoughts are connected to our internal experiences but are influenced by many external factors. External influences can include cultural programming (e.g., formal education, societal norms), family, social/work interactions,

interactions with nature, and even possibly the collective unconscious. As thoughts surface in conscious awareness, the ego mediates the interplay of motivating desire and valence and makes decisions about what to follow through on, giving rise to intention and action. Here we see that the ego plays a fundamental role, for better or worse, in contributing to intention, the choice of what we want to manifest in our lives.

The intention of the Psychedelic Mindmeld is to join physically and psychically with another person. In short, this means to consciously commit to sharing all of the experience with the other person as equals engaged in a co-creative process. To fully share in the mindmeld is to open oneself up to the other, to where there is no holding back. Similar to creating a piece of art, or other creative exercises, it is about relaxing into a flow state where self-judgment and judgment of the other are dropped. There is no self-censorship, just allowing.

The foundational pillars of intention I recommend using in all psychedelic sessions are love, compassion, wisdom, and healing. Intention directs energy. The intent behind working with these pillars is to create a metaphysical atmosphere of openness and loving-kindness. The atmosphere is the "set" of mental location in the "setting." Because these four pillars are so interconnected, there is no priority among them. While you are not obligated to use any of these pillars, the intention to join with the other person physically and psychically without reservation is mandatory to attain the most effective results of the mindmeld.

Setting intention can be subtle. To offer a personal example of how subtle the act of setting intention is, I will share the story of my first ayahuasca ceremony. At the time, my spiritual beliefs oscillated between atheistic and agnostic. I had read about shamanism but thought it was a practice of wild imagination without meaningful substance. A friend had told me about an impending ayahuasca ceremony. I attended out of curiosity, given my background interest in world religion and my reading on shamanism.

The shaman was Canadian and had been trained in Peru for several years under the tutelage of a famous Peruvian shaman. The ceremony had all the trappings of Amazonian tradition, including smudging and *icaros*—traditional ceremonial songs and chants.

We started by sharing our intention for the ceremony. I knew from my reading on shamanism that intention was important, so I pondered it deeply beforehand. When the shaman asked me what my intention was, I shared with her it was to experience more joy. She asked me if I didn't experience joy, to which I replied I did, but I just wanted to experience more. She immediately asked me a couple more questions and then told me she thought I had a blockage toward spirituality. It was a direct challenge to my ego. But it took me less than a minute to contemplate what she had said, and I had to agree. I had grown up in a fundamentalist Protestant home, and at an early age I rejected the dogma forced upon me, including any notion of spiritual engagement. My study of religions was intended only to assuage my ego's fear of eternal damnation in hell after the message had been repeatedly drummed into me by my father and the Church. I also had a master of science degree and strongly believed in the efficacy of scientific empiricism and the Newtonian-Cartesian paradigm of the mechanical world.

Based on the recommendation of the shaman, my intention became to open my heart to spirituality. I stated this to the group, but a large part of me was completely skeptical of what awaited. I drank the ayahuasca, returned to my seated position, and waited. I was so skeptical of the experience I refused to close my eyes as I did not want to let my imagination create "false" imagery behind my closed eyelids. I just stared at the shadows on the wall across from me in our darkened setting. I purposely did not reinvoke or further contemplate my intention once the meditation started because I did not want to create something with my mind through a preoccupation with an idea.

Although the room was dark, there was enough ambient light that I could make out the shadows on the wall in front of me, which were gaining a life of their own as they began to sway and bleed down into the floor. Suddenly, to my immediate right, and in front of the shaman sitting next to me, a portal opened up in the floor. It was similar to a black hole but had swirling greenish-yellow fractals playing in its darkness, dropping into the void below the house. I was shocked but had read about how it was possible to enter portals. Immediately my mind started racing: How do I enter the portal? Do I physically get up and step into it? Do I use only my consciousness to enter it—but how would I even do that? Was it my portal to use, or was it for the shaman?

The answers didn't matter because what soon greeted me was a human-sized praying mantis. It stood right in front of me. The insect reached out its front legs and started performing open-heart surgery on me with its claws. I was so startled I didn't move. Strangely, it all felt like it was supposed to be happening. Any initial fright or resistance I had fell away as I began to feel this wonderful, blissful, loving energy entering my chest cavity.

The whole experience lasted only a few minutes. When the praying mantis had completed the energetic surgery, it closed up my chest and disappeared as suddenly as it had arrived. I was dumbstruck. What just happened to me? That was over fifteen years ago. What seemed like a simple statement of intention radically changed my life. My heart has since completely opened to spirituality in ways I never dreamed possible.

Another aspect of intention can include invocation. Invocation is not uncommon in shamanism and some types of magic and psychic work in which participants invite discarnate beings from other realms of reality to help direct the experience. Examples include the Cosmic Christ, archangels, deities, spirit guides, ancestors, and so forth. Discarnate beings can help guide the journey and direct your experience to the one most favorable for your spiritual development. However, I do not recommend trying this until you have successfully mindmelded several times. First, just working with one person can be more than enough. By introducing other beings you increase the complexity of engagement exponentially. It is exponentially more complicated because not only are you navigating all that is surfacing for you and the other person, but you are also now navigating the invoked *and* the relationship the invoked has directly with the other person. For each additional character arriving, this web of complexity grows exponentially.

The other consideration is that other beings often arrive spontaneously anyway. For example, while mindmelding with John* years ago, his Chinese ancestors showed up unexpectedly. They shared their blessings with us and moved on.

During psychedelic or nonpsychedelic sessions, whether I have been mindmelding or not, all sorts of beings have shown up, including many of those described earlier. The point is, just allow what is meant to arise, and with experience, you can try to be more directive about what may be invoked. Here the recommendation is to slowly work toward accepting increasingly complex and strange phenomena. The more the unexplored territory is explored, the greater the comfort with pushing the envelope into deeper realms of consciousness.

One final recommendation on intention is to not get caught up in trying to create too particular an expectation or outcome. The focus should be on process, not outcomes. You should keep your intention for the journey at a high level, with no excessive grasping. If there is too much specificity, there is the possibility of bondage to the expectation and of not allowing a greater opening and penetration through the layers of the mind for what is meant to arise beyond the ego's desire. When an expectation that is too specific is not met, the result is disappointment, which equates to suffering. It is better to focus on just entering the mindmeld without a specific destination, or to deal with a particular trauma, or to reach a particular blissful state. Trust your deeper intuitive self to guide the experience, bringing to the surface what needs to be worked on, processed, or reveled in.

Robert Monroe (1985) developed an affirmation for out-of-body experiences that fits our purpose well (p. 26). I have adapted it for the Psychedelic Mindmeld. The affirmation addresses the general intention

---

*Names of Psychedelic Mindmeld participants (co-*melders*) have been changed to protect privacy.

of the mindmeld and emphasizes a safe set and setting. When you feel ready to invoke discarnate beings, the last paragraph includes a general invitation to other beings for help and protection with emphasis on psychic and spiritual safety. But first, a word of caution: please do not invoke dark entities. We are porous and vulnerable. Such invocation is psychically dangerous and may cause unforeseen harm. There is enough destructive energy and archetypal evil in the world. We do not need more. I recommend both participants state the following affirmation together before starting the meditation.

I am more than my physical body. Because I am more than physical matter, I can perceive that which is greater than the physical world. Therefore, I deeply desire to expand, to experience, to know, to understand, to control, to use such greater energies and energy systems as may be beneficial to me and constructive to me and to those who work jointly with me. I deeply desire to connect telepathically with my co-melder in the Psychedelic Mindmeld to share in love, compassion, healing, and wisdom.

Also, I deeply desire the help and cooperation of all beings who want to participate and share their love, wisdom, and experience with us. I ask for their guidance and protection from any influence or any source that might provide me with less than my stated desires. Thank you.

RITUAL

Ceremonies of all kinds, from shamanic plant ceremonies to church ceremonies, involve rituals. Rituals provide structure, rules, and *intention* for action in preparation for entering the sacred and for how the ceremony will run. Rituals help people prepare for ceremonies and know what to expect. As described above, making ground rules around set and setting are loosely comparable to performing ritual.

Rituals often incorporate a combination of themes, such as sound (e.g., chanting, song, music, blessings), visual aesthetics (e.g., colorful, artful clothing, jewelry, art), lighting (e.g., candles, colored lights), smells (e.g., incense), totems (e.g., power objects, healing sticks, feathers, idols, crystals), and space (e.g., church, a tepee, altars, a clean and decorated room).

The mindmeld is not a ceremony. However, as a free-flowing and creative exercise, there is nothing to stop people from creating or using rituals. For example, people may start the session using the traditional ceremonial practice of smudging. Smudging usually uses some form of incense to clear negative energy from individuals and the space being worked in. Some people may want to start the session with prayer, chanting, or playing of musical instruments, like a drum, rattle, or even a guitar. Rituals can be playful but should help galvanize the intention. Because ritual contributes to the mindset of the participants, it can be a useful tool for starting a session. So, if the intention is to work with love and healing, for example, think about what chant or mantra would contribute.

A simple way to judge whether a ritual is useful for a mindmeld session is simply to ask whether or not it enhances the session's effectiveness. Notice how creating a ritual is also an ego-based activity in this context. The ego wants to be in control. Working with ritual is a way of creating continuity and a sense of protection and security. There is nothing inherently wrong with this, but observe its nuances and be careful not to get trapped by the egoic game of forcing your rituals on others when doing this work. You are protected in this work through your own integrity and purpose. As such, be open to the co-creative design of ritual following the general guidelines for set and setting presented in this and the following chapter.

The mindmeld already pushes the boundaries of exploratory psychedelic work, so the priority is creating a safe container for set and setting in which to do the work, helping the ego fall from its place of prominence. Once you and your partner have agreed to a plan, stick to it and deviate only through agreement. Rituals can help put people at ease leading into a session. Given how profound and unpredictable the sessions can be, encouraging a sense of ease and relaxation at the beginning is helpful.

Once in the meditation, all distracting elements should be dropped, such as putting aside drums and rattles. The one exception is tools to contribute to healing work. For example, I leave healing crystals on the bedside tables in case I am drawn to use them during the mindmeld. The same could be said for tuning forks or other similar tools. But any use of healing tools should occur when the body is driven to use them beyond the conscious choice of the mind, lest the ego begin to lead the narrative.

MENTAL STATE

One's mental state, particularly one's emotional orientation, on the day of the session is important to assess, but not so much that one becomes preoccupied with it. Apprehension and nervousness arising from fear are normal; you are about to journey into unknown territory. Emotional states are constantly shifting. What will arise in your experience once you are working with a psychedelic is likely to be different compared to your state of mind immediately before.

Self-assessment can be difficult, but some simple things to consider are:

- Do you feel reasonably well rested, free from excessive fatigue?
- Do you feel healthy or have a looming sickness?
- Do you trust who you are about to work with?

Excessive stress or fear may result in an unpleasant experience. Conversely, a relaxed, curious person in a warm, comfortable, and safe place is more likely to be open to experiencing awe and wonder. But emotional states are not certain predictors; one can start the session relaxed and comfortable, and then shift into dealing with difficult emotions arising from the unconscious.

Trust yourself and your intuitive abilities, dropping any preconceptions, personal barriers, and limiting beliefs. Tune in to your adventurous, curious multidimensional self, opening to expansive telepathic shifts in your awareness. Be open to receiving from your partner.

You should also tune in to your connection to your partner. Are there any outstanding misunderstandings or conflicts between the two of you? If so, be aware these can become exaggerated during a mind-meld session, possibly leading to negative states and loss of trust, as discussed more fully in chapter 13. As such, quickly check in with your partner to ensure you feel comfortable and strong in your relationship before the session.

An open mind can keep things in perspective. For example, while likely unwanted, an unpleasant or strenuous experience can produce insights, learning, and meaning in one's life. Ironically, the challenge with having blissful and profoundly beautiful mystical experiences is that they can leave a person wanting more and struggling in their return to the mundaneness of day-to-day living—but even in this struggle there is room for insight and learning.

HOW OFTEN SHOULD I ENGAGE IN MINDMELD WORK?

A question related to set is how often people should use psychedelics. This question is often asked. Many have offered prescriptions varying from never, to once in a lifetime, on key occasions (e.g., coming of age, marriage, facing death), a few times a year, once a week (e.g., the Santo Daime church originating in Brazil), or several days in a row, the latter of which shows up in some shamanic traditions. When the answers are this diverse, nobody *knows* the answer. In this regard, each person has to figure it out themselves.

Figuring out how often to engage in the mindmeld, in particular, is potentially even more challenging because of how intimate the work is and how overwhelming it can be, sometimes making it more demanding to integrate the experiences afterward. But to work with the mindmeld is to learn by doing and becoming, not by contemplating and rationalizing, so it does require repetitive engagement. Through engagement comes insight and wisdom.

I have found the following insight about making meaning helpful for myself. If we accept that a major driver of human purpose is the pursuit of meaning, Peterson (1999) offers a way to help us answer the question of interval:

> Meaning is the most profound manifestation of instinct. Man is a creature attracted by the unknown; a creature adapted for its conquest. The subjective sense of meaning is the instinct governing rate of contact with the unknown. Too much exposure turns change to chaos; too little promotes stagnation and degeneration. The appropriate balance produces a powerful individual, confident in the ability to withstand life, ever more able to deal with nature and society, ever closer to the heroic ideal (p. 468).

This statement offers a good baseline for determining how often to engage in this work. There is a need to find a personal balance between often enough and too often. There is a need to engage in the work often enough to connect to the benefits of shared healing, gaining profound insight and wisdom, seeing progress and personal growth, and avoiding personal stagnation and degeneration. But there is also a need to not engage so often as to risk adverse personal chaos possibly manifesting as psychosis, dissociation, avoidance behaviors, problematic insomnia, distress, or excessively imbalanced energy in the body, thus leaving one feeling ungrounded. Ideally, you do not want to be in a state where you cannot function and meet your daily responsibilities to family, community, and occupation.

Figuring out your baseline, however, is not easy because to do this work is to completely let go and enter spaces where it seems the ego will never reform, as it is lost in dissolution with little or no reference to one's body. In this state, there is an element of psychosis, although it is a state one has entered voluntarily. These spaces are intimidating to the ego. And yet somehow, these experiences are readily accepted at a soul level as the nature of things.

A person also has to survey all the other things going on in their life to strike the right balance. Excessive stress at work or in relationships or dealing with health issues, as examples, all need to be taken into account. Know there are no absolute right or wrong answers.

Thankfully, the answer to the interval question can show up while working with psychedelics. Psychedelics have a way of pushing people to take a break if they have gone too far, giving them a chance to make meaning of their experiences and potentially integrate the lessons into daily life. Such direction to take a break can manifest in a vague manner, such as a challenging trip so overwhelming that the person decides to take a prolonged hiatus from psychedelics just to recover. The message can also be more direct. Years ago in Wyoming, I met Rex, who had smoked N,N-DMT (dimethyltryptamine) more than two hundred times in less than five years. When I met him he was taking a prolonged break from DMT because the aliens whom he regularly met with told him to stop smoking DMT and integrate his DMT experiences into his lived reality.

The body also develops a tolerance when one is regularly taking some psychedelics, like psilocybin and LSD. The result is a diminished response to the drug as the body adapts to its continued presence. Signs of tolerance are another indication longer breaks should be taken between sessions.

8

Establishing
the Setting

Establishing the setting of the physical and social environment and logistics for the Psychedelic Mindmeld is a critical part of preparation. To start preparing for the mindmeld, I recommend both participants read this book and then compare ideas and notes with each other from their reading. You can also use "Appendix A: The Flow of the Psychedelic Mindmeld Session" to help prepare for the session.

A briefing between participants in advance of the session is critical. A joint briefing will prepare each participant to understand what should happen before the session, what to do during the session, what may occur during the session, and what to do if something goes wrong. The briefing sets up a common understanding and is intended to create a safe container for the experience. The briefing should set the ground rules and establish boundaries for the session and participants. Completing a briefing ahead of time can help avoid major and unnecessary misunderstandings, such as perceived violations and psychological projections. Results of poor preparation could be traumatizing to one or both participants, potentially undermining the long-term relationship between the two.

Discussing and understanding the sharing of physical and psychic energetic contents, as described in chapters 10 and 11, should be incorporated into the preparatory briefing of the psychedelic session.

Participants will then have fresh clarity on how to engage with each other in the mindmeld and have a mutual understanding of the broad range of possibilities that may arise during a mindmelding session.

Set was discussed in the previous chapter to help prepare the mindscape for entering into the Psychedelic Mindmeld. In this chapter, setting is discussed as part of the briefing as it describes the preparatory necessities of the environment and logistics for the session.

Setting can profoundly influence a session. Variation in setting is capable of activating different and unforeseen aspects of an individual's unconscious. As such, there is a need to be very conscious of setting. For our purposes, the setting should be safe and secure, evoke support, reassurance, and trust, and be nourishing. This framework for setting reinforces the importance of finding the right partner to engage in the mindmeld, as discussed in chapter 6. This framework should also guide the preparation of the setting.

A discussion of setting leads to establishing ground rules between participants for the interpersonal and physical environment. Ground rules help facilitate the safe use of psychedelics but are particularly practical for the smooth and safe flow of a mindmeld session. Below is a list of points to help establish ground rules before the session, and these are discussed in turn through the rest of this chapter.

1. Days before the session
2. Personal hygiene
3. Transportation logistics
4. Start time
5. Location
6. Type of psychedelic and dosage
7. Music
8. Safety protocols
9. Sexuality and establishing physical boundaries
10. More than two people
11. Intent for the second half of the session

DAYS BEFORE THE SESSION

There are no hard-and-fast rules for preparing for the days leading up to a mindmeld session. Some shamanic ceremonies can be very prescriptive (e.g., abstinence from sexual activity, alcohol, and drugs, and avoiding a list of specific foods), while others are not. Through observation and experimentation, I have found the following to be a good list of recommendations:

- Avoid alcohol and other mind-altering substances (e.g., short-acting antianxiety medication, opiates, amphetamines, cocaine) for at least forty-eight hours as they constrict consciousness and can undermine psi performance (Metzner, 2005; Kelly, 2011, p. 272). I also recommend not using alcohol and other potent drugs in the days following a session because it can shut down any newfound awareness after these experiences, dulling the positive aftereffects and slowing any additional healing and insights received from the session.
- Avoid caffeine the day of the session as it promotes attention and focus, undermining psi performance (Kelly, 2011, p. 270).
- For at least twenty-four hours, avoid heavy meals and fermented foods, such as red meat, cheeses, kimchi, and sauerkraut.
- Have a light breakfast.
- It is an option to fast for twenty-four hours in advance of the session, which can potentiate the psychedelic effects and reduce nausea for those more susceptible to it.

PERSONAL HYGIENE

People should aim to be scent free. When working with psychedelics, the senses often become hyperaware. Scents can be distracting, and many people have sensitivities to certain smells. While people may choose to smudge with sage or another plant, commercial perfumes should be avoided. If a person smokes, their clothes should be washed to prevent smells, especially as commercial tobacco smoke is filled with toxins. For some, body odors may be distracting. Because you are working close to someone else, having a shower or bath before a session is recommended.

Having said this, when entering a session, things may happen outside your preferences, which is the nature of life. The best practice, in this case, is to work with meditative techniques encouraging equanimity for what is out of your control and you don't like, such as the other person releasing gas or vomiting.

I once worked with a woman whose husband smoked. Though faint, I could smell the toxic fumes in her clothes. It was distracting and made me slightly nauseous. But there was nothing to do about it as the session had already started. I brought my focus inward and observed the queasy sensations in my stomach. Within less than thirty minutes, we were dropping into the mindmeld and the smell didn't bother me anymore.

TRANSPORTATION LOGISTICS

The logistics of transportation to and from the session must be agreed upon ahead of time. The session is likely to be held in a person's home, so only one person is likely to have to be concerned with transportation logistics. People working with long-acting psychedelics in high doses should not drive themselves home on the day of the session. If the session is done early in the day, people may *feel* fine to drive in the evening, but they shouldn't. *Feeling* fine and *being* fine are different things. Before driving, participants should wait at least eighteen hours (preferably twenty-four hours) to pass from the beginning of the session. This means arrangements need to be made for one person to stay overnight or use a taxi or friend to drive the person home. Staying the night is a good option because it allows both participants more time to debrief the session and ensure they are both in a good mindset when parting from each other.

START TIME

When working with long-acting psychedelics, I prefer to start the session early in the day, usually by noon. Some psychedelics are active for up to twelve-plus hours. While psilocybin mushrooms are generally reported to be active for only four to six hours, I usually feel the effects for up to ten hours. By starting early, you are more likely to get a good sleep and not upset your circadian sleep rhythm. While there is no guarantee of waking up feeling completely fresh and well rested the day after an intense session, going to bed at a reasonable time increases the odds.

Some shamanic traditions wait until sundown to begin ceremonies. While this makes sense for their intentions, I find it better to work earlier in the day to be fully awake for the experience and avoid the fatigue associated with staying up all night. But again, there is no hard-and-fast rule here.

LOCATION

Choosing a safe, secure, and private location is necessary for a successful mindmeld session. I offer the following guidelines:

- The location should be relatively soundproof. Loud outbursts, such as toning, singing, shouting, yelling, or screaming, are possible. If such outbursts occur, you do not want concerned neighbors knocking at the door or phoning the police.
- Clean the location: it is always nice to use a clean bathroom and not be navigating dirty dishes and dust balls. A clean space equals a clean mind.
- Have purge buckets for each person in case of the need to vomit.
- Have stable tumblers of water for each person for hydration.
- Turn off all phones. Phones should be easily accessible for emergencies but not used during the session as they are a distraction and undermine the commitment to the work.

- Lock the house doors. You do not want friends or neighbors bounding in unannounced.
- The visiting driver's keys should be hidden. While extremely rare, someone may panic in a state of paranoid delusion of feeling trapped and want to leave early and drive away. For obvious reasons, this is very unsafe. I know of one sitter who took these precautions, and a participant still found her keys, drove away, and was in an accident, and the sitter ended up in jail.

The room you are working in also has to be prepared. You will want to work with a queen-sized bed at a minimum or a similar-sized space if you are working on the floor.

The room should be dark but with enough ambient light to maneuver safely. I use black lights and candles for ambient light, creating a beautiful hue in the room. (If you use candles, make sure they will not be at risk of getting bumped over if you start moving around and that they can burn themselves out without damaging anything.)

Because psychedelics sometimes lead people to feel chilled for parts of the session, ensure the room is warm. Warm blankets are optional, but once bodies begin to move, they should be set aside if they impede movement.

Clothing should be comfortable and loose. I prefer a T-shirt and shorts, to make movement easier than when wearing full pants. I have found skin-to-skin contact more effective for energetic work, though not necessary when engaging in sharing physical energy. Psychedelic or abstract artwork on clothing is optional, but decisions like these should be made by the person who will look at the clothing, not the person wearing it.

Jewelry should be taken off. Fingernails and toenails should be trimmed to avoid accidental scratching when engaged in physical bodywork.

If there is a need or desire to separate from your partner and take a break from each other, having a second private room with somewhere to lie down is a good idea. Ideally, the space should be within shouting distance from the other room in case of emergency for either person.

Another consideration for location is the atmosphere you will be in during the second half of the session. As you will likely move around, it's nice to have an aesthetically rich setting to enjoy and relax. Ideas to consider are lighting (e.g., lava lamps, LED lights, gourd lamps, Turkish lamps, or candles), art (e.g., psychedelic digital/fractal art; abstract, impressionist, or surreal art; mandalas; Buddhist thangkas; sculptures; carvings), natural elements (e.g., collections of minerals of various shapes, textures, and colors; exotic seashells; plants and flowers), or the use of incense (e.g., acacia, agarbatti, copal, frankincense, myrrh, Palo Santo, sage).

TYPE OF PSYCHEDELIC AND DOSAGE

Determining what psychedelic to use and how much to use is a critical part of the process. I suspect most psychedelics can be used to access the mindmeld, as they generally can be used as tools to dislodge the ego from its executive function. According to a handful of research studies on self-reported psychedelic experiences, the range of people who have had some form of psi experience (most commonly telepathy) when using psychedelics is 10–83 percent, depending on the study (Luke, 2019). I have had telepathic success with psilocybin mushrooms, LSD, ayahuasca, mescaline, and 5-MeO-DMT. Anecdotal stories and self-selected survey results reported from around the world identify significant numbers of people who have used these psychedelics and had telepathic experiences. Ayahuasca is even referred to by some as "telepathine" because of its capacity to induce telepathy. According to the research, additional psychedelics with the potential to induce a range of telepathic experiences include cannabis (Tart, 1993), ketamine, and 3,4-Methylenedioxymethamphetamine (MDMA) (Luke, 2019).

My preference is either mushrooms or LSD because they are long-acting. While nausea is not unusual for mushroom users, it is rare that people vomit. Ayahuasca, on the other hand, often leads people to vomit, which can be distracting to those working closely in partnership with another; however, if users are comfortable with this possibility, ayahuasca is a potent medicine for this type of work

5-MeO-DMT is arguably the most powerful psychedelic on the planet as it is the most consistent for inducing nondual states of consciousness and profoundly processing blocked energy in the body. As such, it is also the most potent for inducing one-on-one psychedelic therapeutic work. Considering working with 5-MeO-DMT is to consider another way of working with psychedelics. Using 5-MeO-DMT may be the most likely option to lead to an energetic mindmelding experience, but less so for shared consciousness where both participants are mindmelding at a psychic level and sharing a story. Moreover, the 5-MeO-DMT experience is very intense and brief, lasting only minutes. The experience is rarely visual or dualistic in the sense that there is a subject and object-generating story. Because the experience is so intense and short-lived, with a likelihood of being nondual, the approach to working with the energetic mindmeld is significantly different compared to working with other psychedelics. In some ways, it is so different that it requires its own description, which is beyond the breadth of this book. If you plan to work one-on-one with others with 5-MeO-DMT, I highly recommend reading Martin Ball's material, as suggested in chapter 4 under the heading "Nondual Energetic Therapy."

So, when choosing a psychedelic, be aware of its unique qualities and open to what it can teach you. The psychedelic plants, in particular, want to be conscious participants in the process; they offer their intelligence to help us. Consider giving thanks to the plants before each session.

When it comes to determining dosage, it is more art than science. Responses for people using the same dose of a particular psychedelic vary tremendously, resulting from complex psychological and biographical factors, psychic factors, and constitutional or biological/energetic factors. This is where prior work with psychedelics is helpful as a baseline to help you figure out what will work best and recognizing that individuals working with the same psychedelic and the same dose from session to session can have considerably different outcomes.

You want to take enough of a psychedelic to dislodge the ego from its executive function but not so much that your brain is overwhelmed (e.g., taking a "heroic" dose) and you struggle to remember what happened during the session, resulting in a dissociative response. Sometimes, when not taking a high enough dose, the experience can become little more than a prolonged struggle of egoic resistance (the proverbial "bad trip"). Here there is not enough force from the psychedelic to help act against the ego to relegate its executive position and penetrate the layers of mind.

Over time, the more experienced you are with this type of work and the various meditative techniques outlined in this book, the lower the dose you will likely need. People with less experience and strong ego structures tend to need higher doses.

Because we are ultimately trying to relegate the ego, I often have participants do one or two individual 5-MeO-DMT sessions in the weeks preceding a mindmeld session. As mentioned earlier, 5-MeO-DMT can energetically open people up for more expansive experiences with other psychedelics, including energetic and psychic openings in the mindmeld.

To get started, I recommend the doses below for the Psychedelic Mindmeld, but personal discrimination should be the priority. Also, the dose can be difficult to determine, as potency is hard to gauge with psychedelics, such as ayahuasca (different brews have varying amounts of the active psychoactive ingredient N,N-DMT), mushrooms (different species have varying amounts of psilocybin and psilocin), or the amount of LSD on individual tabs versus liquid LSD. Crystalline DMT and mescaline also have hydrochloride (HCl), sulphate, and freebase versions, each with different potency (my recommendations are based on HCl versions).

- Ayahuasca: Minimum dose: one ounce (30 milliliters) to one-and-a-half ounces (45 milliliters). High dose: two ounces (60 milliliters).
- LSD: Minimum dose: 200 to 300 micrograms. High dose: 500 to 600 micrograms.
- Mescaline (HCl): Minimum dose: 400 to 500 milligrams. High dose: 500 to 800 milligrams.
- Psilocybin mushrooms: Minimum dose: 3 to 4 grams. High dose: 5 to 7 grams.
- 5-MeO-DMT (HCl): Minimum dose: 20 milligrams. High dose: 25 to 30 milligrams.

It is becoming increasingly popular to stack, or mix, psychedelics, such as taking LSD or mushrooms with MDMA. Considerations include timing for ingesting each dose of the mix and adjusting/titrating dosage during the session. I recommend starting with just one psychedelic when working with the mindmeld. If there is an interest in stacking psychedelics, I recommend to first try stacking individually before trying it in the mindmeld.

MUSIC

Inducing holotropic states of consciousness by using music is an ancient technique. Over the millennia, shamans, yogis, Christian and Buddhist monks, Sufis, and many others have used music to enter holotropic states to connect to spirit and healing. For example, the sonic drive of percussion instruments like drums can act as a carrier wave to transport participants and sustain them in the journey. According to Michael Harner (1990), shamans sometimes refer to their drums as the "horse" or "canoe" that transports them into the shamanic worlds (p. 51). In many of these traditions, music alone is used to enter holotropic states without psychedelics. Sometimes dance, either free-flowing or ritualized and choreographed, is added or other forms of movement or ritual are, but the point is music plays a fundamental role in the journey.

For our purposes, music is a tool to help the ego-mind let go and surrender to the experience. Music can both subtly relax and distract the mind from its incessant chatter and internal dialogue. As such, music can help people overcome psychological defenses and impasses and contribute to surrendering to the experience (Grof, 2019a, p. 362).

I recommend starting the session with music. Everybody has musical preferences, so personal preferences should be given due consideration. A common selection for psychedelic sessions is instrumental music, such as Western classical, Indian, or Sufi, with instruments such as the sitar, tabla, and harmonium. Usually, music with consistent rhythm and beats that are trance-inducing is best. The music should have a minimum of lyrics, especially if they convey meaning and can push people in a particular direction, distracting them from simply letting go into the experience.

Modern examples of modalities that use music for trance-inducing emotional and psychosomatic healing include 5Rhythms, Ecstatic Dance, and Holotropic Breathwork. These modalities usually work with thematic playlists that have an event arc of introduction, the buildup to a midpoint, and then a slowing to a conclusion.

In Holotropic Breathwork, developed by Stanislav Grof and Christina Grof (2010), the sessions begin with dynamic, flowing, emotionally uplifting, and reassuring music. As the session continues, the music gradually increases in intensity and moves to powerful rhythmic and trance-inducing pieces. Toward the midpoint, often an hour and a half in, when the experience typically culminates, "peak" or "breakthrough" music is introduced. Selections range from sacred music, such as masses, oratoria, requiems, and powerful orchestral pieces, to dramatic film soundtracks. In the second half of the session, the intensity of the music gradually decreases with the use of emotionally moving, uplifting, and heart-opening pieces. To end the session, the music has a soothing, flowing, timeless, and meditative quality.

5Rhythms, developed by Gabrielle Roth (n.d.) in the late 1970s, follows a similar style of progressive musical elements composing a dance session: (1) Flowing, (2) Staccato, (3) Chaos, (4) Lyrical, and (5) Stillness.

There are plenty of resources online to help one put together good playlists. Spotify, for example, has psychedelic and 5Rhythms playlists. My preference is to work with the music of Prem Joshua.

I recommend experimenting, including working with music on and with it off. Having a backup playlist is a good idea in case the flow doesn't work. The challenge is that you want to immerse yourself in the experience and only use the music as a tool, not letting it distract you from going deeper.

A final consideration is agreeing on music volume. For psychedelic sessions, some prefer louder volumes to aid the ego in releasing its grip, while for others, loud music is too jarring.

There is a lot of choice of how to work with music and what to work with. Choose purposefully.

SAFETY PROTOCOLS

It is critical to plan for safety. Safety exists on two planes: (1) physical safety and (2) perceived safety.

For *physical* safety, having access to phones is essential for emergencies. The participants should agree beforehand on what defines an emergency. For example, if someone feels abused or irreconcilably "lost" during the session, they should be able to phone a friend or family member to come and pick them up. If there is a health emergency, there should be agreement to phone 911; this can be complicated because the psychedelic you are using is likely illegal, and this may cause hesitation about calling authorities for help, even though someone's life is on the line. Each person should give the other person an emergency contact number for a reliable person to offer support in case of need. Ideally, the emergency contact will understand the range of complex phenomena that may occur in psychedelic sessions to help ensure they don't overreact.

Establishing safety protocols in advance is crucial because when you are engaged in the work, you are unlikely to think straight and problem-solve real emergencies effectively and efficiently. In this context, inexperienced people should consider having a third person sit for the session who does not take any psychedelics and can provide a safe and objective container for the experience. A sitter needs to be qualified. Being qualified means having prior experience with psychedelics and being aware of all the strange possibilities outlined in this book. Ideally, the sitter should only observe the session from a distance and should avoid any engagement, including talking, unless medically necessary.

If there is a sitter, one added consideration is to have them video-record the session. If there is little movement or vocalization during a session, there will be little to review. But if there is physically energetic work, a review of the footage can be a helpful reminder of how the work was done and where. If the energetic work clears blockages in a person's body, the footage can highlight areas for future work by other health professionals, such as a massage therapist, acupuncturist, visceral manipulation therapist (gentle manipulation of the viscera to promote optimal mobility among organs), osteopath, etc. If sessions are recorded, there needs to be agreement on how the footage will be stored (or deleted,) and with whom it can be shared.

Having each participant familiar with basic first aid is recommended. Other simple things, like knowing where the fire extinguisher is, also promote safety.

Ensuring the *perception* of safety among participants is more complicated. Waivers to address medical conditions and concerns about any form of injury are optional but may not carry any weight in the context of certain psychedelics being illegal. While preparing for physical safety helps create an environment of safety, trust is even more crucial.

An essential facet of establishing trust is consent. Under no circumstances should people engage in the mindmeld without prior consent nor should they be under any pressure to participate. For people with a history of physical or sexual abuse, physical and psychic sharing can be particularly intense and possibly triggering. While people who have gone through these traumatizing episodes may have a lot to gain from this process, they are also the most vulnerable and may warrant abstention from participating. "Appendix B: Psychedelic Mindmeld Agreement of Intent" is a consent form template for the mindmeld for your consideration.

An aspect of ensuring safety is setting clear boundaries for confidentiality. Because most psychedelics are still illegal, there is vulnerability in their use. The strangeness and personal contents of sessions are often very private. Discuss and be clear about what may be shared with others, including the specifics of who the "others" are. Clarifying what specifically can be shared about the particular session should be broached again during the debriefing to ensure mutual understanding.

SEXUALITY AND ESTABLISHING PHYSICAL BOUNDARIES

Related to safety is the establishing of physical boundaries. It is likely both people will notice a movement of sexual energy when moving toward the mindmeld, and this can be hazardous territory. It is necessary to be aware of the flow of sexual energy, discuss it, and set boundaries. A strict and absolute boundary in the mindmeld is no sexual contact.*

By our nature, we are sexual beings. We have deep sexual drives to procreate. Sex is also pleasurable. We also have a drive in our psyche toward union and integration. These drives can give rise to sexual desire and consummating connection. Sexual drives can also result from a reenactment of early attachment dynamics and

---

*In the case of long-term couples, there should be a discussion of sexual boundaries before each session where sexual engagement may be an option, although sexual engagement will likely distract from engaging more deeply telepathically.

childhood wounds, early sexual violations, depression, and underlying needs for physical contact. As Grof (2008; 2009) as well as Grof and Grof (2010) describe, when working with psychedelics or Holotropic Breathwork, the desire to act on sexual urges can often function as a psychological defense and avoidance of deeper trauma, possibly linked to painful and frightening dependence on a feminine figure or some form of abuse.

According to Fisher et al. (2012), sexual thoughts surface nineteen times on average per day for men and ten times per day for women. As most men and women meet various people they tend to immediately assess attractiveness and desire: hot or not. Because of preferences, this mechanism is so fast it usually doesn't register in the case of not finding another person attractive. But as soon as there is the possibility of finding the other attractive, the impulses from the radar become more apparent and are especially noticeable if you physically shift your head or body to get a better glimpse. Sexual desire during the session can feel very compelling. Physical proximity and the onset of the psychedelic are likely to exaggerate feelings of sexual desire. I make these observations because awareness of sexual energy often arises in the mindmeld.

It is commonplace at the beginning of the session, usually within the first half hour of meditating, for sexual energy to emerge for one or both participants. This movement of sexual energy does not seem to depend on the gender or sexual predisposition of the participants.

I identify as a cis-straight (heterosexual) male (he/him). But in doing mindmeld work with men, I have been surprised at the fluidity of sexual energy and feelings of attraction. For me, sexual energy does not reach the point of sexual desire to have intercourse with another man but can elicit desired physical closeness. While many people can feel comfortable with the fluid nature of sexual feelings, some may develop a fear of changing their sexual identity, which could create an unnecessary but immediate crisis to work through. When working with people of your preferred gender, the desires can feel more compelling.

It is vital to discuss the nature of sexual energy during the briefing. Sexual energy exists and is an integral part of being human. Each participant therefore needs to cope with it. The more open participants are about discussing it, the less taboo the feelings become and the less shame and guilt there is surrounding sexual desire. The discussion itself seems to act like a partial antidote to sexual energy.

If and when a sexual desire arises, the more effective antidote is to look inward and to meditate and observe the sensations and how they connect to the desire. Ask yourself: From where in the body is the passion coming? Do not deny the existence of the desire. Let the challenging sexual material surface, witness it, and let it flow and dissipate—all without physically engaging with your partner beyond continuing to hold hands. Let the sexual energy propel you further into the trance that can become the mindmeld.

Usually, as the psychedelic begins to take stronger effect as more time passes, the movement to different sensations and visualizations is quick. In most instances, feelings of sexual energy are fleeting, lasting only seconds to minutes. Sexual energy may arise later in the session, but then, return to the same observation technique, and again, it will pass.

Again, a critical boundary in the mindmeld is no sexual contact. To physically engage sexually risks crossing ethical and moral boundaries and can easily lead to tricky emotional states and possibly to accusations of sexual assault. If there is consent for adult sexual contact in the moment, any form of approval while using psychedelics is tenuous and should not be accepted.

The challenge is that when engaged in sharing energetic physical contents, there can be a lot of physical contact—which is not sexually driven but may include brushes with the genitals. Contact does not mean groping or fondling, which has obvious adult sexual content and should never happen. A few examples can illustrate the tricky challenge of physical engagement and how genitals can get in the way.

Physical engagement can vary from simply having one hand on an arm or leg to something approaching a full-body massage where both bodies are fully engaged in moving energy. On one occasion, I physically worked with a woman for five hours straight. At one point, my body was stretched over hers with my head between her feet and my feet at her head. We were both grasping each other's feet. Yet, with torsos bound to each other, neither of us was sexually stimulated.

Later in the same session, the woman was lying on her back with me sitting on her torso, my knees straddling her lower ribs. I was working her right arm, which was outstretched, with my left hand, but bracing myself with my right hand partly on her breast. Again, there was no sexual stimulation.

When working with a man, my hand went from working on his torso to his thigh. Along the way, my hand brushed his genitals. When the body moves energy beyond the conscious mind, these "bumps" can happen. It is crucial to discuss these possibilities in the briefing because if either participant is uncomfortable with their genitals being touched (not groped or fondled), they should not try this work.

Another possible sexual challenge is if one person feels compelled to start fondling their own genitals. While ideally this should not happen because of the intent to observe sexual sensations and let them pass without acting on them, if a participant can't help themselves because they are absorbed in rapture, the other person needs to decide to either sit through the experience, not engaging the other person, or leave the room. I don't recommend trying to intervene in an attempt to stop the person as interference may create traumatic effect, especially if the person fondling themselves or masturbating is responding to deep regression and the surfacing of past traumatic contents; by letting them act out, they can have a powerfully corrective experience, possibly healing long-lasting psychological trauma (Grof, 2008, p. 160).

Another sex-related challenge is that one person may take all their clothes off. While for obvious reasons this is not recommended when one is already in close physical contact with another, I recommend discussing boundaries around nudity in the briefing. If both people do not have an issue with nudity, then there is little likelihood for a problem. (I still recommend not getting naked because people may reflect on the experience after the session with unforeseen guilt or shame, or they may project the same onto the other participant in an accusatory way.) If one participant has an issue with nudity and the other person decides to undress during the session, it is fair for the detractor to ask the other person to put their clothes back on. If the person refuses, a "safe" room needs to be available for the participant to go to and be alone.

A final point to make on sexual boundaries is the consideration of nonsexual physical touch when relaxing after physical and psychic energetic exchanges in the mindmeld. This distinction should be made in the briefing for what participants are comfortable with and not, establishing strict ethical rules and boundaries. For example, hugging another person can be very rewarding to both participants by elevating dopamine, oxytocin, and serotonin, all endogenous chemicals known for happiness, relaxation, improved mood, and lower levels of depression. Some people are not open to physical embraces such as hugging; in cases like these, they probably should not try the mindmeld because of its physically intimate exchanges. But most people accept hugging as normal. On the other hand, a more lasting embrace, like cuddling each other, is often more complex for people. Yet after having gone through what can be a heroic exchange of physical and psychic contents, it may be comforting and consoling to relax in each other's arms for a few minutes.

One of the most natural ways for humans to calm themselves is to embrace another person physically. To embrace is to share intimacy more consciously, being more awake to meeting primal needs of being touched, comforted, validated, needed, loved, and appreciated. In this context, physical contact can be highly rewarding. But physical embrace can lead to a slippery slope where this intimate connection can lead to kissing and more. Here, physical embrace can create vulnerability and be triggering. It is possible to cross boundaries, resulting in broken trust and antagonism with longer-term adverse outcomes.

The ego can also quickly become engaged in judging physical intimacy, which can later create false stories of shame, guilt, or attachment. This issue is more likely to arise if someone is in a romantic relationship with another person. If people are in romantic relationships with another or others, it is wise to consult them on what they need the physical boundaries to be. The challenge of attachment is one of the traps participants can fall into, which is discussed in more detail in chapter 13. To help avoid this trap, be aware of it and set clear boundaries in advance of the session for acceptable physical contact between the waves of energy work and shared consciousness. "Appendix B: Psychedelic Mindmeld Agreement of Intent" provides suggestions to help both participants set clear intentions and boundaries going into a mindmeld session.

MORE THAN TWO PEOPLE

Working with more than two people is an option but is not recommended. Every time you introduce one more person into the mindmeld, the relationships get exponentially more complex. Not only do you have to be aware of your surfacing material, but you also have to be aware of and prepared to work with the material of the others. This may include navigating the relationship of the interactions shared by each other possible dyad in the group independently of you. Such complexity is only for the most adept. If you plan to try this, I recommend each person work with each other individually first in a mindmeld dyad before working together as a group.

The potential for exploring the power and profundity of the hive mind is mind-boggling. I have heard anecdotal reports of group telepathic experiences in psychedelic ceremonial settings (e.g., ayahuasca and peyote ceremonies) and *communitas* experiences in raves and concerts. Various authors report "tribal telepathic understanding" (Nuttal, 1970) and telepathic group mind (Leary et al., 2007; Wolfe, 1968). But I am unaware of ongoing attempts to induce such hive-mind connections intentionally or of any research into the phenomenon.

PLANNING THE SECOND HALF OF THE SESSION

The psychedelic journey has an arc of experience based on the psychedelic chemically cycling through the body from ingestion to completion. The four phases in the arc are: (1) ascent, (2) peak, (3) plateau, and (4) descent. Usually, the final phase lasts the longest, through the second half of a session, regardless of what psychedelic is used. For our purposes, the first half of the session is to: (1) relegate or transcend the ego in the ascent, (2) enter the mindmeld in the peak, and (3) maintain it in the plateau. As the psychedelic begins to slowly wear off, usually around the midpoint of the session, the ego starts to regain its executive function and usually trumps efforts at mindmelding.

If the mindmeld is the primary purpose of the session, then what happens in the second half of the session in the *descent* really falls to the participants' preference. There is a long list of possibilities to consider, highlighting the various ways of engaging with psychedelics described in chapter 4. Make plans in advance so you don't have to make decisions on the fly. Plans can change, but if plans aren't made in advance, it is easy to avoid doing more challenging things like continuing meditation.

Below I list several options for the second half of the session, but there are two things I recommend after the first half of every session:

1. List in bullet points the highlights of the experience, particularly anything seemingly shared in consciousness, to discuss during the session debriefing. Because you will still be under the influence of the psychedelic, don't worry about details. You can wait until

the session is wrapped up to journal. Even if you don't journal, the short, bulleted list can be a helpful reminder of how powerful your experience was as time passes and memory fades. A helpful tip for memory recall is to practice labeling your experiences as you are having them using keywords related to memorable moments, names, locations, themes, or emotions (e.g., "Dog," if your pet dog shows up; or "India" as a location; or "Love" or "Sadness" as emotions). You can also try lying entirely still with eyes closed, possibly with the same music playing as at the session's peak, and eliciting/ remembering your emotions from the session.

2. List and track any points on the body where physical work was done or where you felt profound sensations, vibrations, or movement. While the energy needing to be processed from any particular area may be resolved, some areas of the body may require further intervention, which should be monitored.

As the egos of both participants begin to reform toward the end of the session's first half, there will be an increasing temptation to discuss each other's experiences. Discovering what was energetically and psychically transmitted can be exciting. But the ego can easily get caught in discussion, and hours can quickly pass when more meaningful activities can be played with and enjoyed, while talk can wait. Waiting also helps you avoid influencing the other person's experience when the power of suggestion is still strong while partially under the influence of the psychedelic. Too much talk can also short-circuit the experience and bring everything back to "normal," which wastes the session. So, wait to compare notes and debrief until the session has ended and you have written a summary of your experience.

Additional options for the second half of the session are:

- Continuing the meditation. When working with long-lasting psychedelics like LSD or mushrooms, continuing to meditate for another two to four hours can be rewarding. As the psychedelic wears off, more effort is required to sit in stillness. But similar to standard forms of meditation, this offers an excellent opportunity to observe the ego and its ongoing desire to do something. As such, it is a great time to practice stillness, peace, and equanimity. By maintaining deep relaxation, it is possible to train oneself to enter deeper states of meditation and holotropic states without psychedelics while in this intermediary zone of the psychedelic wearing off. You may also want to try experimenting with Holotropic Breathwork (see chapter 12) to reengage a deeper holotropic state as the psychedelic is waning.

- Doing yoga.
- Sharing massage, which may include massaging deep tissue knots identified earlier in the first half of the session.
- Dancing.
- Chanting or singing, or simply humming or whistling. Repeating om, or mantras, can be a beautiful, soothing exercise.
- Playing musical instruments, like drums.
- Listening to music.
- Artwork: painting, drawing (e.g., mandalas), collaging, sculpting, or a free flow of another form of artistic expression to capture highlights from the first half of the session.
- Looking at artwork (e.g., psychedelic digital art or other abstract images).
- Reading poetry or religious, philosophical, or spiritual texts.
- Journaling or creative writing. This exercise can include problem-solving a professional or work challenge.
- Working with tarot cards to find deeper meaning in the day's session.
- Discussing personal psychological challenges. While this is usually best postponed until the end of the session, some people find it rewarding to discuss therapeutic topics that they may not otherwise broach when they are not under the influence of plant medicine. While this can be risky territory, peer support for working

through personal challenges related to the session or to more general topics in life can be rewarding.

- Eating tasty fruits and vegetables or other whole foods can introduce a heightened gustatory experience. An equally valid option is to fast for the remainder of the day; fasting can be a reminder of the seriousness one brings to the work and is healthy for the body.

- Having a hot or cold shower or bath.

- Going for a walk in nature is an option but not necessarily recommended until near the very end of the session. Connecting to nature can be profound when working with psychedelics but can introduce logistical challenges. For example, I had a friend go for a walk and faint in front of passersby. What started as an enjoyable experience suddenly got complicated. The person who fainted almost hit her head on a tree, which could have resulted in a concussion. Not being completely lucid also increases the possibility of tripping and getting injured. In this case, the risks are not unlike those for being intoxicated with alcohol. (Going for a walk in an urban setting is likely to be overwhelming for anybody on high-dose psychedelics.)

Engaging in any of these activities can be enjoyable. Choosing what to do should be reasonably fluid based on what participants agree to do.

When planning for the second half of the session, consider preparing the overall environment. For example, ensure you have yoga mats if you plan to do yoga. If you plan to do art, have art supplies already out.

Whatever is agreed to for the second half of the session, a general ground rule is for people to remain near each other. I once had a participant leave the house to go for a jog. I stayed in the house and ended up worrying most of the time about his safety. While this was an exercise for me in letting go of control, the other person broke the ground rule of staying together. As a result, I have been reluctant to work with this person since.

As the session ends, participants may want to somehow close the session. This can be as simple as sharing gratitude with each other and any discarnate beings who participated. More complex rituals can be introduced based on the participants' preferences.

With the preparatory work of set and setting addressed, we can now explore how best to enter the Psychedelic Mindmeld.

9

Entering the Psychedelic Mindmeld: Meditative Techniques

As described above, there are three key phases of the psychedelic journey in the mindmeld: (1) the *ascent*, in which the ego is relegated, (2) the *peak*, when it is possible to enter the mindmeld, and (3) the *plateau*, when you try to maintain the mindmeld. The first meditative technique, "Stillness and Breath," is to help settle the mind and body and initiate the relegation of the ego. The second and third techniques, "Opening the Heart" and "Surrender," are to continue the process of relegating the ego and initiate the mindmeld through the final stages of ascent and on to the peak. After discussing engagement in the mindmeld and what is shared in it in chapters 10 and 11, three additional meditation techniques are described in chapter 12 to help maintain the mindmeld during the plateau of the experience: "Being the Witness," "Holotropic Breathwork," and "Being the Bodhisattva."

The meditative techniques I am suggesting will range in effectiveness for people depending on the correct set and setting, inclusive of the type and dosage of psychedelic, and each participant's prerequisites, biographical history, and overall personal constitution and intuitive capacity. Both participants have to relegate their egos for a full sharing of energetic physical and psychic content. If you do not succeed, seek to let go, and let go . . . again and again. Be prepared for setbacks and obstacles. It is critical to continue the use of self-discipline and optimism, never giving up. Success comes to those who believe in the power of telepathy. In my experience, while volition and intent toward allowing a shift in consciousness and letting go of the ego in the meditation is needed, grace also plays a role in dropping into the mindmeld. As such, the deeper you can let go of your small "self," the "I," the ego, the further you drop into the mystical where grace lies in wait for you and telepathic connections are made possible beyond focused volition.

In my own efforts, I have successfully mindmelded with around half of the people I have worked with. For those I have worked with successfully more than once, there is no guarantee the mindmeld will work again in another session. While I can consistently relegate and transcend my ego, many others cannot. When the other person remains caught in their ego, I can still do physical energetic healing work on them, but the work is more unidirectional. Here I can intuitively feel into the other person. And while I assume they unconsciously share physical and psychic content with me, they are usually unaware of doing so. For example, I have seen dozens of lifetimes of others, yet they are unaware of their journey through multiple lives.

There are no hard and fast rules for the meditative techniques I lay out below, only recommendations. The methods are progressive but not necessarily linear. The more one does this work, the more one becomes accustomed to the flow of the mindmeld, engaging, disengaging, and reengaging using the various meditative techniques. I encourage you to experiment and discover what works best for you. You may also want to research and practice lucid dreaming, shamanic journeying, out-of-body experience, or past-life regression techniques to help in telepathic engagement. The techniques I outline are a starting place for you to progress into personalized methods best suited for you. Persistence and perseverance can be instrumental in opening your intuition and creative entry points to telepathic connections.

To get started with the mindmeld, perform any adopted ritual, such as smudging. Then, once each of you has taken the psychedelic, take three to five minutes and sit opposite each other, holding hands, and stare quietly into each other's eyes. This may feel uncomfortable at first, but reach into the other person through the portal to their soul. Seek to observe and become their experience, setting your intention to telepathically mindmeld. Once you conclude this exercise, turn on your music playlist. Then, lie side by side on a comfortable bed or mat. Hold hands with the other person. (Physical contact is not necessary for a telepathic connection but helps facilitate focus, physical presence, intuitive physical assessment of energy in the other person, and intimacy of the relationship.) Close your eyes. Observe your busy wandering mind. Being apprehensive and nervous is expected; you do not know what will happen next, but you know you are entering the unknown, and no matter what happens over the next few hours, there is no escape. I have been doing this work for years and feel nervous before every session. Addressing anxiety is one reason why meditation is a valuable skill to develop. It helps you relax. So, now let's get into the specifics of the meditation techniques.

MEDITATIVE TECHNIQUE: STILLNESS AND BREATH

I discussed the nature of ego in chapter 7 because it is both our ally and our foe when doing this work. The ego is our ally because it can help direct our conscious choice to do the job with intent and engage in meditation; it is our foe because it will not want to let go of its control at the decisive moment of penetrating through to the unconscious mind and through to nondual clear light mind. To start, we need to use a meditative style that is engaging to the ego but slowly and subtly let it fade into the background as the psychedelic contributes to chemically and psychically shifting the mindscape. For this reason, the initial meditative technique requires complete physical stillness. This includes avoidance of any talking. When the body is still, stillness is brought to mind, allowing it to journey to the deeper layers of consciousness. Chuang Tzu states: "To the mind that is still, the whole universe surrenders" (in Waley, 1934, p. 58).

Movement is a distraction in meditation and is usually related to the fear of the ego penetrating through its very nature. It is equally the ego's (aka the monkey mind's) compulsive nature to always be doing something, like commenting on something, wanting to be in control, or desiring satisfaction. Each itch or muscle discomfort becomes an excuse to move. As soon as the body moves, the ego escapes from sitting with discomfort. There may be an initial fear of stillness and being exposed to feeling certain sensations long avoided. But if you can bring curiosity to bear on what is happening inside of you—to the fear itself, to the nature and flow of the sensations, then fear can be trumped, and things will shift positively. To help the mind avoid grasping at movement when discomfort arises, simply observe the sensations as they arise and dissolve. When you are engaging yourself in this way, you are involved in your emotional regulation, calming yourself to go deeper into the meditation.

Here, meditative training like that practiced in Vipassana is helpful. This Buddhist practice is to sit completely still and bring equanimity, mental calmness, and composure to discomfort and the desire to move. To help settle the ego into stillness, slowly scan the body from head to foot and from foot to head, back and forth, observing how the sensations, both comfortable and uncomfortable, never stay the same but are constantly changing, sometimes becoming more uncomfortable, more comfortable, more sensation, less sensation. The more you can tune in to the body, the less you will identify with the ruminations of your mind. You will become increasingly anchored in the present moment. Someone who cannot lie completely still is unlikely to enter the mindmeld.

A similar and slightly simpler technique to calm the mind is focusing on the breath and the sensations of the breath coming into and leaving the body. You can be specific with your focus, from the sensations of the air passing through the nostrils or on the back of the throat to the chest rising and falling. I make it an ongoing practice to return to my breath and bodily sensations throughout the day, a method of being centered and present in the *now* moment.

Either of these techniques will help calm and quiet the mind and the nervous system. It is then possible to increasingly let go of egoic concerns like anticipation, expectation, prejudice, apprehension, fear, or personal issues. The more this process unfolds, the more the ego relaxes and allows for the powerful tool of the psychedelic to help dislodge the ego from its preeminent position.

As the psychedelic begins to take effect, you may see fractal imagery. The feeling of your body's weight and spatial awareness may shift. Often at this stage, the ego-mind can become more agitated as it sinks into the murk of the surface to the middle layers of the unconscious mind. Thought can become increasingly disagreeable and uncomfortable. It can feel as if your thoughts are discordantly banging against a wall. This stage may be fleeting but also feel like an eternity. In real time, it is likely only to last between a few minutes and up to an hour. It's rare, but if the psychedelic dosage is too low or the person has a well-armored ego, this struggle can last for the duration of the session.

As the ego-mind struggles in the agitation of losing control, the body, as an extension of the executive function of the ego, will want to move. The ego will use any number of tricks to distract you from subjugating its executive function. As mentioned, the chief of these tricks at this point is moving the body. Itches, minor aches and pains, and fidgeting can all forcibly push their way into your field of awareness. You may desire to urinate; check yourself to see if this is really needed. Just observe these sensations and do not succumb to movement. You may be tempted to talk; don't. Keep returning to the technique of observing the breath and avoid moving any part of your body.

Ironically, in using these techniques, the ego is still doing. Here we are simply trying to relax the grasp of the ego. The ultimate thing to do is nothing. The more you can sit in the joy of simply being and in the moment of now, the more likely an authentic self-expression of energy will surface. The power of divine intuitive, creative force can then lead to the manifestation of the mindmeld, where each individual's unique inner configuration and patterning will commingle and interpenetrate with the other. The following technique, "Opening the Heart," helps us access this divine intuitive force.

MEDITATIVE TECHNIQUE: OPENING THE HEART

As the intensity of the psychedelic trip amplifies, it is time for the meditative focus to shift. The technique I describe here is not necessarily required. A mindmeld can occur quickly if both egos dissolve early. However, as the psychedelic begins to take hold and you feel like you are getting distracted or overwhelmed by your own experience to the exclusion of the other person, it can be good to aid the direction of your intent toward mindmelding with the other person. To do this, focus your awareness on your heart and imagine it opening, visualizing it on the canvas of your mind's eye. See it and feel it pouring loving energy out toward the other person. Use all of your senses to reach out and feel into their experience of receiving your love. Share yourself with the other. Let yourself drop into loving intimacy. Let the intention you have planted within your unconscious to connect energetically at a physical and psychic level with your co-melder rise into awareness. You may also try tracing the energy you are opening from your heart, through your arm, and your hand into your partner's hand, then up their arm and into their heart. Alternatively, you can focus on breathing out loving energy to your partner. Keep concentrating on deep interconnection. Another alternative is to visualize your "third eye" of extrasensory perception in the center of your forehead. Imagine a silver cord growing out from your third eye and moving over the face of your co-melder to their third eye. Once the cord is connected, send pulsing, loving light energy through the cord to your partner to initiate the telepathic mindmeld.

In the inner exploration, it becomes increasingly apparent love is an ingredient in the alchemical mix to help overcome any fear you may face on the journey. When you reach out from the heart, it fosters connection in the mindmeld. Love is the antidote to the control and domination of the ego. If the ego leads you down a fearful path of self-preservation, fomenting alienation and separation in duality, then love as a choice for a deeper connection to the other person can help you make psychic contact with the other. Through the mindmeld you can experience yourself in the other person and as the other person. When you transcend your sense of separation in the experience, your feelings of connection and caring for the other person can amplify, fueled by deeper awareness and concern for them.

One of my introductory experiences to the mindmeld was through the intention of sharing heartfelt energy with my friend Jude. While my consciousness had previously entered the body of another person while on ayahuasca, I had no real idea of the potential depth of the mindmeld. For me, the concept still played in my mind like science fiction.

Through various synchronicities, I attended an ayahuasca ceremony in the Mexican jungle while travelling with Jude. I was planning a recreational trip to Mexico when a shaman contacted me and told me they were holding a ceremony in the same place I was traveling to. I had never been to the location before, and the shamans had never held a ceremony there. What made this incredible was that Jude was interested in trying ayahuasca but did not want to try it in our hometown out of fear of risking his professional reputation.

It was a large ceremony of around thirty participants, three shamans, and two helpers. The first two nights for me were uneventful. A couple of hours into the third night, and again little was happening. I was disappointed and frustrated, primarily because of the synchronicities bringing my friend and me to the ceremony. Jude had spent the whole time being sick while on the ayahuasca and complaining about his experience. His struggle wasn't surprising to me as he was an alcoholic and struggling with profound traumas, and I believe the medicine was working to heal his body and mind. All the same, I found myself asking why I was there. The simple answer was that I was concerned about Jude's alcoholism and its negative impact on him, his family, and his friends. I had urged him to try ayahuasca to possibly help with his addiction, which he rarely admitted was a problem.

Up to this point, my intention for the ceremony had been a vague notion of healing for myself. But as I pondered my intention, it shifted to meditating on sharing a loving, openhearted energy with Jude. Within minutes of changing my intention, I felt a rush of energy rise through my body. My right arm jerked and swiftly grabbed the left side of his head. He did not resist. My arm began to shake. The vibration moved up my arm and into my whole body. All of me began to tremble and shake. Tears started streaming down my face, and an outpouring of grief overwhelmed me. The energy flowed through me for about half an hour.

Gradually the trembling eased, and the crying ceased. I looked to my right and saw a dark, earthy, wormy energy begin to work its way through my hand and up my arm. My ego reacted with fear as the black mass reached my shoulder. I sought to cast the energy off into a void in the universe, with apparent success. But partway through this process fear got the better of me, and the flow stopped.

The next day I asked Jude what his story was. He told me that when we were psychically joined, he experienced the first deep, cathartic release of grief about his young daughter dying many years before of a disease from which he could not save her, despite being a doctor. I told him I had felt his grief flow through me but without knowing the nature of the trauma. Once he told me his story, the energetic flow made sense to me.

I learned many things during this ceremony, but the most salient was how profound intent could be, not only in initiating the mindmeld, but also in prematurely ending it when I became fearful of the dark, earthy energy flowing into my arm. To be clear, I did not physically withdraw to stop the mindmeld, but the fear arousal was enough to stop it. In other words, it was not a conscious choice to stop but an unconscious one. This distinction is important because it highlights how there is both a conscious choice or intent of engagement and an unconscious choice of engagement—or disengagement. As such, for two people to engage in the Psychedelic Mindmeld, both must choose to connect psychically and energetically at the conscious and unconscious levels. The conscious intention is the verbal agreement to join in the mindmeld between participants. What happens afterward relies on the unconscious, once the ego is shunted from its dominant position.

If working with your heart is new to you and this method is not working, try shifting your awareness to listening to the other person's inner experience instead. Listening may start with noticing the other person's breath or hearing them fidget. Try entraining your breathing with theirs. Perhaps, you can feel their heartbeat pulsing from their hand to yours. I have found this subtle shift in "listening" awareness can immediately drop me into attunement with the other person, thus initiating the mindmeld. Here you are trying to place yourself in their experience, putting yourself inside them.

If you find this exercise trying and you keep getting distracted by your thoughts, return to observing your breath and calming yourself to step into surrender.

MEDITATIVE TECHNIQUE: SURRENDER

As you drop further and further into ecstatic experience, the ego has begun to let go. Psychedelics are potent tools to open the floodgates to the inner universe forcibly. Where there is resistance to the opening of the unconscious, it is generally in fear of the unknown, in fear of change, or in fear of uncomfortable, bare emotional states lying in wait under the surface. And, at the moment, it really can feel as intense as if you are about to die physically. Of course, what is dying is just the ego, and it is not really passing. It is simply being relegated or transcended. But again, in the moment it will not usually feel this straightforward.

Ego relegation or dissolution is necessary to penetrate the deeper layers of the mind that are vastly more expansive than the ego can manage where relegation is into dualistic states of consciousness and dissolution is into nondual states. Ego relegation or dissolution is needed because it helps us let go of our conditioning. It helps us let go of the density of the material realm. Our body is then allowed to shift energetically, beyond the physical constraints identified by the ego, into higher states of energy where energies in the body are enabled to flow more intuitively and freely.

I have had several full-blown ego-death trials where I thought I was going to die physically. In one instance, I was lying naked on the bathroom floor after using the toilet, where I said goodbye to my body. In another case, I returned to a "past life" where I was shot while in a B-52 bomber during World War II, died, consciously went through the whole decomposition process, including rigor mortis, and had my flesh rot off my body. But in each case, these deaths transformed into something glorious, either with me journeying to other dimensions or planets or with a greater connection to the Divine. After awakening from the bathroom floor, I directly communicated with "God," connecting to an infinite divine force. After decomposing—after I was shot in the bomber—my heart opened into a fully blooming lotus flower.

Over the years, I have found relegating or dissolving the ego does not become more predictable. Sometimes the transition comes as second nature, and other times it feels like imminent physical death. Sometimes it's easy, and other times it's horrific. It can also feel as though there are orders of the ego dying: the individual ego or the passing of the archetypal ego originating from the collective unconscious.

Disintegration and dissolution of the small ego-self can feel completely overwhelming. The ego's default is to harden its defenses to preserve the status quo of its self-image. Resistance is the ego wanting to maintain its illusion of control. But resistance against the waterfall of the opening induced by the psychedelic only leads to increased discomfort that can feel like drowning. The only way out is through, which is to let go and into the flow of the unknown. To surrender is to take a leap of faith that everything will arise as meant to be brought into greater awareness, both of darkness and in light. To surrender is to let contrivance, clinging, and attachment wash away. It is to open oneself to vulnerability. To surrender is to release oneself to something beyond our known selves and conscious thought: to the unconscious, the soul, the collective unconscious, or a much larger universal intelligence. To surrender is to courageously drop into the void of not knowing. When we open ourselves to the void of the unknown, we open ourselves to learning what we are ready to be taught and are capable of understanding. When we expose ourselves over and over to annihilation, we find the indestructible within us.

Surrender can be as easy as relaxing and voluntarily letting go of any sense of control. Cares and distractions fade. To surrender is to tune in to humility. It is to sit in the presence of oneself and the other. There is nothing to do and nothing to prove. It is not unlike letting yourself fall asleep and into dreaming.

The concept of surrendering into "being" is abstract and can be hard to understand from a practical perspective. "Being" can sound static, but like all states of consciousness, it is a living process where we are constantly engaging with what is. Welwood's (1997) words help guide us more directly toward experiencing *being*, leading us in the direction of surrender:

A simple way to glimpse the nature of your being is to ask yourself as you read this, "Who is taking in these words? Who is experiencing all of this right now?" Without trying to *think* of an answer, if you look directly into the experiencer, the experiencing consciousness itself, what you find is a silent presence that has no shape, location, or form. This nameless presence—in, around, behind, and between all our particular thoughts and experiences—is what the great spiritual traditions regard as our true nature. . . . (p. 3).

To consistently drop into being is to be in the flow of surrender and the flow of allowing. It is to be awake and open.

Sometimes, when my ego fights the experience, it can feel like repeatedly banging my head against a wall. It hurts, and it's annoying, and in the throes of the banging, it is challenging to step back and ask why I am even doing it. But eventually, the fight becomes so exhausting that my ego just resigns and gives up. Capitulation is when egoic contraction lets go to surrender and transforms into spiritual expansion.

When ego dissolution is not forthcoming and there is a feeling of being stuck, try bringing curiosity to the part of you that is fearful by asking, "What part of me is afraid?" Or try reaching beyond yourself and ask, "Show me what I need to know." Ultimately you are asking yourself to reveal something within your consciousness, but it is a way for the ego to reach beyond its limited self-identity.

As the mediation deepens and the mind and body relax, the ego lets go. But strangely and ironically, the body can now feel compelled to move. This impulse is very different from the physical distractions created by the ego. The body is driven to move from beyond the conscious choice of the ego-mind, which is generally preoccupied with either moving the body to become more comfortable—fidgeting—or, as an extension of drives, to "do" something, either where conscious choices are being made or in reaction to the environment (e.g., flight, fight, freeze, or fawn responses to external stimuli). Ball (2009) describes how this internal drive to move, occurring beyond the ego, does not have a "personal" quality but rather can feel like one is moved by forces outside of oneself (p. 82). For the uninitiated, it can seem as if you are possessed because your body is moving beyond conscious choice. But the ego is still present, although farther in the background. With some effort, it is possible to bring the ego back into its higher executive function and stop the movement. When doing this, it becomes obvious the body was not, or is not, inhabited or possessed by another being. The movement is simply one's energy authentically expressing itself.

So, if the body begins to move without conscious intent, it is time to let go and let it roll. In my case, it took over thirty ayahuasca ceremonies before my body began to move on its own spontaneously, but this varies widely from person to person.* The spontaneous movement and engagement of physical energy are discussed in detail in chapter 10, but for now, know this movement can be a signal of entering the mindmeld. As the ego dissolves, the mystical arises. This stage can be a complicated transition. I do not recommend stopping physical processing at this stage, as it will only strengthen the ego's resolve to avoid such states. The ego will want to grasp at doing something; if this is the case, there is a need to surrender even further. Engagement in the mindmeld means to completely let go, offering yourself to the psychedelic, your energy, and the other person's energy. In this process, there is no holding back and no personal censorship. There is no room to be self-conscious; getting caught up in being self-conscious is a fear-based constriction of the ego.

Another possibility is to get lost in your own personal "trip." There is nothing wrong with whatever surfaces. Go with the flow, for it is in the flow that you may meet the other person and share psychic experiences. This is the sharing of psychic consciousness discussed in chapter 11.

A final consideration for reaching into surrender and the mindmeld is the possibility of using joint hypnosis. Hypnosis itself invites surrender. I have not tried this technique, but Charles Tart (1967), psychologist and parapsychologist, began exploring this technique working with LSD in the late 1960s to explore "unusual subjective experiences." In one of his studies, test subjects were jointly hypno-

---

*In my experience, the fastest way to accelerate the process of moving into fractal energetic yoga is to work with 5-MeO-DMT, although not everyone will be "moved" in this way.

tized while using LSD. Both test subjects reported a "merging" and telepathic connection. Using such a technique adds a layer of complexity, including the need for high levels of trust, and experience with hypnosis. For those with the skills and exploratory drive, this technique appears promising.

The preceding sections provide meditation tools to help enter the mindmeld. Once your ego has been relegated, you are on the cusp of entering the mindmeld.

10
Sharing Physical Consciousness

The mindmeld is a telepathic union in which energetic physical* and psychic contents arising from consciousness can be shared. In this telepathic union, co-creation is involved in the transfer of—and, possibly, the total symbiotic absorption in—the contents of shared experience. The shared contents can also be modified or processed by participants, including psychic and physical energetic discharges. To understand what is shared is to explore the nature of physical energy as manifested in the human body and the nature of psychic energy as it arises in the conscious awareness of the human mind. By first understanding the contents of physical and psychic energies, we can better comprehend what we are working with and sharing in the mindmeld.

While we will explore the phenomenon of physical and psychic energies independently in this and the next chapter, at the outset we must realize both are interconnected. Taking a holistic approach, Carl Jung (2017) describes it as follows:

> The distinction between mind and body is an artificial dichotomy,
> a discrimination which is unquestionably based far more on the

---

*Some people may describe the psychic sharing of physical energetic contents as a form of clairvoyance because of the overt connection to a physical state of affairs.

peculiarity of intellectual understanding than on the nature of things. In fact, so intimate is the intermingling of bodily and psychic traits that not only can we draw far-reaching inferences as to the constitution of the psyche from the constitution of the body, but we can also infer from psychic peculiarities the corresponding bodily characteristics (p. 85).

Therefore, the mind and body are so interwoven that we can consider the two to be an energetic composite where the two exist together and simultaneously, directly and indirectly, influence each other in psychobiological relationship. Many researchers have made this distinction in biology, cymatics, epigenetics, neuroscience, medicine, and psychology.

THE HUMAN ENERGETIC SYSTEM

Albert Einstein's theory of special relativity expresses that mass and energy are the same physical entity and can be changed into each other, which is summarized in his equation $E = mc^2$. In this equation, the mass (m) of a body times the speed of light squared (c^2) is equal to the kinetic energy (E) of that body. This equation reveals that everything in the universe is energy in constant movement and transformation of light, vibration, frequencies, and waves. Nikola Tesla and Max Planck reached the same conclusion during their life's research (Laszlo, E., 2016).

In this chapter, I explore the human body from the point of view of its being energy. At its simplest root, the body is electromagnetic radiation or light. Science will substantiate this much. But as we go further, I will make esoteric assertions based more on subjective observation of experience, which is difficult to prove empirically. At the same time, I am not making these assertions in a vacuum. Instead, they are based on the insights of the Eastern and Western wisdom traditions, inclusive of hermetic, shamanic, and yogic traditions, various healing modalities, and insights from psychology and different medical professions. My assertions are also based on my experiences, which I briefly share.

As a human being, you are a being of energy. As Ball (2017) observes, the human body "is an energetic construct that perceives energies of the surrounding environment, produces energy internally, and processes energy via self-expression, and through interaction with elements of the surrounding environment" (p. 129). The Hermetic tradition through the *Kybalion* shares a similar insight: "Every thought, emotion or mental state has its corresponding rate and mode of vibration. And by an effort of the will of the person, or of other persons, these mental states may be reproduced, just as musical tone may be reproduced by causing an instrument to vibrate at a certain rate . . ." (Three Initiates, 1912, p. 85). Tolle (2006) takes a similar view saying, "Thoughts have their own range of frequencies, with negative thoughts at the lower end of the scale and positive thoughts at the higher" (p. 146). We can take these points to mean that thoughts vibrate in the body, affecting the physical self. The biofield anatomy hypothesis goes further with the suggestion humans have an energetic biofield shaped like a torus extending approximately five feet to all sides of the body and three feet above the head and below the feet. The hypothesis is that the biofield contains the record of all of our memories, embedded as energy and information in standing waves within this structure (McKusik, 2014, 2021). From this perspective, thoughts, emotions, sensations, perceptions, and states of consciousness are all forms of moving energy in and around us.

As a manifestation of energy in form, we are always moving. Even if our body sits still, all internal systems continue to move, from our blood flowing to our stomach digesting and our lungs breathing. From inception in the womb to death, we are energy in flow. One could argue this flow of energy has no beginning or end as we are made from stardust—leptons, hadrons, baryons, fermions, bosons, quarks, nucleons, electrons, molecules, atoms, light, waves, dark matter, and so forth, continually being recycled in life and death. To speculate on the origins of stardust is to explore such theoretical concepts as the Big Bang or the creation myths of world religions.

Whatever the truth of origin, my simple point is we are energy. So, when I talk about sharing energy as it manifests in physical form and sensation, we can more easily relate to what is happening in the mind-meld, even if we do not fully understand the dynamics of this exchange.

As a physical form, the human body is a complex energetic system. It comprises intricate subsystems, including the skeletal, muscular, respiratory, endocrine, immune, cardiovascular/circulatory, urinary, integumentary, reproductive, and digestive systems. These systems, in turn, function through interactions with organs, nerves, tissues, cells, bacteria, electrical signals and waves, various chemicals, molecules, and much more. These systems interact in such complex ways that their behaviors, including their relationships with each other, are extremely difficult to understand because their complexity is so challenging to model scientifically. As such, it is hard to understand dependencies and feedback loops among the systems, how they are self-organizing, and how they adapt to change. Behaviors and properties can also emerge in any one human system, appearing to only be possible with their interaction with the more comprehensive whole and not in isolation. Human systems can also act with nonlinearity, where the change of the output in the system is disproportionate to the change of the input (e.g., doubling the dose of a drug in a patient rarely evokes a doubling of the expected response).

All of the systems in the human body cooperate at such a high level that it is difficult to fathom. The achievement of the human body, life in action, far exceeds anything humans have ever created. These systems in the body have to work together to respond to changes in the environment—including temperature changes, diet, level of activity, and exposure to threats to the body, such as toxins and diseases—often working to repair and heal bodily systems. The physiological process, or organizing intelligence, that seeks to keep the variety of functions in the body within set limits for optimal functioning and maintaining life, including such things as body temperature and fluid balances (e.g., blood sugar and oxygen levels), is called homeodynamics. Homeodynamics ensures the free circulation of life energy through multiple channels in the body. For instance, this can be through nutrients in blood cells such as oxygen, carbon dioxide, hormones, glucose, amino acids, vitamins, minerals, and fatty acids, among others in a long list of other chemical and electrical exchanges in the body. Homeodynamics can come into conscious awareness through our feelings, our interoception, prompting us to take corrective action. For example, if I feel cold, I will put on warmer clothes to warm my body. If I feel hungry, I will eat, or if thirsty, I will drink. If I feel sad, I may go to bed and rest, exercise, or socialize, depending on my predisposition. If I feel seriously physically or mentally ill, I will likely go to the doctor for diagnosis and prognosis. Reaching into how we feel is where discernment, directed and mediated by the ego and its longing for control and safety, with such faculties as intellect and memory, helps keep us alive.

Homeostasis, on the other hand, is a relatively stable equilibrium or coherence in the body's physical, chemical, and energetic conditions resulting from the interactions of the interdependent systems described above. When these systems are in homeostasis, the body can perform effectively, ensuring optimum internal conditions for survival, including physical health and healing. Homeostasis also promotes peak mental health, which contributes to infusing and rekindling our life force. We know we are in homeostasis when we feel energetic, healthy, and content, are engaged in life, and are socially connected. The mind and nervous system feel at ease (Hanson, 2013). Homeodynamics is an inherent life force within the whole bodily system, supporting order, structure, function, and resiliency with the aim of homeostasis.

Brennan (1988) describes how the human body lives in a sea of energy, which is the energy existing throughout the whole of the environment around us. The body constantly interacts with this energy and metabolizes it as the energy moves through the body, which is generally felt as emotion. The greater the flow of energy in this interaction, which includes the optimal flow of energy through the internal human systems, the healthier we are. We feel better physically, emotionally, and spiritually. On the other hand, illness in the system is often caused by imbalanced energy or blockages in the flow of energy. A simple example of recognizing what an energetic blockage in the body can feel like is going for a massage and spontaneously crying partway through without any connection to a "story"; this is a release of emotionally blocked energy. In more dramatic form, disease, or the inability to fight and recover from an illness, can result from a lack of flow and resilience in the human energetic system. Beyond causing disease, a lack of energy flow can also distort our perceptions and negatively impact our emotional state, undermining a more positive experience of life.

The human mind is a receiver, perceiver, and transceiver of psychic content within the sea of energy where the body lives. As mentioned above, the body and mind are interconnected. The body then responds to psychic information. As osteopath Jean-Pierre Barral (2007) describes, "Our brain records all the emotions and tensions we encounter and redistributes them in our body according to their intensity, setting off superficial or deeper reactions that range from dysfunction to actual illness" (p. 209). Grof (2009) and Hanson (2013) both separately point out that this effect is particularly heightened in childhood when the brain is in a stage of hyperlearning. Issues from this time—such as abuse, oppression, neglect, rejection, deprivation, abandonment, humiliation, bullying, discrimination, family tension, burdensome secrets, financial hardship, injuries, disabilities, and illness—cast a long shadow. Making this picture more complex, thoughtforms are energetic. So, habitually negative thoughtforms negatively impact the body's physiology (Brennan, 1988, p. 93; Hanson, 2013). Egoic issues of patterns of illusions, projections, distortions, and attachments also contribute to increasing negative energy in the body. Negative thoughtforms driven by egoic dysfunction, unconscious trauma responses, and unexpressed emotions mean that everybody has stuck and incompletely processed energy they carry in their bodies (Ball, 2017; Walker, 2013). Stuck energy can have an impact on the body that can manifest physically and symptomatically, usually in connection with stress hormones, such as adrenaline and cortisol. In response to stress, the brain discharges these chemicals through the nervous system where, when in excess, they can overwhelm and negatively impact the body. Consequential issues can include headaches, promotion of inflammation, muscle or joint tension and aches, thinning bones, chronic fatigue syndrome, problems with bowels or sexual function, cancer growth, cardiovascular and metabolic problems, elevated blood pressure, anxiety, depression, and so forth (Maté & Maté 2022; Scaer, 2014).

Barral (2007, 2014) has written books describing how people tend to struggle throughout their life with one organ or body part as a weak link in their overall visceral (autonomic) nervous system, which contributes to defining their personality. Stress, for example, will target predisposed vulnerable areas in the body. Physical or mental trauma/injury or sickness/disease can create additional vulnerabilities. Barral (2007) states:

> Not only do organs react to emotions, but an organ's reaction can determine a behavioral pattern. Take the intestine, for example, which is often related to psychological rigidity and a cleanliness phobia. When a person with a fragile or weak intestinal system is going through a crisis, he or she may suddenly go on a cleaning binge or get angry at people over nothing (p. 4).

Biological responses to stressors are adaptive for emergencies and are meant to help bring the body back into homeostasis. If struggles are resolved, symptoms are likely to dissipate or disappear. But when chronic stressors are present without resolution, stress chemicals can become trapped, or blocked, within the autonomic nervous system. Over the long term, if the human vehicle surpasses its compensation limit or tolerance threshold, this can produce harm and even permanent damage to the body, often leading to chronic illness (Hanson,

2013; Levine, 2008; Maté, 2012; Maté & Maté 2022; Scaer, 2014; Walker, 2013).

Psychiatrist Ivor Browne (1990) theorizes that traumatic contents that overwhelm a person in the moment of the trauma are energetically stored in the body, creating an energetic signature of isolated incidents of trauma in the body. Because the nervous system is initially overwhelmed, the individual cannot fully consciously experience, process, and integrate the experience at the point of trauma. The internalized stressor then exists outside of time in an unstable state in the body. Unless and until the energies of the internalized trauma are fully experienced, it will continue to exert its negative effect indefinitely on the person, potentially contributing to inhibition and constriction of the personality. Using the appropriate therapeutic techniques can help the person surface traumatic memories and their associated physiological energies over time in a safe and controlled environment to be more fully experienced emotionally and physically and thus processed and released.

Based on decades of research, Grof (1976; 2008; 2009; 2019a) describes how the psychodynamics of our unique perinatal, biographical, ancestral, racial, and past-life contents leave energetic traces and blockages in our physical bodies. For Grof, these energetic, unconscious contents can, throughout our lives, cluster within our physiological being into constellations of memories (and associated fantasies) with similar basic themes, attracting and containing similar elements. Each constellation is accompanied by strong emotional charges of the same quality. These constellations can influence how we perceive ourselves, others, and the world. They also affect how we feel and act.

Grof (1976; 2008; 2009; 2019a) refers to these constellations as COEX systems (systems of condensed experience).* COEX systems can be either negative (condensed unpleasant emotional experiences—

---

*Grof's (2019a) theory of COEX systems is similar to Jung's concept of "complexes," being constellations of psychological elements, including ideas, opinions, attitudes, and convictions clustered around a nuclear theme and associated with distinct feelings (p. 231).

generally connected to emotional problems, unresolved conflicts, repressed material, or traumas) or positive (condensed pleasant emotional experiences). Given the nature of pervasive human suffering, negative COEXs are dominant. Examples of themes in COEXs include fear, abuse of trust, fury, grief, loss, and abandonment. Feeling into a negative COEX at an emotional level can elicit such states as panic, depression, loneliness, disgust, guilt, helplessness, depravity, sexual excitement, self-hatred, or general aggressive tension. Somatic symptoms associated with these emotions can include, for example, nausea and vomiting, breathing difficulties, various cardiovascular complaints, profuse salivation or sweating, sudden diarrhea, or intense pain in multiple parts of the body.* Positive COEXs can elicit the opposite, such as feelings of optimism, joy, radiance, and bliss.

These COEX systems are constantly in flux. We are all subject to them. Each of us has a unique history and will have varied constellations of contained emotional content within ourselves. Individual COEXs can selectively influence a person's self-perception, thoughts, feelings, and somatic processes. At the same time, these COEX systems are all connected to the broader complement of emotions that we as a species can experience and hold, including our unique relationship to archetypes—the timeless, primordial principles, patterns, and configurations underlying and informing the fabric of the material world and the collective unconscious.

Each COEX system carrying a negative charge has a unique defense system representing potential energetic blockages, discussed throughout this chapter and the next. Working with psychedelics as therapeutic tools makes it possible to bring to the surface a range of energetic

---

*For those familiar with the work of Eckhart Tolle (2006), the equivalent of the COEX is the "pain-body": an energy field of pain living in the cells of the body and left behind by strong negative emotions not fully faced, accepted, and released. While the pain-body can result from trauma, much of it is created by the ego and a false sense of self. The pain-body is also connected to human suffering in the collective psyche of humanity (p. 142); unlike Grof, Tolle does not reference the equivalent of "positive" COEXs.

blockages, including those associated with unique COEX systems. Psychedelics help circumvent constricting human defense systems, opening blocked energies for processing, resolution, and integration, which are discussed in the next section.

Shocks, physical and mental traumas, and negative emotional disturbances from this lifetime and possibly from ancestral lineages, previous lifetimes, and the collective unconscious all leave their mark on the human energetic system. The takeaway is that when the body and psyche are in homeostasis, the body is more likely to be healthy and filled with vitality and purpose. When the body and psyche are in dysfunction, the body may suffer physical or mental illness or be more vulnerable to sickness. Physical and psychosomatic symptoms can then indicate blocked energy trying to emerge.

Traditions like Vedanta and Chinese Medicine have developed sophisticated and holistic systems of exercise, diet, meditation, and healing practices (e.g., acupuncture, massage, and use of plant medicines) to maximize human health and address sickness. They use terms like *prāna* and *qi (chi)* to describe vital life force energies. The underlying principle of these traditions is the same as described above: for the human body to be healthy there needs to be a maximal flow of unobstructed vital energy throughout the body.

It also appears to be the case that the more unobstructed the flow of energy is in the body when entering holotropic states, the more easily the body can shift into higher energetic states and penetrate more deeply into the mind and stabilize these deeper states. Here again, we are presented with how the body is an energetic system and entity connected to the energetic psychic contents of mind and consciousness. The following section discusses healing and homeostasis through movement and releasing blocked energy while using psychedelics. This movement toward healing and homeostasis simultaneously contributes to purifying the body's energy so it can more effectively and efficiently enter deeper and more radiant states of consciousness, making it easier to access and sustain the mindmeld.

HEALING AND HOMEOSTASIS THROUGH MOVEMENT AND RELEASING BLOCKED ENERGY

As described in the previous section, the body can store energetic blockages from trauma and from negative, ego-generated energetic patterning. Several more factors can also undermine health and homeostasis in the body. Physical injuries from impacts, but also from repetitive strain, where there is a gradual buildup of damage to muscles, tendons, and nerves from repetitive motions, can contribute to knots in the body. A lack of exercise or poor posture can contribute to constricting and undermining the performance of many systems in the body. Vulnerability or weakness in some bodily systems resulting from physical heritage, including genetic makeup, may undermine functional resilience and adaptability and contribute to energetic blockages. Poor diet (e.g., consumption of alcohol, processed foods, excessive sugar and unhealthy fats, etc.), exposure to toxins (e.g., commercial tobacco smoke, household cleaners, prescription and over-the-counter drugs, gasoline, pesticides, etc.), exposure to particulates (e.g., air pollution, wood or cannabis smoke), and hazardous electric and magnetic fields in the environment may also undermine homeostasis and contribute to dysregulation of systems in the body. Homeostasis can protect against these things, but when the body is overwhelmed by a constant barrage of these negative inputs, it becomes more susceptible to diseases, including cancers, virulent bacteria, and viruses. Retreating or contracting from feeling unwanted emotions through drug use (including legal pharmaceuticals) and other numbing and suppressing activities can further undermine homeostasis in the body.

Energetic knots or blockages can restrict the body's ability to maintain healthy homeostasis and thereby limit the capacity of its systems for optimal function and self-healing. There are many *conscious* homeodynamic options to help address energetic blockages in the body. While there is no room to provide an exhaustive list with full explanations, examples include: physical exercise and movement, including dance and stretching (e.g., 5Rhythms, Tensegrity,* qigong, tai chi, yoga); breathing techniques; cold water therapy; grounding; meditation styles leading to somatic release (e.g., Vipassana); acupuncture; massage (e.g., visceral; sacral cranial); osteopathy; energetic healing (e.g., healing touch; Reiki); eye movement desensitization and reprocessing techniques; somatic psychotherapy (e.g., somatic experiencing; sensorimotor psychotherapy); and naturopathy.

For our purposes, the focus is on using psychedelics as tools to help process, release, and completely discharge blocked energies, or COEXs, in the body. This work can be done alone or in the mindmeld. To understand the movement of energy in the body while on psychedelics, I first describe what can occur at the individual level to help us better understand what can happen in the mindmeld between two people.

As the mind penetrates deeper levels of consciousness when working with psychedelics, the body shifts and can be propelled into what feels like higher, more radiant energetic states. Shifting states of energy can loosen the energetic impurities from one's mental, emotional, and physical being, which are again all connected in the energetic matrix that is you. As stuck or knotted dense energy is loosened, it readies itself for discharge.

There are several *unconscious* homeodynamic ways the body can process energy when working with psychedelics. When the ego is transcended, unconscious homeodynamic drives enable the body to release tension or energetic blockages. The types of energetic releases encompass vibration, purging, vocalizing, and movement, including fractal energetic yoga (spontaneous, subconscious physical movements). This movement of energy can blend with felt experiences of catharsis or abreaction, relieving emotional armoring and emotional distress (e.g., repressed grief, shame, guilt, anger) from the body via uninhibited free expression. As the denser energies are discharged from the body,

---

*Tensegrity (or magical passes), which includes a variety of intense bodily movements, was developed by the shamans of ancient Mexico and summarized by Carlos Castaneda (1999) in the book *Magical Passes.*

a clearer and more robust energetic platform is established. This new energetic platform decreases hyperarousal, allowing the body to move toward homeostasis more effectively. This purification work presents an energetic solution to an energetic problem. It also creates momentum for progressively reaching more profound states of consciousness, sustaining them, and remembering them over time when working with psychedelics and meditation.

Vibration is a common way for the body to discharge stuck energy. This phenomenon can occur throughout the body or be localized to certain body parts during a psychedelic session and can range from waves of energy to tremors, twitches, and flailing limbs. Fluctuations between feeling hot and cold during a psychedelic session are subtle symptoms of energy being dislodged and processed within the body. At its rare extreme, it can manifest as convulsive seizures. I have seen people pound the floor with all of their limbs with such overwhelming intensity it seemed as though they were going to break either themselves or bust holes in the floor. In these cases, by personal account, they were processing long-held and intense anger. More often, these are cases of abreaction where an emotional release is attached to a direct incident or story of trauma. On the opposite end of this vibration spectrum, waves of blissful energy can flow in pleasurable ways and reach the intensity of a full-body orgasm, similar to what can be experienced on MDMA. These are all normal ways for the body to process and discharge energy when working psychedelics in higher doses.

In all cases, there is nothing to do but observe the flow of energy and movement. Any attempts to control what is happening, whether purposefully exaggerating the movements, slapping hands, shaking them, or fidgeting, are egoic efforts to accelerate the process to avoid extended discomfort. Attempts to forcibly still the body once it has started releasing energy can result in feeling nauseous or more anxious. Trying to manipulate the process undermines the body's inherent homeodynamic capacity to heal and move toward homeostasis. If someone continually tries to manipulate or avoid the process, it is a symptom of an overactive ego; the only way through is to surrender. While this work can be exhausting and overwhelming, you need to trust the process, trust your body, relax, and let go. Ball (2017) states: "Your only job is to stay relaxed, neither trying to augment nor diminish the vibrations, and, to the best of your ability, let the energy sort itself out naturally and unimpeded" (p. 102).

If your co-melder starts kicking and flailing in the mindmeld setting, it is time to get up and give them space. If they are not in danger of hurting themselves, do not intervene. Be compassionate and patient as a helper. There is nothing to do or say now; just be the witness. Your calm witnessing presence will provide validation, solace, and comfort to the one struggling. To hold space for your co-melder is to avoid judging their experience or trying to fix something. Holding space is an exercise of co-regulation where your calmness can positively affect the physiology of the other person by nonverbally encouraging them to mirror your experience unconsciously. (Co-regulation can similarly occur in the mindmeld when one person calmly approaches uncomfortable psychic contents, encouraging the other person subconsciously to witness the challenges instead of negatively reacting.*) Once your co-melding partner settles down, return to lying beside them and holding hands. Avoid conversing about what happened until after the session, other than perhaps acknowledging the person just went through something big. It is then time to settle back into meditation.

Purging (i.e., vomiting) is another possible physical release of stuck energy when working with psychedelics. Not releasing the resistance of the ego itself can cause nausea when avoiding release into the full energy of the erupting experience.

While purging is less likely to happen when working with LSD or magic mushrooms—even if mushrooms have a reputation for nausea—it is more likely with ayahuasca, peyote, or 5-MeO-DMT. Either way, it

---

*Of interest, the most recent neuroscience identifies how, in relationships and through our interpersonal actions, we co-regulate each other at a physiological level, which is traceable through brain function (Barrett, 2020).

is easy to accommodate by having buckets and towels available to help with cleanup. If someone is prone to vomiting, it is wise to have access to a shower and bring an extra change of clothes. There is nothing to be ashamed of or embarrassed about if making a "mess." This, too, can happen as a practical result of working with transforming stuck energies in the body. And, while vomiting is uncomfortable, it is normally followed by relief and possibly new realization or the ability to go deeper into the meditation. Relief follows on the heels of letting go of something. In this respect, it is simply releasing held energy that is not serving the individual, not unlike vomiting after eating something with harmful bacteria.

While highly unusual, there are stories of people emptying their bowels or bladders. The same guidelines apply: have a spare set of clothes and access to a shower. Again, there is nothing to be ashamed of. People are likely to find relief in letting go and may even find humor in such a release—although this may take time to realize. At its more extreme end, people have wallowed in their "messes," transforming held beliefs of what is disgusting and shameful into something natural and beautiful, as another part of the Great Divine to be embraced (Ball, 2017, p. 98).

Another form of energetic release when working with psychedelics is *vocalizing*. Vocalizing comes in many types, varying from talking to chants, singing and whistling, glossolalia (speaking in tongues), and xenoglossy (speaking a real foreign language a person has never learned). Producing tones is also common. A further possibility is producing other sounds, like clicking, gurgling, purring, and growling. When vocalizing becomes intense, people can scream, wail, and cry. Laughter, which can range from joyous to maniacal, is also a form of vocalizing. These are all valid forms of release. Vocalizing, especially when attached to emotions like anger, grief, or sadness, is more likely to be cathartic discharge, a general cleansing of emotional energies without a specific source of trauma. Whether catharsis or abreaction, it is all about letting things go. Again, there is nothing to do but surrender and allow the process to unfold.

When vocalizing, there can sometimes be an interplay of the ego as it often tries to regain its dominant position when relegated by the psychedelic, especially after the apex of a session. Ball (2017) points out that some forms of vocalizing can be more of a commentary on the person's experience driven by the ego than authentic, energetic release. Ego-driven dialogue tends to be narrative, exclamatory, or sometimes pleading and desperate (p. 87). It is the ego's attempt to extricate itself from the possibility of dissolution. The threat when working toward the mindmeld is getting trapped in distracting conversation and undermining the mindmelding process.

Vocalizing from a nonegoic state usually manifests as a deeper and richer tone than everyday speech. Speech usually becomes more formal, without contractions, slang, or informal terminology. The person's typical character is not present, so their speech, or things like laughter, will not conform to their usual patterns or characteristics. This expression is unlikely "possession."* Instead, Ball (2017) states, "they are merely speaking from a place of energetic authenticity where the ego is not present to filter and shape the expression of energy" (p. 87).

This is undoubtedly the case for me, where I often vocalize in deeper tones with messages I would not usually blurt out. For example, I have spontaneously said, "We are Aquarius!" immediately after coming out of total nondual absorption in a mindmeld using 5-MeO-DMT. Another example is shouting "We are all one!" during my first fractal energetic yoga experience at an ayahuasca ceremony. I have also thanked various iconic figures, such as John Lennon, Aristotle, Plato, Mozart, archangels, God, and even the Moon at length in song, all the while doing fractal energetic yoga. Or, I have described what is energetically happening to the other person while engaged in a mindmeld and physical exchange; this is rare, and I suspect it results from the other person needing comfort during the energy work. In all these examples, my voice dropped an octave lower, with a slightly robotic or electronic resonance.

---

*I explore the unlikely possibility of possession in chapter 13.

Demonstrative outbursts can also take a different direction. I was working with Delia, who released pent-up anger toward God. While the movement of divine energy was ramping up in the mindmeld, she spontaneously shouted, "I hate God." After the session, she described her resentment toward God as having two antecedents: one was in response to the horrors committed by the various churches of "God," including supporting wars, genocides, sexual molestation, and mind control, and the other was the challenge of being human and separate from God. But by releasing this anger, she soon settled into her energy and the Divine within.

Vocalizing can express what a person is feeling and authentically experiencing. If a foreign language is unknown to the person but is spoken coherently, the person may genuinely convey something from the collective unconscious. If there is incoherence, such as trying to communicate in their native language but being unable to articulate words clearly, it may represent the confusion the person is in or simply reflect confused thoughts. A healthy approach is to avoid becoming attached to the phenomenon. Speaking in tongues may cause a person to feel unique or special, which is an egoic-generated storyline. Ball (2017) warns if the person becomes attached to the phenomenon, their ego may try to make it happen again. On the other hand, without attachment and with more presence and grounding, there is usually a shift in energy into coherent language in subsequent sessions (p. 88).

Ball (2017) also points out how the ego can even co-opt authentic vocalizations and expressions of grief or sadness. An energetic release through screaming or crying can subtly move from authenticity to self-indulgence to be seen and heard. This distinction occurs if someone is shouting out or crying and the energy is processed and discharged, but the person continues to act out through a conscious willfulness, perhaps in self-pity or self-absorption (p. 89). There is nothing inherently wrong with this happening. But suppose we want to bring more awareness to ourselves and our actions. In this case, we can learn more about ourselves, our mosaic of egoic parts, by bringing the witness to bear on how manipulative the ego can be in configuring our energy in this way. Watch for these subtle shifts in tone and witness the change of personality. Vocalizing should be considered a normal part of the mindmeld session. But if you notice the other person is starting to narrate mindlessly or is babbling at length about their experience, it is fair to redirect the person to their internal experience to relax, such as focusing on their breath or meditating on their heart center. A gentle reminder that it is unnecessary to talk could be enough to shift their focus: "I know you are having an intense experience. You don't have to talk right now. We will talk about your experience later. Try focusing on your breath."

I have found the ego's engagement in these types of energetic releases exists on a continuum, as the ego's position of relegation can vary from nascent to complete dissolution, from a surfacing presence to fully lucid and in control. In the mindmeld, we strive to relegate the dominant role of the ego, but there is nothing wrong with its interjection. Just be aware of it. By being the ongoing witness to the ego, we can better understand it, which helps us better understand ourselves. It is easy to judge the ego, but ironically it is just the ego judging itself. Bringing awareness to the ego is to bring love to the ego and more love, acceptance, and compassion to ourselves—and by extension, to others.

Grof's research (2008) into LSD psychotherapy and Grof and Grof's work (2010) with Holotropic Breathwork (without the use of psychedelics) are valuable proxies to understand further and normalize the process of these types of homeodynamic energetic releases. Grof describes how LSD research and Holotropic Breathwork participants discharge pent-up physiological tensions through profuse sweating, tremors, twitches, facial contortions, violent shaking, coughing, gagging, and vomiting. Physical movement can be more complex, consisting of animal movements like climbing, flying, digging, crawling, slithering, and so on. The release of blocked emotions can also be discharged through crying or screaming. Other types of vocal expression include speaking in tongues, or unknown foreign languages, baby talk, gibberish, chants, singing, or animal sounds.* From my journeys with psychedelics, working with others, and attending plant-based ceremonies, I have witnessed or experienced all of these possibilities.

The practice of *Inner Fire* is another proxy for understanding homeodynamic energetic releases while also validating improved health and homeostasis when using psychedelics. Indian yogis refer to *Tapas* or *Kundalini*, Tibetan yogis to *Tummo* or *Dumo*, and Taoist yogis to *Huo*, while varieties of shamanic tribes use their own words for working with inner heat or fire. Practices use meditative breathing, visualization techniques, and, occasionally, yogic movements to change the thermoregulation within the body. The intent is to burn away impure psychophysical constituents and residues, thus vanquishing emotional afflictions. Here, purposefully induced stress on the body and mind can create tension that strengthens the organism, similar to many forms of exercise. The practices stimulate the sympathetic nervous system, heightening arousal and cognition. These practices improve the human endocrine and immune systems and psychological resilience. The desired longer-term result from this alchemical interplay of immolating psychosomatic impediments is joyous illumination, bliss, clairvoyance and other psychic abilities, and the clarity of pristine awareness, or clear light mind—*Nirvana* (Arundale, 1938; Baker, 2019; DeGracia, 1997; Eliade, 2004; Metzner, 1998; Mookerjee, 1986; Tirtha, 1979; Yü, 1970).† While Inner Fire practices generally do not include a lot of physical movements, I have included a description here to further illustrate how techniques that do

---

*Grof (2008) accounts for much of these discharges as processing perinatal trauma in the unconscious, which can reach into cycles of death and rebirth in the collective unconscious. Some of these expressions may also be the surfacing of deep instinctual tendencies and conflicts.

†Gopi Krishna (1967) provides warning of working with these inner energies due to potential adverse side effects. Side effects can include levels of psychosis, paranoia, insomnia, headaches, and other painful physical symptoms; to work through these effects requires practicing equanimity, and may require working with practices like meditation, yoga, tai chi, and bodywork as an extension of working with the energetic phenomena described throughout this book. I, and the people I have worked with, have not had any of these side effects to date, but I suspect others could.

not use psychedelics, such as breathwork, can similarly contribute to processing and releasing energetic blockages in the body and also contribute to homeostasis and higher states of consciousness. When a variety of techniques have so many similarities in the movement of energy and the outcome, it helps us triangulate our understanding of the body as an energetic vehicle requiring ongoing maintenance to ensure its highest performance and capacity to reach high states of being.

Some of these expressions of energy can also be seen in clinical therapeutic practice, which indicates how available this phenomenon is when people are allowed to relax into a deeper part of themselves and express themselves safely and openly, releasing pent-up energies. In psychology, personality changes are referred to as "switching," where vocal and body expression changes can occur when working with traumatic contents in therapy. In some therapeutic settings, patients may activate distinctly different emotional and physiological states as they work through their trauma. For example, they may change their tone of voice and speaking style and manifest different facial expressions and body movements. Dr. Bessel van der Kolk (2015) notes how people exhibiting these personality changes improve if both patient and therapist appreciate the roles these different states have played in the patient's trauma survival (p. 241). This insight signals the value of mutual validation as we witness the surfacing, processing, and releasing of each other's energetic contents in the mindmeld. The wonderful thing about doing the mindmeld work one-on-one is that each person creates space for the other to drop deeply and fully into their experience. Usually, in most ceremonial settings, any extended movement or loud vocalizing is considered disruptive and often shut down, which is an unfortunate limitation when working with larger groups.

FRACTAL ENERGETIC YOGA AND HEALING THROUGH MOVEMENT

Energy can be released and discharged more fluidly when working with psychedelics, provided the ego has been relegated from its executive function. Bodily movements can involve yoga-like position holds (e.g., similar to *asanas*) or graceful movement from one position into another, similar to tai chi. Limbs can articulate with the hands moving through *mudra*-like positions, where the hands contribute to the discharge of energy throughout the body. The face and eyes can fully engage in movement and expressions, often with the tongue protruding from the mouth. As described earlier, some people in the psychedelic community refer to this flow of energy through fluid bodily movements as fractal energetic yoga, while others may refer to it as kundalini yoga.

To define "fractal energetic yoga," I break it into two parts: "fractal energy" and "yoga." "Fractal energy" refers to the human being as an energetic form and can be considered a mathematical construct existing in a sea of infinitely complex, patterned, and moving energy, living in space-time, in which it fits as a fractal or a measured nongeometric unit. Simultaneously, the human as a fractal energetic unit is one and the same as the rest of the theorized universal energy field, where everything is ultimately connected as one massive hologram. This is similar to universal consciousness being metaphorically referred to as the ocean; each person is consciously aware as a drop or wave in the ocean, each with its uniqueness in space-time, but is never separate from the whole. Etymologically, "yoga" means to unify or join with the Divine. As a practice, yoga, including physical movement, and meditation, is a path for transcending the ego-self. Accordingly, "fractal energetic yoga" refers to intuitive and energetic, patterned, homeodynamic physical movements of the human body, unobstructed by the ego, working to bring its multifaceted systems into divinely intended energetic homeostasis.

In fractal energetic yoga, consciousness is given greater freedom to authentically manifest beyond the constraints of the ego and tune the body in an amplified fashion (Ball, 2009). The underlying energetic constructs of reality, beyond the limitations of the sensing human vehicle and ego, are given free rein to clear the system, not unlike cleaning built-up deposits on gears and chains in a complex, well-used machine. It is as though all of the body's complex systems, unchained from restraints imposed by the ego, are enabled to cooperate optimally in the divine organization, as they were meant to, through their own recalibration and reconditioning.

Here I emphasize that bodily movements are authentically arising when the ego is relegated and not exerting control over the body. Authenticity is unmistakable when the body is moving beyond conscious choice or input. While on the surface it may initially feel like something else is moving you, there is no "other" pulling the strings; there is no form of possession. The only thing moving you is your divine energy, as released from the ego's dominant reign and allowed to move freely. With some effort, the conscious ego-mind can intervene and regain conscious control. When this happens, there is no sense of something leaving the body, thus confirming all the energy in movement is authentically yours.

In fractal energetic yoga, there is a continuum of experience with symmetry. The degree to which the movements are symmetrical versus asymmetrical has a lot to do with the relative relegation of the ego. For example, when one is in absolute absorption in infinity, or the nondual "God state," the movements are all symmetrical and mirrored by both sides of the body with no cross over of the body's center line. Complete symmetry most often happens when working with the powerful psychedelic 5-MeO-DMT. When working with less powerful psychedelics, like ayahuasca, LSD, or magic mushrooms, there usually is more conscious awareness where the ego is less likely to be fully transcended. While the body's movements can still be symmetrical, there is expected to be a broader variation toward asymmetrical movement. These movements are still connected to the intuitive drive of the body to move toward health and homeostasis as though acting in primordial energetic form. In this case, the body can be standing and move into dance-like movements, reflecting something like tai chi, qigong, the Balinese monkey chant (*kecak/ketjak*), Javanese dances, the Hindu dance styles of Kathakali of the Malabar coast, the Manipuri dances of Manipur in Assam, or Japanese Kabuki, embodying beautifully flowing symmetrical and asymmetrical movements. All these movements can occur without the user's previous knowledge of them. In my case, I had no previous exposure to yoga at the time when my body started spontaneously moving into symmetrical yoga-like poses.

Grof (2008; 2009; 2019a) has reported these occurrences in his research on LSD and Holotropic Breathwork, where people assumed some of these postures and gestures without any former familiarity with them. Other researchers have found relationships between using psychedelics and kundalini experiences, including both bodily movements/physiological energetic shifts (e.g., shivers or tremors moving up and down the spine, displaying spontaneous motor movements, such as dance) and more general kundalini phenomena like ego loss, psychic abilities (e.g., telepathy), and out-of-body experiences, among others (DeGracia, 1997; Thalbourne, 2001).

By way of comparison, reports were made by Lee Sannella (1987) of yoga practitioners from Hatha, Tantra, and Taoist traditions experiencing spontaneous yoga-like movements—without psychedelic use. Similar reports of spontaneous yoga-like movements among participants come from kundalini traditions (Mookerjee, 1986; Tirtha; 1979). In these cases, the involuntary movements originate from *kundalini-shakti* or "serpent power," which Hindus conceive of as a form of impersonal psychospiritual energy or the energy of consciousness. For Taoists, the energetic origin of movements is from *qi*. The !Kung people of the Kalahari Desert in Botswana refer to *n/um*, which, incidentally, for the !Kung is also connected to psi abilities, such as telepathy (Katz, 1982). In the 1980s, Sannella (1987) interviewed a long list of people with little or no connection to a spiritual tradition but who often had some form of meditation practice. Some of those he interviewed identified having spontaneous "kundalini awakenings," many of whom experienced spontaneous yoga-like movements unknown to them.* These additional examples reflect the same style of cleansing of the body as fractal energetic yoga, which points to this psychospiritual energetic cleansing as being universally accessible, with or without psychedelics. The intuitive movements of fractal energetic yoga, or spontaneous kundalini yoga, transcend personal and cultural differences, even if certain traditions create their own defined practices, labels, and narratives around the phenomenon.

It is tough to draw many conclusions about the particular positions possible in fractal energetic yoga because as they manifest, they are unique to the energetic matrix of each individual and how their system needs to express and process energy. The movements themselves also seem to have infinite variation. Because of this, many of the movements will not be seen in yoga or tai chi textbooks, but some will, and there is definitely an overlap with these other systems. Either way, there is no need to seek or create "spiritual" ideas or impose traditional interpretations on the movements; the movements are simply an innate processing and clearing of energy from the human vehicle.

I have had a registered massage therapist with training in osteopathy and yoga watch hours of footage of my independent sessions of fractal energetic yoga. Her insights were profound. She watched as I worked energy through my body with both asymmetric and symmetrical movement, sometimes massaging various parts or working pressure points on the multivariate energetic meridians in the body. From her perspective, asymmetrical movement could be more healing for the body than symmetrical movement as it encourages increased firing of neural synapses, leading to improved neuronal connectivity and more varied stretching of the internal organs and fascia.

She could diagnose blockages in different body parts by watching my movements. She could even predict postures and things like vocalization before they occurred. For example, I would adopt yoga-like

---

*Similarly to psychedelically induced phenomenon, people experiencing a kundalini awakening can begin opening to past-life memories, spontaneously speaking in tongues, or chanting unknown songs or sacred invocations or mantras.

positions, including twists; she could foresee the freeing up of impinged space and energy in the lungs and the integration of earlier postures, leading to vocalization.

My sessions often lasted for hours, and in each case, she pointed out how the movements became more fluid and sometimes more complex as the session progressed and reached its apex and conclusion. With greater flow, sophistication, and difficulty of the poses, there was a greater sense of integration from the early parts of the session. (Of interest, this same woman can perform the same style of fractal energetic healing as I do on others, but intuitively, without using psychedelics.)

I have occasionally experienced fractal energetic yoga without using psychedelics. Given the preceding descriptions of energetic exercises, it should be no surprise I have dropped into fractal energetic yoga during a Holotropic Breathing session. It took two-and-a-half hours of controlled breathing before it started, and it only lasted a few minutes, but it was enough to demonstrate other practices could initiate this self-healing modality. On another occasion, I was working with Niall, an energetic psychic healer, when I broke into fractal energetic yoga. He led me into a trance state to have me explore past lives. I found myself as a Tibetan monk in northern India hundreds of years ago. I visited a Hindu temple, met a guru, attended ceremonies, and later became a teacher in my own right. After being cremated, I journeyed to the heavens, arriving at a building holding the Akashic Records, a storehouse of all universal experience—every thought, feeling, and action throughout all time. Inside I was greeted by the archangel of healing, Raphael. Upon meeting him, I started fractal energetic yoga, which continued for several minutes.

Ball (2014), an aficionado of fractal energetic yoga, has described how after working with psychedelics for years, predominantly with 5-MeO-DMT, he would spontaneously break into fractal energetic yoga without their use. He was eventually able to consciously initiate fractal energetic yoga, turning it on and off at will, but still as a series of spontaneous movements beyond conscious choice, reflecting his energetic state at the moment.

While slightly different from fractal energetic yoga, dance styles like those of the whirling Sufi Dervishes (*Tanoura* in Egypt; *Dhamaal* in Pakistan) and 5Rhythms Dance, can induce trance states where the body begins to dance itself. In the sacred Tibetan Buddhist Cham dances, the dancer is "danced" by the deities who dance through them; here, the adept imaginatively identifies with a conjured divinity to transcend the limited mind (Baker, 2019, p. 43). In all these examples, there is the potential to transcend the ego and allow the free movement of energetic expression of the body, enabling healing and increasing the potential to reach ecstatic states.

ENGAGING PHYSICALLY IN THE PSYCHEDELIC MINDMELD

So, where do all of the manifestations of moving and releasing energy fit within the mindmeld? Given that the mindmeld is a cooperative and co-creative exercise, the intention is to have both participants relegate their egos and share in the engagement of these energetic releases. Each movement of energy and release becomes an opportunity to witness the healing experience of each other. But with the mindmeld there is a sharing that can go much further.

At its peak of possibility, there is a shift toward direct physical engagement with the other person, which is much more profound than the individual experience of energetic processing and discharge. In the mindmeld, bodies are attracted like magnets to each other, where one will begin physically working on purifying the other's body and energetic field. This can become a fractal energetic dance where it is possible to switch roles back and forth—all beyond conscious volition. This process begins similarly to fractal energetic yoga, but the movement is directed to clearing energetic blockages in the other person. Each person can become the conduit for the other's healing by dislodging blockages they could not release. When this happens, joint healing can occur. This work helps to restore the energetic flows in either or both bodies.

In this full engagement, all aspects of the body are brought to bear—physical, mechanical, and chemical factors, along with the more subtle electromagnetic elements of vibration (frequencies and waves), in every cell and organ, all contributing to the healing process.

When this engagement starts, just allow your body to magnetically trace the energetic draw or pull into the other person's body, regardless of where it goes. Trust your body to apply the correct pressure and force to unwind the other person's knots right to their source.* If the other person is in complete surrender, they will intuit your movements are following a perfect line of processing. Many people have commented on the preciseness of the work: the physical work was exactly what they needed. People then asked how I knew how to do it. The answer is simple: our energy fields know, not the ego-based conscious self. There is no story, just an authentic, energetic dance of processing and releasing.

At the same time, the person may be dissociated from your discharging of their energy. In hindsight, they may connect it to personal story. This scenario happened with Luke. I held his hand and traced his energy through his palm, up his arm, and into his torso. Somehow, I poked something deep, and a massive shock wave bounced back through me. My tongue was forced to the floor of my mouth. I suddenly felt like I was drowning. I wondered if I had stepped beyond what I could handle but reminded myself of the role of the bodhisattva (described as a meditative technique in chapter 12). I continued to hold his hand. The energetic flow was so intense my torso jumped up from the bed into a sitting position, and I started screaming. I coughed up lots of phlegm, spitting it onto the bed and floor. The purge continued for several draining, horror-filled minutes. Hours later, Luke commented on

---

*Barral (2007) describes how well-trained osteopaths can "locate the weakened physical element in an ailing person through manual contact. They will let their hand glide over the patient's body with a pressure equal only to the weight of their hand. Their hand will unfailingly be attracted to the problem zone" (p. 14). Here the hand is "magnetized" to the affected area and starts manipulating it to clear it for healing. Increasing numbers of 5-MeO-DMT facilitators who take the molecule at the same time as clients describe working similarly (Ball, 2022).

how he felt disconnected from the purge. I told him the release, from a dualistic perspective, was his, not mine. While slow to respond, he eventually shared that he had taken LSD five months earlier and had a similar experience related to challenging interpersonal issues with his son. He said he was embarrassed by what he saw me doing because it closely mimicked his earlier purge. I told him there was nothing to be ashamed of. The purge was all part of the joint work of the mindmeld.

When engaged in the mindmeld, all of the fractal energetic movements can occur as described earlier. The difference is one body will attune itself to the other body and begin to contribute to breaking up energetic blockages through forms of deep massage or working pressure points and energetic meridians with the hands, using the fingers as needles to drive into blocked areas. Other body parts may also be employed, including the feet, legs, torso, head, and even the tongue. When the body is fully engaged, many parts can simultaneously become involved with the other person in a full-body massage. In most cases, though, there are only one or two contact points. My body, for example, may be in yogic positions where one or both arms or legs are outstretched and the hands are in fluid "mudra" forms, but my remaining limbs are connected to the person in some type of hold or working massage.

This work is similarly reflected in therapeutic touch, healing touch, acupressure, massage, and osteopathy, but not normally with the more extreme engagement of the whole practitioner's body as just described. The healing arts working with the human energy field claim that the energetic vessel of the human body can intuitively find denser frequencies of blocked energy in another body. Here, energy currents flow from "higher" voltages to "lower" ones (Brennan, 1988). When doing this type of mindmelding energetic work, it feels like a magnetic draw to an area of the other person's body to where I simply allow the various parts of my body to follow. Once I am physically connected, it feels like I'm a tuning fork, shifting and clearing the energy in the other person.

Vibration, purging, and vocalization (particularly nonverbal toning) can all shift energy from one body to another. For example, I have screamed through releasing other people's trauma (including accidents and assaults). I have foamed at the mouth, shook, and gasped while releasing blocked energy in a person's lungs, including releasing toxins from the lungs of past smokers that I disgustingly tasted as putrid tobacco rolling out of my tongue. I have profoundly shaken and wept as I have participated in the discharge of other people's grief and sorrow. High- and low-pitched toning has shifted blocked energy in various parts of the other's body. And so forth. If I work with some part of the body where the skin is exposed, I can sometimes see through the skin, witnessing the flow of blood and the movement of energy through the flesh and along bones.

In the mindmeld this process is not unidirectional. Sometimes I can be working on a person's body, only to have them change roles and work on me, and then back again. When I have had people enter my field, I can feel their energy in my body, retuning my systems. This shared exchange rarely happens, as the other person has to entirely relegate their ego and be equanimous with the exaggerated movement of energy through their body and into someone else's. Still, I have found some people can intuitively do this with no prior experience—my wife, Isabel, being one of them. When two bodies play in tandem like this, it is a reminder that none of us are clear vessels and we are all engaged in healing. It also demonstrates the intuitive and divine interconnectedness of giving and receiving healing energy out of pure loving-kindness beyond the infirmities of the ego-mind.

When already working on the other person's body, it is possible to physically let go of them and continue the movement of fractal energetic yoga independently. When this happens to me, my body mirrors the vibrational patterns of the other person as it moves to clear further stuck energy from the transpersonal matrix. Admittedly, this is an intuitive sense of what is occurring, as my body may be triggered by the work on another to begin clearing blockages in myself. If the latter explanation is the case, it is an example of how working to heal others can simultaneously trigger or contribute to our healing. If this happens to you, when the energy has been fully processed and assuming you have moved away from the other person, return to lying beside one another holding hands, and start the mindmelding meditation process again. Save any discussion for later; you are now in the throes of energetic work.

Breaking up and moving stuck or blocked energy in the body while in the mindmeld can be painful and challenging for both people. The one receiving the physical work must relax, breathe, and open into the pain and difficulty without reacting or interfering, although there is always the option to stop, as emphasized further below. The one doing the work has to remain calm, constantly surrendering and allowing the energy and movement to flow, regardless of how strange and demanding it gets. Trust and faith in the process are critical; both grow and mature with more experience.

There should be no holding back, no censoring or self-editing. The mindmeld cannot reach its most fabulous possibilities if the ego steps into the way. Remember, there is absolutely nothing for the ego to do. Beyond surrendering to the experience and each other's energy, there is no plan, no specific procedure. And, in surrender, you have to be ready to feel pain physically, mentally, and emotionally—yours and the other person's. Ultimately, one learns to embrace the pain as part of the purification process. You have to be prepared to be vomited on. You have to be ready to listen to piercing screams, strange tones, and babble. There may be convulsing and thrashing. You may even have to witness the other person act out sexually with themselves. Let these scenarios play out in your presence without your interference, reaction, or any "doing." But also be ready to bask in each other's divine beauty and bliss and share in the sacred wonder of the universe as energies shift and clear.

In the physical exchange of the mindmeld, you can find yourselves physically entwined. The profundity can reach a state where there is no sense of physical separation between you and the other person. You may be aware of the other person's consciousness, but there may be no distinction between their breath and your breath, their heartbeat and yours, or the separation of bodies. I even induced this state purposefully with co-melder, Gene, by projecting my consciousness into the top of Gene's spine while resting my forehead in the said spot, resulting in both of us completely melting into each other in a full nondual state. This symbiosis can last for some time until someone's ego flinches. Then, either one of you may suddenly start gasping for breath, squirming, or wrestling for physical space, which are all potential manifestations of the ego's resistance to the work of letting go and not entering the energetic dance.

When working with psychedelics like mushrooms and LSD, there are often waves of intensity during the experience. These waves are felt in the mindmeld. The energetic healing work is usually taxing. You may go through intense minutes of interpsychic or physically energetic connection with the other person to later find yourself returning to a sense of normalcy. The body has an intuitive way of knowing when to take a break to relax. Sometimes I will be engaged in the work for several minutes, and then my body will disengage. Stepping back can be precipitated by feeling overwhelmed, fearful, or apprehensive. More commonly, however, it is either one or both participants needing a break. These breaks are rest periods for bodies and minds. I have also worked energetically and psychically with people for hours without a break, which is harrowingly intense and exhausting but can also be profoundly rewarding for both participants. Either way, as these cycles occur, there is nothing to do but just rest. When resting, there may be brief moments of lucidity and normalcy where the ego is entirely online. When this happens, just silently return to the initial position of lying side by side, holding hands. Return to the meditation. The more you rest and relax, the more likely it is that the movement of energy will start again.

As an energetic movement concludes, you may find yourself in an awkward physical position. You may be lying sideways on the other person and not have the energy to move. That's okay. Just relax, and eventually, the fractal energy should flow again.

The following is a short example of how beautifully one can slide into relaxation and then move to a closer connection. I had been working on Gene's hip and head simultaneously, with one hand on each, and my body stretched over hers. The energetic flow paused, and I was too exhausted to move, so I lay with my chest over hers for several minutes. I let my awareness drop into my heart beating into hers, breathing into her breathing. The connection grew increasingly adjoining, and after more minutes had passed, the energy rose and I again started moving and continuing the work.

Once the energy is flowing, but there has been a long pause for a break, it is an option for the one doing the energetic movement and work to sit on the other person's front thighs and place their hands on the person's abdomen. Or, you can start with the receiver lying on their stomach and the one doing the work sitting on their hamstrings with their hands on the person's back. Then, relax and wait for the energy to move you to where the next work is needed. If nothing happens, go back to lying beside each other, holding hands.

As described above, this energetic physical work can be physically painful and overwhelming. If onerous psychic contents also arise, people can feel overburdened. It is necessary that if a person is feeling overwhelmed, they can stop the process at any time. As such, an essential part of the briefing is ensuring each participant can say "Stop" at any time. Stopping means both participants must bring their egoic volition and agency back to the fore and disengage from a shared connection, either physically or psychically. In my experience, there is usually a delay of several seconds to stop the mindmeld, particularly when doing physical healing work. The delay occurs because, through meditation and using a psychedelic, the ego has been relegated to a subordinate position. The ego still has volition, especially if there is any sense of subject and object, but it requires conscious effort to return it to conscious control of the body. (When working with 5-MeO-DMT this is much more difficult to do and may not even be possible for short periods because the person is so thoroughly absorbed in the nondual experience.)

Stopping is required when someone says, "Stop," regardless of the circumstances. To not stop is to incur a severe and egregious breach of trust, potentially permanently undermining the relationship and, at worst, leading to accusations of assault.

In this scenario, I work with the same protocol as the Grofs. For Grof and Grof (2010), the only way to stop an intervention is to use the word "Stop." Other commands, like "Leave me alone," "Get away from me," "You are killing me," "Get off my back, you bastard," or "Fuck off," are considered part of the participant's internal drama and dialogue (p. 40). In my case, I also stop the work if the person physically pushes me away, which should also be a standard approach, especially if someone is struggling to verbalize their desires. Alternatively, you may consider using your own safe word to immediately end engagement, so long as a word is agreed to before the session starts.

To interrupt the work before energies have been fully processed, however, is to cause a short circuit, possibly leading to other physical discomforts. When I have been stopped from completing the cycle of work, there is a feeling of disruption, like a blown fuse. But then I usually continue the fractal energetic yoga independently. Those who stop the work prematurely usually regret it in hindsight after the session fully ends, admitting the area being worked on still feels tense, blocked, or inflamed.

A session with Isabel serves as a good illustration. I was working with blocked energy in her shoulder, deeply massaging it. It was causing her a lot of pain she couldn't handle, and she told me to stop. I did, but was left feeling jarred and off balance because the energetic circuit had been broken. Her shoulder continued to bother her in the following days. We discussed the matter later, and she regretted not working through the pain. She told me it felt like energy had been loosened in her shoulder but not resolved. Since then, she has increased her tolerance for deep tissue work, and pain, and has not asked me to stop again.

Grof and Grof (2010) have reported similar challenges when working with Holotropic Breathwork. In the same way as in the mindmeld, the participants remain in complete control of the process the entire time by using the signal "Stop." Immediately, any physical intervention of bodywork by a facilitator stops. However, the Grofs point out that in most cases, the bodywork is correctly applied. Still, more unconscious material is brought to the surface than the person can handle and may be left unresolved for the session (p. 40).

When material comes to the surface and is not resolved at the moment, it may linger for days or weeks after the session. Here there is no right or wrong or anyone to blame. The person struggling with the latent blocked or stirred COEX energy is encouraged to work with it through meditation, therapy, acupuncture, massage, Reiki, yoga, or other forms of energy healing. Another psychedelic session is also an option.

The body is a complex vessel and is never fully clear of challenging energetic debris. In yoga, there is a tenet that you can spend years clearing the body but it is impossible to perfect it. Even if you remove 99 percent of "debris," the last 1 percent will be just as frustrating, or more so, than all the rest to clear. Because of this limitation, the Buddhist teaching of sitting with and observing suffering is valuable; some peace is found in accepting discomfort.

It is worth sharing that not all energetic work connects to difficult blockages. It is also possible to connect to positive COEX's. For example, with Isabel, my hand reached into her bicep and released pure loving joy, where we shared in her bliss together. Twisting my fingers slightly increased or decreased the intensity of the shared joy and laughter.

Although uncommon, I have observed that some people have memory lapses regarding profound, shared physical events. These lapses are brief but are surprising given the intensity of the events. For example, I have deeply massaged tissues on different parts of the body or firmly held body parts, including the head, and even screamed during the discharges. Still, there is no recollection of the deep tissue work or sounds of my voice. I have also vocalized words beyond my egoic conscious mind that are not recalled by the other person, even though they were the only words spoken during the session—things like "We are all one" or "We are all interconnected." Yet, they have a good recall of the rest of the session.

There are a few possible explanations for this phenomenon. First, there is usually such a vast amount of material in longer sessions that it is hard to remember all of it anyway. Human memory capacities are fallible, which we often do not want to acknowledge. We regularly filter out incoming information and forget or re-create memories from our past experiences (Gilbert, 2007). This reality is brutal for the ego to digest when it constantly wants to feel in control, which leads to denial.

Another possible explanation is that much of the material surfacing in a psychedelic session is ineffable, especially when traveling into other dimensions and transcending time, where there is a lack of language to describe the experience(s). The ineffability makes it challenging to remember and integrate the knowledge we receive, given so much of our memory recall is defined by the stories we create through language.

A further possibility for lack of recollection is the brain is simply overwhelmed and suffers amnesia as a protective mechanism. A correlate is the example of concussion, where temporary amnesia is experienced due to overwhelming trauma, even though the person can be fully awake during and following the event. This could be possible in cases where there is episodic memory lapse in the face of intense content during a session. This may be exacerbated through the tenuous link between the psychedelic state and the physical neural network. When working with large doses of psychedelics, which we are doing, there is an overlapping plausible explanation of what are sometimes described as "whiteouts," where the person is so overwhelmed by the psychedelic they forget part(s) of their experience.

A final possibility is a lack of familiarity with the experiences and practice with recall. In this case, the more familiar a person is with the territory, the more likely they are to remember it, especially if they have tools for recall, such as labeling experiences by location, name, theme, or emotion as they occur.

I mention the potential for memory lapse because, while unlikely, it may be a vulnerability some people are not comfortable with. If so, they should not work with high-dose psychedelics. I also want to normalize what can happen so people will not unnecessarily panic from a belief there is something uniquely wrong with them if it happens to them. Video-recording sessions is an option to help address issues associated with memory loss, including unforeseen psychological projections that could result in unfounded accusations.

You may wonder how much physically energetic work to expect in any session. From the work I have done, it is entirely unpredictable. It varies from person to person and session to session, even when working with the same person over time. Although the sessions themselves last hours, assuming you are working with long-lasting psychedelics like ayahuasca, LSD, or mushrooms, the energetic exchanges last anywhere from just a few minutes to several short- to medium-length exchanges to several hours. There is no planning when the ego is not in the driver's seat—just surrendering and allowing.

POSSIBLE RESULTS

There are two categories of possible results from the physical exchange of the mindmeld: short term and long term.

Short-Term Results

In the short term, in the days immediately following a session, there will likely be a noticeable shift in energy in the body, assuming you are someone attuned to and aware of the ongoing subtle shifting sensations in your body. Energy shifts are relatively common after high-dose psychedelic sessions but more common after the mindmeld. It is difficult, however, to draw direct correlations or definitive conclusions regarding energetic shifts from the psychedelic sessions because energy, especially as it is connected to our emotional states, is always shifting.* But there is a significant possibility you may enhance your interoception of feeling new

---

*The same confounding ability to make direct correlations regarding energetic shifts is also true of healing work from other modalities, like massage or osteopathy, as examples.

sensations, or new flows of energy, not experienced before. For example, there may be rushes of energy through the spinal column or tingling sensations you have not previously had in a particular part of your body. Or, you may feel a slight blissful buzz throughout your body. There may also be differences if you were more the "giver" than the "receiver" of the energetic work in the mindmeld. However, I have not been able to distinguish between the two meaningfully. Having said this, more general comments can be made on short-term results.

According to Brennan (1988), to be engaged in activating an energetic healing process is to move frequencies of energy that your energetic field is not used to moving. She claims that to transmit specific frequencies required in healing, your field must vibrate in the same frequency or harmonic. In this healing process, your energetic field will fluctuate like a roller coaster as you constantly transmit different intensities of light energy. Brennan points out that this work will have an impact: "It will be good in the sense that it will speed up your own evolutionary process because changes in frequency and intensity will break your normal holding patterns and will release the blocks in your field" (p. 185). From this perspective, the work may contribute to psychological flexibility, as in being fully aware and accepting of a broader range of emotions and sensations, resulting from the restructuring of energy in the body and the novel movement of energy in connection to another person in the mindmeld. We should also not be surprised at the possibility of greater personal expansiveness resulting from this flow.

At the same time, this work may deplete your energy. For this reason, it is crucial to focus on your overall health. While the healing energy is moving from the "Universal Energy Field," which is infinite in supply, it is the *process* of energy moving that tires the body out. In my experience, I have found session impact unpredictable. It does not seem to matter how subtle or how intense a session is. Sometimes I will feel energized the following day(s), while other times I will feel tired and more emotional. If I feel tired, usually I have returned to "normal" by the second day. But I also give myself space from doing the work regularly, and I won't usually do more than one session every two weeks.

The body can be worked hard in a session. The fractal energetic yoga, especially if it continues for hours, can be tiring. The good news is that you are likely to feel more limber and relaxed the following days, similar to what happens with other forms of yoga.

When receiving physical energetic healing work, especially deep tissue massage, one should be ready to feel sore and sensitive for a few days afterward. Feeling tender is similar to the results felt from any other form of deep massage, especially Rolfing.

In the short term, you should not be surprised if the general processing and the releases of energy do not stop after a psychedelic session, similar to what occurs with most other forms of energy work on the body. For example, I once went for a visceral massage where the masseur massaged my organs. After the session, I spontaneously broke into tears for over half an hour and felt discharges of sadness throughout the next day. Following a near-fatal accident, I often went for osteopathic sessions where the same thing would happen, with emotional lability continuing for up to two days later. Similar results would occur after eye movement desensitization and reprocessing sessions. Many others have similar stories. Again, this work is meant to process and clear what is stuck.

Energetic work, including working with psychedelics as described throughout this book, can lower our protective guards against feeling deeply and increase our awareness and sensitivity to emotional states. In a culture promoting emotional repression, this move toward feeling more deeply becomes more pronounced if a person simultaneously starts a meditation or mindfulness practice. The same can be true when stepping away from excessive distractions or addictions, particularly those numbing or overstimulating the nervous system, such as alcohol, drugs (e.g., depressants, antidepressants, and stimulants), excessive work, exercise, video gaming, gambling, shopping, or unhealthy relationships. Because the mindmeld promotes heart opening, greater self-awareness, and ongoing healing, you should not be surprised to notice more substantial and lasting emotional releases when engaging in this work or having more noticeable emotional reactions to various stimuli outside sessions.

Energetic work can initiate a process of releasing long-held repressed emotions. As blocked energies are released, they can bring to the surface further repressed contents for peripheral discharge and processing (Grof & Grof, 2010, p. 37). For some people, it will feel like the floodgates have blown wide open, and they may feel completely overwhelmed, even debilitated. Discharges can include outbursts of anger, uncontrolled weeping and crying, feelings of anxiety or depression, and more. This processing further frees repressed material and helps the body toward homeostasis. Here we need to remember that all states of consciousness are transitory and play back and forth between emotional poles of what feels good and what we dislike or disown. So, while emotional releases can be overwhelming, especially if they persist for days, weeks, or even months, they will one day exhaust themselves and reach some conclusion, and then transition into something else.

When there is substantial repressed trauma, there will be more to process, which takes more time and may demand serial sessions. Chapter 13, under the heading "Unprocessed Traumatic Material," discusses how to address overwhelming and ongoing energetic releases. But, for now, know that the more balanced we become in the process of discharging traumatic material, accepting the fluctuations in emotional swings, the more integrated we can feel, with greater coherence in our life. And, while I am distinguishing between physical and psychic contents in the mindmeld in this chapter and the next, you can see an overlap in the mind/body connection where emotions are clearly connected to the psyche but manifest as feelings or sensations in the body.

Long-Term Results

Determining the long-term results of the physical energy work in the mindmeld takes time and effort. While I have been doing this work for years and consider myself healthy and have expanded my access to the infinite wonders of consciousness, I suffered a traumatic physical injury in an accident years ago that I continue to work to recover from. The work I have done, which is described in this book, has not been a silver bullet leading to full recovery. But I have improved and remain hopeful of an eventual full recovery.

I have also worked with dozens of people, some of them only once, making it challenging to ascertain long-term results from this work. There is no baseline data, and I have not methodically followed up with questionnaires or surveys for participants on subjective results. However, most of the movements of energy in the bodies of participants, regardless of whether they are shared in the mindmeld or not, are similar to what is reported in yoga, tai chi, and various forms of therapeutic healing touch where there is a release of bio-energetic blockages in the body. We can use these reports to provide insight into how such work can contribute to healing and homeostasis.

Other forms of yoga, and physical movements like qigong, tai chi, and dance, provide us with an indication of the underlying benefits of this physical engagement, which can act as a proxy for helping us understand the benefit of fractal energetic yoga and the physical energetic work associated with it. Physical yoga, including Hatha yoga, Tantric yoga, Tibetan yoga, and tai chi, for example, all engage the body in stretching and balancing exercises. More immediate benefits of these yogic systems include increased blood flow and overall circulation, thus improving the movement of antibodies, leucocytes, lymphocytes, oxygen, and other nourishing cellular factors that contribute to strengthening systems throughout the body; promotion of cell growth; promotion of proper functioning of organs; stimulation of the lymphatic system; reduced stress hormones and reduced anxiety and depression; release of muscle tension and toxins from muscles; increased flexibility and movement; increased muscle strength and overall balance; increased mental and physical energy, including a boost in alertness and overall mood. A broader list of benefits includes prevention, diagnosis, and treatment of disease; releasing stuck energies to improve the flow of life force (*qi* or *prāna*) throughout the body; optimizing health and longevity; concentration and mind control in meditation removing obstacles to spiritual practices; and entering holotropic states, including connection to one's divine nature (Baker, 2019; National Center for Complementary and Integrative Health, n.d.; Mayo Clinic, n.d.; Vishnu-devananda, 1988).

I presume the intuitive movements of fractal energetic yoga, described earlier in this chapter, driven by an internal intuitive compass, can foster the same personal health benefits and resilience and facilitate a greater connection to one's divine nature. It may be possible that the benefits of fractal energetic yoga could surpass those of other yogas because the body is moving intuitively and responding directly to what the body needs, as opposed to following conventions that may not be as optimal for individual needs.

Similarly to yoga, the healing arts of physical and energetic therapies (e.g., acupuncture, visceral massage, osteopathy) work to address blockages in the body and help to bring the systems of the body back toward homeostasis and optimal functioning for balanced healthy living. Examples include reducing stress and anxiety; reducing pain and muscle soreness and tension throughout various parts of the body, including reducing nerve pain; improving circulation, energy, and alertness; lowering heart rate and blood pressure; improving immune function; and increasing relaxation (Barral, 2007; 2014). Thus, the physical movements and energetic work, including deep tissue massage, in the mindmeld should be presumed to foster the same potential benefits of optimizing the body's systems for healing and working toward or maintaining homeostasis. The insights of yoga and other healing modalities highlighted above also indicate the need for ongoing maintenance of the human vessel. Working with psychedelics as psychoactive meditative and energetic tools can contribute.

A further consideration is to track parts of the body worked on during a session to gain insight into what may appear at an energetic level. Various health and energetic practitioners have sought to understand the complexity of the human body and its systems and how parts of the body respond to specific types of trauma and energetic flows. Understanding these peculiarities is beyond the reach of this book, but I offer the following examples for further reference. Barral (2007; 2014), for instance, explores in his books the interpretation of physical and emotional signals in nerves, organs, and joints. Anodea Judith (2004), Barbara Brennan (1988), and Eileen McKusick (2021) each explore the human anatomy and energetic systems and how they hold and respond to trauma. Martin Ball (2017) explores the interpretation of energetic flow through the central parts of the body with the use of 5-MeO-DMT in a chapter in his book *Entheogenic Liberation.*

Ball (2017) describes how a life filled with suffering, pain, judgment, fear, anxiety, frustration, and dissatisfaction can make for a long journey of extensive work to unwind these energetic patterns. But by doing the purification work, you can reach the center of your being, your loving self, and take responsibility for all of your energy (p. 166). Ownership of your energy can include transcending the energetic exchanges you perceive and experience as coming from outside yourself, both "light" and "dark" energies. For Jung (1969), this transcendence, if done consistently, would be the equivalent of becoming an individuated, realized, and aligned being who has taken ownership of and responsibility for their shadow.

Renee (n.d.) provides a more esoteric description of energetic clearing, like that found with fractal energetic yoga:

Emotional clearing is the main process we will experience as we shift through the Ascension cycle. Since emotional pain and energetic imbalances are responsible for our states of dis-ease, many of us will experience physical releases clearing from our body. Some of this energy clearing is dropping density from the karmic, genetic or ancestral soul lineage. Some lightworkers have chosen to clear states of energetic imbalance for the collective or for a specific group. This will feel as movements of energy being transmuted or transited through us, as our spiritual-energetic being may act like a cosmic filtration system for the greater whole.

I add this description without any certainty of its truth. This statement contains beliefs about the soul, past lives, karma, the etheric field and collective unconscious, and an evolution of consciousness. Given the layers of mystery in things like fractal energetic yoga, her assertions may hold truth. Similarly, Monroe (1985) believes that we need to detoxify the body of density of certain particles to help in our ability to journey out of body through various higher dimensions of waves and frequencies. Doing so can help the soul better transition from lifetime to lifetime and evolve spiritually. I have worked to clear my own energetic field, those of others, and the collective field. In doing so, there seems to be a progression where I can access deeper states of consciousness associated with higher dimensions of nonphysical reality, including leaving my body without the use of psychedelics.

11
Sharing Psychic Consciousness

Can the internal contents of our conscious psychic experience be telepathically shared with another? The answer is yes. But how is this possible? There is debate as to whether the human body is a vessel for consciousness or the originator of consciousness. The Eastern wisdom traditions of Buddhism, Hinduism, Taoism (Daoism), and Vedanta, for example, favor the first explanation, while science generally favors the latter. As already described above, there is no doubt that the physical body and its psychic contents interpenetrate each other. But as we will see below, the Psychedelic Mindmeld points us in the direction of something greater than the physical body being the originator of psychic contents. For if psychic contents can be shared, there must be a field beyond the body through which the psychic contents can be transferred or communicated. In other words, if a physical connection is not needed for the psychic transference between two people, then what is the conduit, or conductor, for such transference?

To answer this question is to speculate on our fundamental nature and the nature of the universe. If we are souls-in-body capable of connecting to the world of spirit through dreams and out-of-body experience, then, theoretically, time and space are relative and do not constrain consciousness. For Jung (1969), there is a shared universal conduit through the collective unconscious. For others, it is through the *anima mundi*, or collective imagination (Harpur, 2003).

As briefly mentioned earlier, some Eastern wisdom traditions believe in the idea of a universal energy field. This energy field penetrates everything in the universe. Various Buddhist traditions refer to either *prāna* or *qi*; Tibetan Buddhists refer to *lung*, Hindus refer to it as *prāna*; Taoism refers to *qi (chi)*.

There is also the philosophical idea of panpsychism: the view that the mind is a fundamental and ubiquitous feature of all reality. The *Vedas* similarly refer to *Akasha* (or *Akaśa*), a universal etheric field in which all thoughtforms from all time exist. The storehouse for all thoughtforms is the *Akashic* (or *Akasic*) Records, which, as mentioned earlier, is a library of all the experiences and memories of humans, and possibly all other living things, through all lifetimes. According to Sivananda (2014) this library of thoughtforms can be accessed by all of us.

A growing number of physicists posit that the universe is ultimately unified and integrated, a place in which everything affects everything else. The electric universe theory, for example, postulates the universe is a vast, electric organism (McKusick, 2014; 2021). Theoretical explanations of a unified universe are hypothesized in quantum physics (e.g., the zero-point field, the quantum potential, quantum consciousness, and the Higgs field). Einstein's general theory of relativity references the existence of *aether*, an all-pervading, infinitely elastic, massless medium connecting everything in the universe, often glossed over by other scientists.* Ervin Laszlo (2003; 2004; 2016) argues that the entire universe, as a grand unified field or universal hologram, consciously remembers its experience through infinitely co-evolving quantum consciousness, supporting the supposition of the Akashic Records.

---

*Millennia earlier Pythagoras, Aristotle, Plotinus, and other ancient Greeks similarly used the term *aether*. The Chinese sage Lao-Tse made the same basic insight referring to the *Tao* (or *Dao*). The Hindus reference *Brahman* or *Lila* (Laszlo, A., 2016).

Kelly (2011) and Radin (2006) invoke quantum entanglement to explain the mechanics of telepathy. For Geesink and Meijer, human "bi-directional" communication occurs within a global electromagnetic field via wave resonance composed of universal consciousness experiencing the sensations, perceptions, thoughts, and emotions of every conscious being in the universe (in Church, 2018). This view accepts that energy, space, time, consciousness, and matter are not separate phenomena but are entangled and interact in a vast synchronistic dance in the quantum field. This view is similar to that of Rupert Sheldrake (2009; 2012), for whom the telepathic sharing of psychic contents occurs through morphic resonance within morphic fields. These fields make up a universal database for both organic (living) and abstract (mental) forms. The universal database both influences all connected to it and receives and integrates the experiences and learning of all its members. There is room for sharing psychic contents in the quantum universe because everything is fundamentally interconnected: there is ultimately no separation between consciousness and the physical cosmos.

All these theories point to one thing in common: there is a field or mechanism beyond our physical selves in which consciousness or thought can exist, flow, and be shared. These theories help validate our beliefs that such things are possible. But we can avoid being preoccupied with these ideas or determining which have the greatest merit when our real aim is to *experience* the underlying expansiveness of these theories for ourselves.

As already described, telepathy is a shared state of consciousness between two individuals, but there are several levels of telepathic sharing. When working with the conscious and unconscious mind and memory, it is possible to share the most intimate personal information between two people telepathically. The list includes information about the past (retro-cognitive), present (indicative of present state, or thoughts in the present about the future), or future (precognitive awareness of the potential trajectory of future thoughts) of an individual's mind, inclusive of mental states (i.e., telepathic simulation), and thoughts (Kelly, 2011; Ullman et al., 2023). At the physical and psychic level of the conscious and unconscious, it is also possible to share emotional states through the transfer of kinesthetic sensations (also known as emotive telepathy, empathic telepathy, telempathy, or clairsentience), which is connected to the sharing of the energetic contents of physical consciousness described in the previous chapter. Telepathy at the superconscious level allows us to share access to the collective wisdom of humans, animals, discarnate beings, and a dualistic connection to the Creator, the Divine, or God. At these levels there is a quantum jump in sharing experiences where direct, instant experience or immediate knowing is transmitted from one intelligent energy system and received by another. Robert Monroe (1985), famous for out-of-body journeys and research, refers to this level of telepathy as "non-verbal communication," where large packets of information are instantaneously exchanged in a form of gnosis.

Sharing states of nonduality, or ultimate reality, is the last known destination of the mindmeld. I will explore each of these levels of sharing psychic contents in the following sections, noting the mindmeld using psychedelics is just one of several ways to share consciousness.

TELEPATHY AND THE HUMAN PSYCHIC SYSTEM

The nature of the human psychic system as an element of consciousness is an immense area of study, yet is simultaneously shrouded in mystery. Some of the most fundamental questions about consciousness have yet to be satisfactorily answered. Examples are: Where does consciousness originate? Where does consciousness reside? Does the brain give rise to consciousness? If so, how? This chapter does not seek to answer these questions definitively but rather presents what the human psychic system is capable of with regard to the sharing of consciousness. I encourage you to explore what is possible and draw your own conclusions.

The uninitiated may view shared consciousness as impossible. Presenting what's possible helps normalize and validate the idea. Doing so also provides a map of the known territory and opens up possibilities for further exploration. To engage in this work is to become a cartographer of consciousness. As a mapmaker, you contribute to the vast mapping data bank of consciousness, perhaps even those in the Akashic Records, improving the survey of coordinates and milestones. By entering into deeper states of consciousness and exploring new territory, it may even be possible to contribute to enlarging the territory itself. This latter postulate accepts the possibility that conscious realization is infinite, constantly evolving and expanding based on the experiences of all consciousness in time and space.

To share any form of consciousness with another person is to communicate telepathically. The phenomenon of telepathy, or shared consciousness, is well accepted in Eastern traditions, particularly by Buddhists and Hindus. Swami Sivananda (2014) describes telepathy simply as thought transference* from one person to another. In the same way that sound moves around in space, so thought moves in the mental space, the *Chidakaśa*, or aether of Pure Consciousness, which is shared by all. Eastern traditions point out that telepathy is a part of the natural world and has nothing to do with faith, religious doctrine, divine intervention, spirituality, or the supernatural (Radin, 2018; Sivananda, 2014; Yogananda, 1998). Shamans working with psychedelic plants say the same thing, referencing how they can naturally see into participants' visions during ceremonies and guide them through other worlds (Harris, 2021, p. 21).

Telepathy can happen spontaneously or deliberately. An example of *spontaneous* telepathy would be thinking of a friend who phones you minutes later or thinking of someone when they are in crisis or when they are dying. Mothers and children, twins, lovers, and close friends

---

*Thought transference, or the "transfer of thoughts," can also be referred to as telepathic cognition (Kelly, 2011, p. 98).

can often be telepathically tuned in to each other's consciousness in this way. More broadly, every time we think or talk about another person, we are sending out thought waves toward that person, positively, or negatively, or may be receiving thoughtforms from the other person.

Deliberate telepathy is an intentional sharing of consciousness. Deliberate telepathy is practiced by mediums and psychics when they telepathically tune in to the unseen subtle energies of the person they are reading. Mediums and psychics often refer to clairvoyance as the telepathic ability to share psychic contents using imagery; clairaudience is the ability to share telepathically using hearing. Deliberate telepathy is also used in scientific studies for sharing such things as specific thoughts, images, or sensations between research subjects. But what, more specifically, do we know about what can be psychically shared telepathically? The rest of this section provides an overview of the possibilities from the perspective of different modalities.

In an act known as *shaktipat*, great adepts or *Mahatmas* (great souls) can deliberately transmit their lessons and messages telepathically—sometimes from beyond the grave—to deserving aspirants or yogis in their presence or sometimes elsewhere in the world (Desai, 1979, p. 70; Sivananda, 2014, p. 329). Here, the teacher is an activator, opening the student to what is already accessible in their consciousness. The !Kung of the Kalahari report that a *n/um* master can create or psychically transfer access of the psychic abilities associated with the *n/um* to a student (Katz, 1982). Similarly, shamans are known for imparting teachings by appearing in the dreams of their protégés (Harris, 2021, p. 22).

A mix of spontaneous and deliberate telepathy can occur in dreams. Swami Sivananda Radha (2013) facilitated dream groups who worked closely together for long periods. On some occasions, several members had similar dreams at the same time or even dreamed parts of the same dream. By her claim, she would sometimes dream the other half of a student's dream. For this to occur, both people need to be open to each other with neither dominating the other. In another instance, she connected to a student's dead ancestor who was trying unsuccessfully to impart a message to the student and then employed Radha to help share the news—which she did (p. 112). Similarly, Ullman et al. (2003; 2023) and Radin (2006) have written about the viability of dream telepathy in their books based on their research. In his book *Dreaming Wide Awake*, Brown (2016) explores research into shared dreaming and telepathy through dreams and the use of psychedelics, highlighting compelling evidence for the existence of these phenomena.

Telepathy can also manifest in connecting a person to the collective unconscious or superconsciousness during dreams and meditation, where it is possible to access transpersonal premonitions of future events (Jung, 2011b; Yogananda, 1998).

For yogi masters like Swami Vishnu-devananda (1988) and Sivananda (1994), *siddhis* (physical and psychic powers), such as telepathy, clairvoyance, and clairaudience, among others, are incidental milestones on the path to attaining communion with one's higher self, a state known as samadhi in which, at the final stage, the yogi sees and experiences Brahma (God) everywhere, the equivalent of a nondual state. Vishnu-devananda (1988) describes how *siddhis* are yogic powers that the "real" yogis never care to look upon. Less advanced students can easily be corrupted by the *siddhis* and use them for selfish purposes, leading to the loss of these abilities (p. 260). Buddhist adepts similarly look upon *siddhis*, or psychic abilities, as distractions along the path to enlightenment.

My intent is not to shun the possibility of these truths. Still, given the apparent lower state of human development generally in the world, as defined by these Eastern wisdom traditions, working with the mind-meld can lend to human development. Working together in the mind-meld opens the possibility of co-creatively fostering each other's potency of evolution, where the whole is greater than the sum of its parts. Here it may be possible for our own internal *masters* to step forward to reciprocally unlock doors to higher states of being in each other.

Other examples of telepathic connection include shamanic and out-of-body journeying and past-life regression work. Pat, a shamanic practitioner of thirty years, shared a story with me about a shamanic journey with a group. Pat works with the shamanic teachings of Michael Harner and uses the percussion of the drum, without the use of psychedelics, to drive the journey. In this particular instance the intention was to support the healing of a client. A Tibetan Buddhist monk with long-standing meditative experience, staying at her house, was meditating in a separate room during the session. During the shamanic journey, Pat was surprised and delighted to find the monk directly in the journey into the other worlds, where the two were telepathically communicating. The monk arrived in the journey with humility and respect and sought permission to participate. Pat describes his participation as holding sacred space with a loving presence, sharing his energy in the positive movement of what was already taking place in healing (personal communication, 2022).

William Buhlman (1996), world-renowned out-of-body traveler, has described how groups of people can meet each other during out-of-body experiences by planning a time and place to meet in the nonphysical planes. People compare and confirm their group experiences after returning to their bodies.

Niall, psychic healer and channeler, takes his clients on transcendental journeys into past lives and alternative realities to heal, clear, and balance them. He also introduces them to the guiding messages and gifted wisdom of the ascended masters. He makes a telepathic connection with the individual he is working with through a meditative trance without psychedelics. This connection can occur at a distance, as he works with people worldwide. He says a session's intention is for him and his client to surrender to and follow the guidance of the channeled-in master. Through this approach, they jointly explore the source of and reasons for illnesses, traumas, and karmic entanglements. With the aid of the spirit masters, these suppressing distortions are energetically discharged and dissolved, leading to healing, the opening of the client's psychic gifts, and general transpersonal growth. Niall can, when required, telepathically see and energetically feel what is arising from his client's transcendental explorations. In most cases, the client doing the work with Niall can see him in their internal world of exploration (personal communication, 2022). This has been the case when I have worked with him.

As more therapists are starting to offer psychedelic therapy, either legally or underground, some are simultaneously taking psychedelics with their patients, although usually at lower doses. There are reports from therapists of telepathic connections with their clients in some of these sessions. Therapists claim to feel the emotions of their clients, perceiving where the person is at psychologically, what is present, and potentially what is being avoided by the client. This mirroring can provide the client with an internally felt sense of support they have never had before and allow them to experience through the therapist how uncomfortable feelings can be faced and processed (Jones, 2021). Grof (1976; 2008; 2009) similarly reports clients in psychedelic sessions experiencing periods of fusion with their therapists even when therapists are not taking psychedelics, where they feel a symbiotic union and a nourishing exchange, and where the clients can also "read" the therapist's thought processes, emotional reactions, and attitudes.

As mentioned earlier, telepathy falls into the gamut of extrasensory perception, psi, or psychic abilities in the West. Science has been much slower to support the possibility of psychic exchanges among people, but this is now a rapidly growing field with hundreds of books and articles published on the subject. For example, Sheldrake (2009; 2011; 2012; 2013) has conducted experiments indicating telepathic connections among humans and between humans and animals. Church (2018) has reviewed research highlighting how sending new signals through your brain's neural pathways can alter the energy fields of those around you. Radin (2006; 2018) has gone further, presenting robust meta-analyses of decades of scientific research in favor of various psychic phenomena, including telepathy.

The science of telepathy is not without controversy. It seems every scientific proponent proving telepathy and other paranormal phenomena has as many or more scientists discounting it (Blackmore, 2012).

My purpose is not to prove or disprove the existence of telepathy but to open your mind to the possibility and for you to experience telepathy for yourself. This book is meant to open "the doors of perception" to new forms of second-person or intersubjective experience and personal research.

To be a serious researcher yourself requires being as objective as possible. In this regard, my suggestion when doing mindmeld work is to refrain from having or sharing any specific intent with your partner ahead of the engagement or trying to manifest something other than a telepathic connection. Let experiences bubble up from the unconscious into manifestation without manipulation. When reaching the end of the session, write down your experiences before talking to your partner, then compare notes to see what was shared telepathically in consciousness.*

Again, for our purposes, we are simply exploring what is possible. By sharing what other traditions and science have researched, I want to normalize what is humanly possible for all of us, guarding against those whose egos may inflate "magical" abilities and somehow create the pretense of superiority when we all have access to this potential. I am not enlightened, and I am not advocating for enlightenment or the highest levels of personal perfection. What I am advocating for is to experience our most complete, courageous, honest, ethical, and cosmic selves.

HEALING AND HOMEOSTASIS THROUGH SHARING AND RELEASING PSYCHIC ENERGY

As alluded to earlier, part of being human is facing trauma. Trauma can result from a long list of things, including physical trauma from accidents, sickness, surgical operations, physical abuse, sexual abuse,

---

*Perhaps, once psychedelics are fully legalized, repeatable experiments will be conducted to test shared consciousness while using psychedelics. Outside judges could be used to evaluate trip transcripts, with a statistician applying appropriate statistical techniques to evaluate the judges' work. People could also try sharing "blinded" targets during sessions.

and even challenges in prenatal life and being born. Psychological trauma can result from all of these physical experiences. It can also include emotional abuse, like abandonment, harassment, and bullying (e.g., humiliation or ridicule), and struggles related to grief, loss, and other challenges. Ultimately, trauma is the physiological response to a profoundly distressing or disturbing event overwhelming a person's nervous system and negatively impacting their ability to live their life. Often trauma is accompanied by persistent feelings of helplessness, diminishing one's sense of self and the ability to feel a full range of emotions and experiences. Trauma can rob you of being in charge of yourself, leaving you more vulnerable to feeling overwhelmed, enraged, ashamed, or collapsed (Kolk, 2015, p. 203). Trauma can be acute from a single incident, chronic from repeated and prolonged exposure, or complex as related to varied and multiple traumatic events. Trauma reflects our deepest wounds (Levine, 2008; Maté, 2012; Maté & Maté, 2022; Scaer, 2014).

Grof (1976; 2008; 2009) suggests trauma can penetrate the transpersonal domain of the psyche, reaching into ancestral, racial, collective, and phylogenetic memories. These experiences can seemingly come from other lifetimes (past-life memories) and various archetypal motifs. Examples include being a victim of ancient religious rituals and ceremonies (e.g., blood sacrifice), torture, mutilations, rape, murder, crucifixion, racial hatred, war and genocide, disease, famine, or natural catastrophe; existential struggle in the face of meaningless extreme suffering; or being violated or destroyed by destructive underworld creatures or gods of wrath. In this context, any emergence of a previously unknown traumatic memory (related to the current life or past lives) should be understood as a psychic phenomenon (possibly like dream content and symbolic or archetypal in nature), even though the event may be experienced as "hyper-real." The memory should be treated subjectively and with caution, with the aim of resolving the energetic signature associated with it before one considers solidifying it as a part of one's true personal biographical narrative. Research indicates that often these types of experiences are not based in fact. However, if the memory is particularly egregious, such as sexual abuse, therapy may be indicated to determine how best to move forward and whether any form of action is warranted (Aixalà, 2022).

Trauma can take a heavy toll on the body but also on the psyche. Here, when I refer to the psyche, I am again referring to the energetic force in our psychological makeup that is the ego and the unconscious and more. The psyche strives to bring the human organism toward homeostasis or, as Jung (2011b) has described it, the *individuation process* as the highest sense of unity.* The psyche contains our inner healing intelligence. The psyche, as a broader force from the collective unconscious and a creative and generative principle in the cosmos, strives for wholeness with the ultimate goal of complete integration of conscious and unconscious, or the assimilation of the ego to a broader personality. In wholeness we are self-motivating, self-accepting, and self-loving. When functional, the psyche (and the superego) is responsible for our conscience—a sense of truth and guilt—and connected to universal moral and ethical principles. A traumatized psyche may undermine our connection to a higher and more moral and ethical part of ourselves, as we are more likely to feel constricted, fragmented, and unhappy, potentially projecting this onto others.

The residues of trauma, such as those resulting from PTSD, can become lodged or stuck in the psyche and the body through what Dr. Pierre Janet coined "dissociation" (in Kolk, 2015, p. 180). Dissociation is the splitting off and isolation of traumatic memory imprints. It is a universal, instinctual, and adaptive survival response to the unbearable. Overwhelming contents become fragmented and disowned. According to Janet, thoughts, emotions, and sensations can become stored in the unconscious and the body as barely comprehensible fragments. Candace Pert (1991), neuroscientist and pharmacologist, describes how your subconscious mind is really your body. Peptides are

---

*As described in chapter 1, some consider the psyche to be the emotive and unifying force of the soul.

the biochemical correlate of emotion underlying the body's most basic communication network. This means that emotional memory is stored throughout the body and can be accessed anywhere through the network. Here Pert confirms the mind-body connection and the mechanism for psychological trauma lodging itself in the body. Dissociation prevents trauma from being integrated. When the residues of trauma are not connected in an effective way of associating and drawing the trauma into the ongoing autobiographical narrative of life, the person can begin to feel constricted and stuck. As such they increasingly lose connection to their feelings, their capacity to assimilate new experiences, and possibly the desire to engage in new experiences (Kolk, 2015; Levine, 2008; Walker, 2013).

From a shamanic perspective, dissociation is the equivalent of soul loss, or soul fragmentation, with the same loss of vital energy. This loss is the same defensive mechanism for the consciousness to survive trauma as dissociation, and similarly demands healing.

All the schools of psychotherapy generally seek to achieve two things when working with trauma: (1) directly address the painful symptom(s) and (2) address the underlying cause of the symptom(s). Symptoms are typically managed through therapy, exercise, and physically based treatments. Examples of therapeutic approaches to address trauma include psychotherapy, cognitive behavioral therapy, mindfulness, somatic therapy, eye movement desensitization reprocessing (EMDR), neurofeedback, yoga, dance, and many more. These approaches seek to explain and "cure" the underlying cause of the symptom(s) to help create a more coherent, resilient sense of self for dealing flexibly with the challenging realities of life.*

---

*Symptoms are also commonly addressed with drugs, although these have limits. Pharmaceuticals, such as antidepressants or benzodiazepines, are often used in therapy. But as Kolk (2015) points out, they cannot "cure" trauma, only dampen the expressions of disturbed physiology. They do not teach the lasting lessons of self-regulation. Thus, pharmaceuticals help to control feelings and behavior, but at the cost of down-regulating engagement, motivation, pain, and pleasure, and often with other negative physiological side effects (p. 224).

For our purposes, it is necessary to understand that psychedelics can bring into awareness dissociated trauma, or the loss of vital energies through soul loss. In this respect, psychedelics have the opposite effect of many pharmaceuticals. Instead of blunting emotional dysregulation, they act as "non-specific amplifiers," bringing to the surface and amplifying unconscious material to be processed (Grof, 2008; 2009). Therefore, one must be prepared for traumatic contents to manifest in the mindmeld. When they do, they are to be experienced and witnessed, not avoided or repressed.

Similarly to therapeutic techniques, and some shamanic techniques, the intention in the mindmeld is for the psyche to become increasingly aware of the difference between the now and the past, mainly using the witnessing method of meditation, described in the next chapter. To face trauma in the psychedelic journey and not turn away is to face it anchored in the present and know these terrible events belong in the past, which creates a new and empowered perspective. To meet the horrors of the past purposefully and voluntarily teaches our courageous exploratory spirit it can prevail over threat (Peterson, 1999, p. 170). Here, we assume people cannot move toward integrating and learning from their experiences on their own because they are either hyper-aroused or shut down. But in the mindmeld, with support from their partner and, possibly, discarnate beings, they may overcome their psychological rigidity and move toward mental plasticity or psychological flexibility. They may find strength to open up to new ways of quietly observing themselves in their struggles. If the psyche can sit with the discomfort of the traumatic residue in the mind and body, the stuck energies can begin to discharge through catharsis or abreaction. Vital life force energies that have been fragmented can then be restored. This shift can bring the integration of past with present, enhancing the person's means of learning and relating. New thought patterns can then emerge, potentially shifting negative, self-critical narratives toward more positive and empowering ones, like loving self-acceptance. With conscious, witnessing awareness or meta-awareness, one can even practice consciously shifting or reframing thought processes that are not serving to ones that do. For example, I have sat with dark thoughts and sensations, with others, in a mindmeld but then subtly turned my awareness to my heart center, and together we observed the darkness transform into a blissful outpouring.

In recovering from trauma, Kolk (2015, p. 203) describes the importance of reestablishing a sense of ownership of your body and mind where you can know what you know and feel what you feel without becoming overwhelmed, enraged, ashamed, or collapsed. As he describes it, this requires:

1. Finding a way to become calm and focused
2. Learning to maintain that calm in response to images, thoughts, sounds, or physical sensations that remind you of the past
3. Finding a way to be fully alive in the present and engaged with the people around you
4. Not having to keep secrets from yourself, including secrets about the ways you have managed to survive

In this context, the mindmeld, with its attendant meditation methods, should be seen as one of many therapeutic tools to help us move in the direction described by Kolk. But remember, psychedelics rarely offer an instant fix, and healing is often nonlinear.

Beyond trauma, humans are also confronted with the existential challenges of facing our own "demons," which can interact with our traumas. Tsultrim Allione (2008) points out that all humans are faced with the egoic struggles associated with fear, greed, aggression, temptation, ignorance, confusion, anger, self-hatred, shame, loneliness, longing, addiction, grief, and loss. We are also confronted with the universal wound faced collectively by the human species: the certain death of everyone and everything we love, including ourselves. Over a lifetime, suffering seems to outweigh joy. Most suffering is fed by our drive to seek pleasure and happiness and avoid pain and depression. The way through these struggles, our personal demons, according to Allione, is to recognize them, give them visual form from our unconscious, face them, and fearlessly and compassionately feed them what they want to satiation so they lose their power.

All the difficulties associated with trauma and existential challenges can arise in the mindmeld. In sharing psychic content, there is an inherent camaraderie of facing challenges and working through them collaboratively. In this way, there is a transpersonal partnership of engagement through recognizing and giving form to each person's challenges—facing them, feeding them, and releasing them from consciousness. This process can be both unsettling and scary but also bring relief and healing, including a restoration of vital energy. Working through trauma can also be a meaningful experience by uncovering more profound levels of meaning and relating.

Kolk (2015) describes how being validated by feeling heard and seen is a precondition for perceiving safety (p. 301). Feeling safe strengthens the nervous system, potentiating healing. In the mindmeld, there is a shared emotional honesty. Such openness can be frightening when there is nowhere to hide once a psychic connection is made and traumatic or dark thoughts are exposed. But as both people sit in stillness with what is presented, feelings of shared safety can be forged as each person holds space for the other while also holding space for themselves. Validation can be a part of the flow of shared psychic contents as each person thoroughly experiences the feelings of the other in the mindmeld, all while the other person knows the sharing is occurring. This shared movement enhances empathic ability insofar as both people can simultaneously feel one another's emotions. More commonly, empaths can pick up on other people's energy fields and feelings, but the other person usually is unaware of the sensing arising in the empath. In the mindmeld, there is an opening to being known at each other's core; each person bares themselves to the other. Each person can drop any sense of shame or pretense in this space. At its most profound, it is possible, when sharing psychic contents, to witness the awakening of dormant qualities in the other's personality that have remained repressed due to trauma or a lack of validation and an inner sense of safety. Here the mindmeld offers the opportunity to foster greater self-confidence, unlocking doors to individuation.

To provide an illustration of this type of psychic connection, I was in a session with Delia, a woman who had been married for years. At the onset, I could detect shadowy aspects within her, including internal resentments toward her husband, layers of self-hatred, and grief and loss of a relative. What is more interesting is she realized I was intuiting these emotional contents and wanted to hide them out of embarrassment from an internal sense of shame. And, yet, I was simply the witness accepting all content. She intuited my acceptance and settled further into our sharing, showing her strength and courage to reveal her inner experience. Soon the inner floodgates of our emotional and spiritual selves opened. Our session went from there and turned into a five-hour, nonstop, shared energetic healing session of deep body and tissue work of release and discharge and connection to the Divine. The session ended with mutual recognition of witnessing a deeper part of who we were in the other. She later commented on how the cathartic session improved her intimacy with her husband.

In another session, I mindmelded with Ben. At the peak of the experience, I met him at his heart. Ben later described how he felt like I had penetrated the core of his being and held his heart with a loving embrace. I experienced his loving wholeness, resonating with the beauty at the center of all of us.

When two people come together in the mindmeld, they can jointly work to heal each other. Resolving difficulties in the mindmeld can lead to increased emotional balance, potentially resolving unconscious emotional problems. Concurrently, coupled with the physical purification process described in the previous chapter, purifying and healing the mind at the psychic level can lead to sharing superconsciousness, jointly entering the heavenly realms, and experiencing the Divine All, which is the subject of the next two sections. Rumi states: "When inward tenderness finds the secret hurt, pain itself will crack the rock and, ah! Let the soul emerge."

SHARING SUPERCONSCIOUSNESS IN THE PSYCHEDELIC MINDMELD

When working with psychedelics, multiple levels or dimensions of reality can present themselves at the psychic level. To reach into the collective consciousness beyond one's self is to enter superconsciousness or the transpersonal. As described earlier, other names for this level are the astral plane, nonlocal mind, primordial thought, archetypal or daemonic realms, the supernatural, and the *anima mundi*—the Soul of the World. Here there is an elevated sense of connection to all life, nature, and the order of the universe, where the infinite microcosm of fermions, bosons, and dark matter interpenetrates the infinite macrocosm of the multiverse, all of which is the metacosm or *totality*. To access this space is to explore the borderlands between the unconscious mind and clear light mind and discover a more expansive and boundless universe of the total being.

Indra's Net is a famous metaphor for the fractal nature of the universe in Hindu and Buddhist cosmology. Belonging to the deva Indra, the Net hangs over his palace on Mount Meru as the *axis mundi*, the connection between celestial and earthly realms. At every vertex in the infinite net, there is a jewel. And when peering into any jewel, the reflection of all the others is there to behold. A timeless hologram of the universe is thus created. Here everything is interconnected to everything else. Space-time becomes relative. Primordial cosmic principles become accessible, such as the creative potential of the Big Bang singularity and the universe's grand design, and conversely, the primordial destructive principle of apocalypse—the Big Crunch—and complete annihilation.

A similar concept to Indra's Net is the Divine Imagination. In *Imagination*, all of reality, including the material universe, and all manifestations of consciousness, through all actions, thoughts, and dreams in all time and space is accessible to everybody. Underlying this concept is the notion that the universe is dreaming and we are all dream characters within it; we are a jewel in the dream net. These concepts give birth to the possibility of exploring infinite realization in the aether of the universe through our minds and jointly sharing this exploration in the mindmeld.

What is found in the territory of cosmic etheric space? What maps do we already have? Many courageous souls have journeyed deeply into the Divine Imagination over the millennia. The literature from the centuries of exploration is vast. I briefly describe some of the general maps shared by others to help us better understand what is possible and where we can play together in the field of dreams in the mindmeld.

I start with shamanism. Shamans generally describe the cosmos as having three realms: an upper world (ethereal), a middle world (a holotropic version of our biosphere), and a lower world or underworld (shadowy and earthy). These worlds, each with distinct levels and discarnate beings, are all connected by the *axis mundi*. Depending on the culture, this axis is represented by symbols like the Tree of Life, columns of smoke, ladders, or staircases (Eliade, 2004; Harner, 1990; 2013). Shamans enter these transtemporal worlds by "magical flight"—akin to out-of-body journeying—using a combination of psychoactive plants and a range of rhythmic dancing, breathing techniques, percussion, chanting, or sensory isolation, such as meditating in a dark cave. Extreme physiological interventions may also be used, like fasting, sleep deprivation, dehydration, and the infliction of severe pain.* They transcend natural laws such as time, gravity, and space to communicate and interact with plants, animals, spirits, and divine information, and they occasionally act as a psychopomp (an intermediary between the living

---

*Many native tribes around the world have used similar techniques to induce holotropic states for rites of passage ceremonies conducted at times of biological or social transitions, such as childbirth, circumcision, puberty, marriage, menopause, and before death. Similar rituals are also associated with initiation into warrior status, acceptance into secret societies, calendric festivals of renewal, and healing ceremonies (Grof, 2019a, p. 12).

and the dead and a guide for the soul transitioning from physical death of the body). They may shapeshift into various animals or have experiences of identifying with or being plants or inorganic matter, like a crystal, volcano, or mountain. They may even have sexual relations and offspring with spirits in these other worlds (Hancock, 2007). With the help of spirits (inclusive of the full range of discarnate beings), they also diagnose and treat physical and mental illnesses. In the case of spiritual illness, where a person has lost or had stolen a fragment of their soul or essence, usually through some form of physical or psychological trauma, the shaman journeys to the other worlds to retrieve it. Upon return, they reintegrate the fragment into the person to help make them whole again (Harner, 2013, Ingerman, 1991; Waya, 2004).

What can appear in lucid dreams, out-of-body experiences, or astral projection (including remote viewing) overlaps with shamanism. Lucid dreaming involves entering different worlds and dimensions during sleep. Out-of-body experience or astral projection involves entering similar alternate realities or astral planes while sleeping or consciously awake using trance meditation methods. These two techniques diverge in the initial stages. In lucid dreaming the mind is cast inward within dream imagination where worlds are highly malleable, whereas in astral projection the astral body leaves from the body into a dimension of the physical plane or material universe where one can observe and interact with, but not significantly change or affect, reality. However, the more one's awareness penetrates into the frequencies of superconsciousness, the more these two techniques converge into similar experiences. In both cases, for the adept, there is a high level of volition and agency, where they journey through space-time and can create and transform objects, people, situations, worlds, and even themselves in nonphysical realms (Bruce & Donaghue, 2013; Buhlman, 1996; Monroe, 1985; 1994; 2001; Ziewe, 2015). Here, the journey's intention is more varied and versatile compared to shamanism; shamans are generally less interested in transforming these worlds, instead focusing more on learning from them for purposes of healing, divination, hunting magic, or gaining power, such as gaining control over spirits (Eliade, 2004).

The astral universe of lucid dreaming, or astral projection, is as infinite as the imagination and ranges from the frivolous to the sublime (LaBerge, 2009). Natural laws can be transcended, as in shamanic realms, and the full range of discarnate beings can be present. It is also possible to have a complete ego (shamanic) death experience, explore past and future lives, receive previews of one's future life, or have perinatal experiences. Some have also traveled to other worlds, cartoon-animated realities, different planes or dimensions of realization, or parallel universes, interacted with passed souls, met highly evolved beings, interacted with deities and demigods, and communicated with the divine Self. It is also possible to connect to the collective unconscious and be exposed to collective suffering (e.g., disease, famine, war, genocide) or collective healing and profound shared bliss. These approaches for journeying all share similar reports of personal and spiritual growth, self-integration, improvements in the quality and depth of life, and transcendence (Brown, 2016; Bruce & Donaghue, 2013; Castaneda, 1993; Hancock, 2007; Holecek, 2016; LaBerge, 2009; Twitchell, 1967; 1987; Willson, 1987; Ziewe, 2015).

Similar reports have been provided by people who have had near-death experiences (NDE) (Atwater, 1994; Brown, 2016; Moody, 2015; Ring, 1980; 1989; 1992; Ring and Valarino, 1998). For obvious reasons, individual NDE maps of alternate realities appear more limited compared to people with years of experience traversing alternate realities through shamanic journeying, lucid dreaming, journeying with psychedelics, and so on. Still, they can be equally profound in their impact on a person's life. Taken as a whole of combined narratives, they share many common traits, such as life reviews, encounters with discarnate beings, positive and terrifying, hellish encounters, and out-of-body experiences, which can include visiting transcendental realms.

A similar phenomenon to the NDE is the shared-death experience (SDE). In an SDE, one person journeys into physical death, while the other person consciously joins but returns, similar to acting as a psycho-pomp. Like the mindmeld, an SDE can include empathic shared experience during the final moments before death and after physical death, as well as jointly journeying to other realms similar to those experienced in NDEs (Moody & Perry, 2010; Peters & Kinsella, 2022; Shared Crossing Research Initiative, 2021).

There are also reports from different cultures worldwide of psychics or mediums relaying or channeling the journeys of souls after death. According to these reports, souls describe, through psychic medium-ship, venturing to different "planes" of existence, similar to those summarized above, where one can encounter a whole range of worlds and discarnate beings (Laszlo, A., 2016). Similarly, there are studies of people, most often younger children, describing their "intermission" memories between lives, such as choosing and viewing parents before being conceived in the womb (Newton, 2002, 2009; Ohkado & Ikegawa, 2014; Tucker, 2005).

There are volumes of reports of lucid waking encounters with super-consciousness or the daemonic realm. Here I am referring to spontaneous events where people experience alien or faery abductions and are taken to other domains or to spaceships, where they interact with an assortment of discarnate beings, such as phantom animals, elementals, angelic beings, and aliens. These experiences again overlap with those described above (Hancock, 2007; Harpur, 2003; Harvey-Wilson, 2000; McKenna, 1991).

In the case of world religions, different spiritual worlds, such as heavenly realms, purgatory, and hellish realms, come to life in various scriptures, each with its nuances. Religions such as Judaism, Christianity, Islam, and Zoroastrianism have stories of an assortment of angels, giants, demons, and mystical creatures (e.g., the serpent in the Garden of Eden). Hindus and most Buddhists recognize limitless nonphysical realms, discarnate beings (e.g., deities, devas, demigods), other intelligences, and disparate states of existence. In the scriptures of world religions, engagement in superconsciousness usually occurs spontaneously. A discarnate being communicates through visions or dreams. It is also likely that some adepts used psychedelics (e.g., *soma* is described in the Hindu *Vedas* as a psychoactive concoction; in the Zoroastrian *Avesta*, the same drink is *haoma*; the Greek Eleusinian mystery schools used psychoactive plants in their sacred potion *kykeon*, which plants were likely shared with Jews and early Christians) (Grof, 2019a; Hancock, 2007). Baker (2019) and Crowley (2019; 2023) have separately amassed evidence indicating psychedelics were used by the ancient adepts of Vajrayāna Buddhism. Allegro (1970), Brown and Brown (2016), Muraresku (2020), and Shannon (2008) have all separately postulated that cults using psychedelic mushrooms, or a mix of psychoactive concoctions, founded Judaism, and Allegro and Muraresku argue the same for Christianity.

The psychedelic journey can overlap what is described above, accessing the same cosmoscape of superconsciousness. Parallels include transcending natural laws, the existence of multiple worlds and dimensions, access to the collective unconscious, the possibilities of a multiverse, and encounters with a vast array of discarnate beings (Bache, 2019; Brown, 2016; Grof, 1976; 2008; 2009; Hancock; 2007; Metzner, 2015; Metzner & Darling, 2005; Metzner, 2006; Strassman, 2001; Strassman, et al., 2008). Experiences can include identifying with or transforming into the experience of being animals or plants. This can occur at symbolic levels, simulating experiences of directly being the animal or plant, or having phylogenetic memories of evolution as the animal or plant. The same can happen with identifying as other people: either connecting to others at a symbolic level, such as with the leadership qualities of Genghis Khan or the spiritual attributes of Jesus Christ or Buddha; reliving experiences of a past life; living the experience of a dead or living family member, friend, or acquaintance or the experiences of an entire group of people, such as becoming the whole of the Jews who were persecuted over the centuries or the Muslims during their pilgrimage to Mecca; or connecting to phylogenetic memories of the human species. Penetrating the microcosm and macrocosm, similar experiences of becoming aware of molecular, cellular, planetary, or extra-planetary consciousness are also possible. Mediumistic phenomena can occur when there is communication with deceased persons, as well as forms of spirit possession (Grof 1976; 2008; 2009). Levels of volition and agency when using psychedelics for journeying and engagement seem to depend on years of experience, similar to lucid dreaming, astral projection, and meditation. Dosage also affects volition and agency, and higher doses usually reduce volition and agency.

Personal reports in the literature of voyaging into the cosmos, whether using psychedelics, employing other specific techniques, or occurring spontaneously, point to an infinite array of territory to be explored. While some maps of experience may appear to contradict each other, it may just be that all experiences hold truth and may speak to the highly complex nature of reality. It may also be that language is an impediment to understanding, where, for example, an "alien" being may be the same as an "elemental" or "faery," or at least closely related. Interpretation and definition of experience, especially through the projection of cultural and personal beliefs and biases, contribute to distortions in nuance. Nuance in the experiences themselves may be affected by a person's character if they superimpose additional layers of their idiosyncratic unconscious projections into their experience (Ziewe, 2015). In this regard, Buhlman (1996) describes how nonphysical environments* are thought-responsive; when we enter nonphysical dimensions, thoughts, both conscious and unconscious, interact with and restructure the energy around us, which can cause immense diversity of experience dependent on the observer. Similarly, Kelly (2011) points out that long-term memory impacts our perception of psi phenomenon. Memory provides reference points for our brains to consciously have the experience and try to make meaning out of it; this helps us receive information and process it, but it can also cause distortion and possibly confabulation.

---

*Nonphysical environments are the supportive energy structures that at a quantum level create physical reality and can be entered and manipulated through out-of-body states of [super]consciousness (Buhlman, 1996).

Questions abound on the nature of the phenomenon of other dimensions and discarnate beings. Are they creations of our mind and limited to the physical matter in our brains? Are they individual and unique phenomena, each with their own identities and purpose? Or are they the imaginings of the Great Divine, along with the entire material universe? For many people, the subjective experience of encountering separate beings offers proof of the hypothesis of "dualism": the existence of a soul or spirit capable of leaving the body and surviving death. It may also be that our relationship with other beings is symbiotic, where our thought stream influences the "other" and they do the same to us. Theories abound on these ideas, and the debate may never reach a conclusion satisfactory to all. Ultimately, these debates do not matter to us regarding our endeavor of the mindmeld. I offer no definitive answers to these debates. Here, I am only surveying the possibilities of what can be jointly explored.

To share superconsciousness in the mindmeld is to meet each other in any of the experiences described above. As such, we can jointly venture into archetypal realms, other worlds and dimensions, and meet other beings. In these realms, we can encounter ourselves together as archetypal universal symbols, such as the Christian cross, the ancient Egyptian ankh, the lotus flower, or the Taoist yin-yang, or archetypal characters like the healer, the adventurer, the hero, the king, the queen, or the demon. Others encountered can include the long list of discarnate beings mentioned earlier, such as aliens, ex-galactics, elementals, entities, plant teachers, spirits, spirit guides, spirit animals, therianthropic beings, souls, ancestors, devas, deities, angels, demons, and monsters. We can share the experience of being a plant, animal, molecule, nebula, or galaxy. As time and space are archetypal, they can be encountered and transcended, as can the archetypes of subject and object in duality, as I discuss in the next section.

In the following paragraphs, I offer a few examples of jointly journeying into other realms in the mindmeld. The first example is of Isabel using mushrooms. As we transcended our egos, we met each other, floating out of body in a black void. This connection and meeting spontaneously occurred without intention, as if guided by the unconscious or the soul.

When we arrived we had volition, as though the ego's function had been transcended to get to the realm but resurfaced capable of directing the experience once we were there. I took the lead and started introducing Isabel to the souls of other living people we knew. There was playfulness in my choices. As someone came to mind, their soul, or higher self, became visible. We didn't interact with the other souls but simply observed them. The first soul was a friend who had suffered profound childhood trauma, struggled with narcissism, and was a chronic alcoholic. He appeared to us in a jail cell. His personal struggle and self-imprisonment were palpable. Our hearts empathized with his dark condition. The next soul was a psychic-energetic healer we had both seen for healing purposes months previously. She had an energetic signature of loving awareness and radiated beautiful, turquoise-colored light. For us, viewing such polarity of characters in this realm was fascinating.

We then shared a common connection to Gandhi. Again, there was no interaction but an awareness of his presence and glowing radiance, coupled with the iconography of India. We ended the mindmeld in Egypt. After our trip, we both verbally confirmed our telepathic connection and shared experience.

Sharing psychic content can be about the symbiosis of divine loving connection. In another mindmeld session, this time using LSD, I was with John when we collaboratively shared love and healing with the collective unconscious at a transpersonal level.* In the journey, we realized we were long-lost cosmic brothers whose origins were from elsewhere in the universe. In both of our realizations, he was the older cosmic brother, yet he was, in fact, significantly younger than me.†

---

*Here I am describing the lived experience. While clearly open to debate, Bache (2019) hypothesizes that in highly energized psychedelic states the collective unconscious can sometimes be activated, perhaps through a fractal flip or quantum entanglement, and to such a degree that it triggers a collective healing process (p. 136).

†Research by Grof (2008), in which many patients in psychedelic therapeutic settings identify their therapists from previous incarnations, points out that such "past-incarnation" connections are not unusual (p. 100).

In an example of jointly connecting to the archetypal in a mind-meld while using mushrooms, Isabel and I became queen and king. She embodied feminine energy, and I embodied masculine energy. We floated as energetic beings through towering, jeweled palaces blazoned in golden sunlight with purple hues. Nobody else was in this world. We did not have subjects, yet we felt like royalty at the center of our power. We basked in our connection to each other and the wider cosmos in immanent loving glory.

In an example of connecting to extraterrestrial realms, I was working in an LSD mindmeld session with Pan, a close friend. After I had done intense physical work on his abdomen (where I later found out he had parasites), we found ourselves lying on the hallway floor. I had my hand on his head in the classic Vulcan mindmeld position, while his arms were outstretched into the air. We both received downloads of nonintelligible alien information. Pan later described the experience as me working his body like an antenna, and I was the radio receiver. I agreed.

Perhaps it should not be surprising that if living physical beings can mindmeld, it is also possible to mindmeld with discarnate beings in superconsciousness.* In this case, there is an energetic exchange, but my body enters fractal energetic yoga to move energy in the cosmic matrix on behalf of another soul. For example, it is possible to connect to the souls of deceased persons. In one case, I connected to my dead grandmother, and I experienced being her while on a train and felt her fear as she was being forcibly moved by the Communists from Ukraine to Siberia following the 1917 Communist revolution in Russia.

Another similar experience occurred days after a friend of mine, Yann, died. He lived a life filled with great trauma from an early age, and as an adult he sustained a severe injury from an assault. Yann

---

*Communication with disincarnate beings is also referred to as "transcommunication." Here I distinguish transcommunication as more of a communication of thought, versus the mindmeld where there is an energetic exchange and a symbiotically shared conscious experience.

struggled with drug addiction to mute his extreme suffering. While in session, I unexpectedly connected to him days after his physical death from an overdose. My body and tongue twisted like I was somehow contributing to wringing out some of the density associated with his soul journeying into another realm. I offered him a heartfelt goodbye as he journeyed forward. Similarly, I have mindmelded with my deceased father, who has connected with me on several occasions and offered healing for past emotional hurts between us while he was alive, with me responding in kind.

I have also interacted with iconic figures like Gandhi, and John Lennon. With these characters, I somehow engaged in an energetic exchange of clearing lingering density in their fields, necessitating extensive fractal energetic yoga work. I often moved through deep sadness and emotional and physical pain, including crying, loud toning, and complex and physically trying yoga-like positions. Sometimes these exchanges included sharing joy and loving-kindness. I also received unintelligible downloads from them.

These experiences have generally been extremely intense and often strenuous to go through. While they are cathartic, they are also overwhelming and have repeatedly made me question why I keep working with psychedelics. Nevertheless, each of these experiences felt like I was transmuting something unresolved of "theirs," giving the experiences a strange sense of purpose and meaning. In these instances, I recognize how fantastical these claims are. I do not hold them tight, and I consider them possible projections of my unconscious or connections to archetypes.

Jurgen Ziewe (2015) has for decades journeyed to many realms of superconsciousness using meditation, lucid dreaming, and out-of-body experiences. He has encountered and interacted with thousands of human souls in other realms. From his years of experience, he reports: "When the relay station and filter, which is our brains, stops functioning [in physical death] and the body is returned to its individual atoms, our conscious and subconscious mind become our new external reality" (p. 22). Thus, who we are in this life is who we similarly experience after death. Ziewe posits that after death occurs there is a constant shifting of conscious states in the ethereal or nonphysical realms, where a dominant energetic persona embodied at the soul level can continue to develop and evolve. Here, consciousness can be drawn back to incarnate realities, other worlds, or dimensions associated with a particular state of mind, where the evolution of conscious states can progress, meaning we can interact with the dead and mutually contribute to each other's evolution.

I have also had mindmelding interactions with archetypal figures like the Cosmic Christ and the Buddha, where I receive personal healing and a loving transference. In one example, I lay floating in a pond of lotus flowers while a Buddha sprinkled me with rose petals. In another example, while meditating for five hours, but without using psychedelics, the Cosmic Christ came forward and cleared me of the extreme anxiety I had been struggling with for several months after a difficult relationship breakup; of interest, this encounter only happened after I completely "gave up" and surrendered in the meditation. Other times I have felt connected to other beings helping me clear my energy and energy in the collective unconscious, including Buddhist Lamas, the Dalai Lama, Carlos Castaneda, Metatron, Archangels Michael and Raphael, indigo-blue light beings from another planet, and more.

These interactions have sometimes elicited overwhelming gratitude and appreciation for the contributions of different beings to humanity, which I have sometimes expressed through spontaneous songs of thanks and praise. Examples include gratitude for the contributions of Aristotle, Plato, and angelic beings like Metatron, Michael, Raphael, and the Cosmic Christ.

Perhaps the strangest mindmeld I have had was with my future self. During a solo LSD journey, I called out to my future self across spacetime to help accelerate my evolution in my current incarnation. But my future self did not show up. Two nights later I was in a lucid dream and saw myself as a blue-skinned jinn-like figure in a mirror, beckoning me in. I was lying on a carpeted floor, feeling exhausted with the busyness of my surroundings, wanting to exit my body. I energetically reached for the mirror with my astral body and passed through the mirror into an out-of-body experience. BANG, I was in another dimension. The realm was much more vivid and vibrant compared to our waking world, or the realm of my lucid dream. I was floating in a massive hall of grand baroque architecture. The walls were red, white, and gold inlaid with thousands of gemstones and hung with ornate tapestries. I watched my future self fly throughout the room, shape-shifting from being human to spherical and cylindrical shapes. I telepathically felt his (my) joy and enthusiasm as he (I) showed me what was possible in my future in higher dimensions.

It is possible to connect to a broader consciousness in the mindmeld as well. During an ayahuasca journey, I found myself in a magical garden of healing plants whose consciousness telepathically communicated with me. Their petals and leaves sweetly caressed me. The intelligence of the plants in this realm was palpable. I was shown the power, majesty, and genius of plants as the consciousness of Nature interpenetrated its loving presence within me. It was an honor to be brought to this beautiful garden.

In the field of superconsciousness there can often be an awareness of a power greater than oneself: the Divine, God, or Creator. These are big terms holding lots of baggage. But the experience of Divine Presence is discernable. When meeting this presence, I have been moved, in the same way as in fractal energetic yoga, to bow down in gratitude and a depth of felt prayer to acknowledge its vast, infinite, living self. This experience is like being prayed through, where I became the prayer. Prayer is fully embodied in prostrated gratitude and humility. Compassion emanates from the depths of absolute unity and love. One senses divine perfection, where there is no dualistic pretense of right and wrong. One is of the infinite fingers on the hand of God. This connection occurs in duality, where subject and object still exist in superconsciousness, yet reaches toward the infinite of the nondual.

SHARING THE INCREMENTS OF
NONDUAL STATES OF CONSCIOUSNESS

As one penetrates nonduality, personal history and story become irrelevant. The "I" having and creating stories dissolves. Any ambitions and cravings for wealth, fame, prestige, and power are shattered. But what is a nondual state of consciousness? In the simplest of terms, nonduality refers to the loss of distinction between subject and object. On the surface, this explanation appears to refer to one possible state of consciousness. And, yet, there are several increments, or orders of magnitude, to this state of consciousness.

Volumes have been written about nonduality in Eastern and Western traditions, including Advaita Vedanta, Hinduism, Buddhism, Taoism, and the mystics of Judaism, Christianity, and Islam. Each tradition has its way of describing these incremental states, often in great detail with many nuances and many different labels.* At the same time, each tradition recognizes these states are ineffable and beyond adequate description.

I keep the description of these incremental states simple, but with enough breadth to give an indication of what is accessible. I am not writing about the embodiment of these states nor trying to place them in any form of spiritual dogma or ideal, like enlightened attainment. A simple map of the possible destinations should be adequate. The exploration of these states is for you to survey.

To avoid language confusion, I refer to tiered levels of experience, using four tiers. Different traditions refer to simply one tier of nondual experience, while others use as many as seven.

---

*The following list samples the diversity of labels for nondual realization: absolute or cosmic consciousness; clear light mind; metacosmic void; supreme self or identity; universal mind; supracosmic or unity consciousness; *advaya*; *alaya-jnana*; Atman-Brahman union; *chittamatrata*; *dharmakaya*; *jnana*; luminosity; *moksha*; *pararthabhavina*; *prajna*; *prajnaparamita*; *ri*; *samadhi* [*asamprajnata*; *kevala nirvikalpa*; *sahaja nirvikalpa*; *samprajnata*; *savikalpa*]; *satori*; *sambhogakaya*; *sunyata*; *svabhavikakaya*; *tathagatagarbha*; *tathata*; *turiya*; *turiyatita*; and *unio mystica*.

As I describe each of the tiers below, it is salient to highlight there is no necessary linear progression through the tiers; each state can occur spontaneously without intention, with or without the use of psychedelics, or without journeying through the lower tiers.

First Tier

In the first tier of nondual experience, there is the presence of unity in duality: the dissolution of polarity. Here all conceivable polarities, contradictory forces, can exist together in experience. For example, it is possible to experience two opposing emotions simultaneously. As such, you can be filled with joyous laughter concurrently with crying with sadness.

It is not unusual as one crosses the precipice from duality into the nondual to experience a flood of feelings of joy, liberation, salvation, redemption, and love. As SantataGamana (2018) describes, "Grace infuses our atoms with immaculate divine happiness" (p. 38). There can be feelings of being cleansed. There is simultaneously a deep intuitive knowingness that everything is connected in unity consciousness. From this state you can look back toward duality from the nondual and recognize the play of Divine Imagination. Everything in the universe is the imagination of God—all of it aware, alive, and interconnected as One.

At this tier, there is a growing unification of individual life force with the cosmic life force. Fractal energetic yoga is, therefore, a first-tier experience of the nondual. Allowing the movement of universal energy to flow through the body, letting it clear blockages and express itself in symmetrical divine patterns beyond the mind, is to engage this energy beyond the limited self in duality. By relegating the ego, there is no separation between the flow of universal energy and the human vehicle. This is not to say universal energy and intelligence are not already a part of all of us and already flowing through us, but to say we are fully opening the reducing valve created by ego when we open ourselves to fractal energetic yoga. Fractal energetic yoga can thereby contribute to opening portals to more expansive levels of the nondual.

As already described, fractal energetic yoga can reach from one body into another in the mindmeld, again beyond conscious volition, where the barriers of subject and object begin to break down. While there may be a conscious awareness of one's body and its connection to another body in space-time in the material realm, the connection itself is nondual insofar as there is no fundamental separation of the individual energy matrices and how they are engaged with each other. There is an enhanced porosity of energy between the two where personal energetic "bubbles" interpenetrate each other.

In the first tier, as duality begins to dissolve, there is less separation between one another. In the mindmeld with your co-melder, it is, therefore, possible to empathetically feel their emotions and be present in their thoughts.

When engaged at this introductory nondual level with discarnate beings, they can enter your consciousness and act out through your body, both positively and negatively, playfully, helpfully and empowering, or aggressively and malevolent. This is often called mediumship, channeling, incorporation, or possession.* Here you assume the identity of the "other" as individual identity blurs and separation dissolves, yet there is usually still an awareness of oneself. Channeling can include physical movement, thought transference, and speech directed by the discarnate being. At the uttermost end of this experience, people can be so engrossed in channeling the "other" that they will not remember the experience afterward.

There have been two occasions when I have welcomed another soul's consciousness into my body, often called voluntary possession. These two experiences occurred after years of fractal energetic yoga, which helped me discern a different experience. I describe these experiences as they were, but I am open to the possibility they were simply an extension of my psyche. The first time I felt that I shared my body with

---

*Luke (2019) describes numerous anecdotal stories from around the world of "incorporation" using psychedelics in his book *Otherworlds*. Falconer (2023) surveys a wide range of possession phenomenon in his book *The Others Within Us*.

another consciousness was when I had been in a mindmeld with Isabel. At some point, I separated from her and began doing fractal energetic yoga on my own. I did not know whether the work was clearing my energetic field, hers, or both. My yoga instructor's teacher, Swami Vishnu-devananda, who died in 1993, then arrived in me. I never met Vishnu-devananda, nor had any devotion toward him. However, the experience itself was of his spirit entering my body. When this happened, he began to play with my body. My awareness of myself was still present, but I observed this other conscious awareness in me. "He" was pleased to be in a body. He began moving my body through intense physical contortions and poses I was unfamiliar with. It was trying and often painful, but there was playfulness and joy that was his. Yet, I lived his playfulness and joy. It was similar to being in a mindmeld, except this mindmeld was with a deceased individual who had agency through my physical being.

A similar event occurred while working with Delia, whose sister had passed away over half a year before our session. The sister who passed had not been into psychedelics but had spent much of her life exploring superconscious realms, mostly through past-life regression work, exploring hundreds of past lives on this planet and others. She was very familiar with journeying beyond linear space-time. She had lived much of her life in extreme pain from chronic back issues and was relieved to die to escape her tortured body.

Halfway through the session with Delia her sister showed up and entered my body. I was awestruck as her sister and I conversed out loud. She was so excited to be in a functional body and grateful that I "let her in," as she expressed in this dual conversation voiced through my mouth. It was strange to feel and hear my mouth uttering her words, with me replying to her through the vessel of my body. The tones kept changing depending on who was talking. Similar to the other experience I just described, my conscious self observed as she began to play with my body, dancing around the house with joy, happy to be in a fully functional body. After less than half an hour passed, she thanked me and left.

Another form of nondual realization I had at the first tier was during an ayahuasca ceremony. A high-profile politician entered my field of consciousness. He arrived as the embodiment of corruption in the oil and gas industry. I instantly reacted with hostility. I had a sword in my hand and stabbed him. But as the sword penetrated him, I found I was stabbing myself. All of what I was experiencing was me. Immediately I realized attacking another was attacking myself. More beautiful was the realization that loving another also brings love to one's self.

Second Tier

As a person further loosens the grip on their dualistic identity at the next tier of the nondual, it is possible for them to identify with the collective experience of entire groups of people while still being connected to their awareness. While there is still a subject and an object in awareness, the dualistic identity of being an individual breaks down. As one's identity disintegrates, one can shift into a collective identity. For example, one may become all mothers or children of the world, warriors of all ages, the entire population of a race or country, or all the inmates of prisons or concentration camps, or, at its far reaches, all of humanity. Yet further, it is possible to experience the consciousness of the biosphere or of our entire planet. Reaching beyond our planet, it is possible to experience being off-world, to be alien species, or to feel planets moving throughout our solar system or the flow of the whole material universe (Grof, 1976; 2009; 2019a). I have experienced many of these second-tier states while meditating with and without psychedelics. One of my favorites was looking at the mountains and sky while on LSD and *drinking in the whole universe*, overwhelmed with joy and gratitude. Another was meditating without psychedelics and feeling through my field of awareness and throughout my body the movement of our solar system's planets.

Third Tier

As a person enters the third tier of nonduality, thought collapses and they lose all sense of subject and object. No longer is there any sense of a "me," "I," "an other," "them," or "they." The ego becomes fully transcended. Here, there is no story. All identification with socioeconomic, racial, national, and cultural identity evaporates. We are one life and all lives. Here no one soul is traveling through time. To experience a past life is to simply experience another point of awareness in unity consciousness where there is no ownership of the past or future but simply an access point transcending time to the unity of one Self.

All experience is a seamless, transparent, reflective wholeness. All formerly existent boundaries are dissolved. There are no perceived boundaries between the experiencer and the rest of the universe. Everything is unified radiance, unified manifestation. Everything is interconnected. The Divine—God—is in everything. And, yet, the experiencer is still aware of there being a material universe. The awareness still beholds all objects in view, including shape, color, and movement, but there is no separation in any of the experiences. Everything is empty, clear, vast, beautiful, and luminous. There is still an awareness of space-time, yet the experiencer is all of space and time. Sometimes while in this state, it is possible to see the energetic matrices of objects, both organic and nonorganic, which can be seen as glowing colored auras or fractal energetic imagery. Bliss reigns in the body. It becomes self-evident that love is the dynamic holding the universe together.

Fourth Tier

The fourth tier of nondual consciousness is complete absorption in the infinite of universal oneness. And, even in the infinite, there is a variety of possible realizations—infinite existence, infinite intelligence, infinite awareness, infinite energy, infinite love. From the following descriptions, informed both by personal experience and by the Eastern and Western wisdom traditions, you can begin to intuit the subtle differences that can be realized at this tier, recognizing that ultimately these experiences are ineffable.

Generally, in the fourth tier of nondual experience, there is a complete loss of connection to the material realm. This loss of reference happens with eyes open or closed; there is no-thing to see. Physical senses go offline. Awareness is nontemporal, nonlocal. Time and space are fully transcended. Subject and object completely dissolve into each other. All becomes featureless, as though one has become seamless in the flow of energy throughout the universe. The observer merges with the observed into the Absolute, the Supreme, the ultimate principle of all Being, God. One's awareness exists in the paradox of being devoid of all content yet all-containing. One is everything and nothing; Being and Non-Being. All "things" neither exist nor don't exist. All is empty; still, emptiness is pregnant with form.

In one case, while using 5-MeO-DMT, I became the singularity of the Big Bang after a radical ego-death. Within seconds of smoking the 5-MeO-DMT, I was no longer aware of material form and did not anticipate returning to human form. I was all consciousness, all energy, exploding outward into a newly created and expanding universe. I was the Absolute. Then, I saw hands in front of me. They were "my" hands. And I returned to ground zero, which was to return to be embedded in my ego-awareness—all within less than twenty minutes.

During another 5-MeO-DMT session, I became the flow of infinite energy of the living and conscious Absolute with no reference to corporeal reality.

At the fourth tier, thought evaporates. There is no objective knowledge. Distinction loses all frames of reference; there is no perception of body, space, or time. Emotional content goes offline. Conceptualization dissolves. There is nothing to judge: there is nothing superior, nothing inferior. All is perfect. Consciousness is only conscious of itself as the unborn, undying, ever-present, ordinary, unbound, infinite awareness. Ultimately, there is no mind, no experience, and yet there is pure presence. All is primordial awareness.

Ball (2017) describes the rapture of a full-blown nondual experience:

[There is] infinite, empty space, sometimes also simply called "the void." This void is both "seen" and felt as the complete dissolution of all sense of boundaries, edges, and limits. This is typical of the full nondual experience: there is no one to see and nothing to be seen, and reality is experienced directly in its immediate unitary totality.

When light is "seen" in the nondual experience, it is with the clear recognition that one is looking at one's self in a mirror. The light is not in any way "other." It is simultaneously seen as God and self, for these are, in fact, identical. There is the clear recognition, "I am that." This can be best understood as looking into the clear mirror of the self. God, the universal self, is a being of infinite fractal energy and geometry (p. 76).*

Immersion in the Supracosmic and Metacosmic Void is to experience the primordial emptiness and nothingness, devoid of form, paradoxically full of all potential as the source of all existence. Concurrently, as one begins to reach across the third tier into this fourth tier of nonduality, one can feel the play of the universe and primordial curiosity, playfulness, joy, and cosmic humor. And, yet one can also touch the deep primordial loneliness and the monotony that possibly instigated the birth of all creation in a craving for "experiences" (Grof, 1976; 2019b).

In the exposure to Absolute Consciousness, we witness the overflowing infinite possibilities of the cosmic source—Universal Mind or Cosmic Consciousness as the loving and creative principle of the universe—giving itself expression in the act of creating the Universe. We can feel how creation gave birth to the possibility that Absolute Consciousness could experience what duality is.

---

*This nondual state of consciousness is what arises in the dreamless state. If a person can meditate their way into the dreamless state as their body falls asleep, and before the dream cycles begin, it is possible to be consciously awake and aware of what is a nondual state of consciousness and to experience infinity with complete transcendence of the body and material realm (Holecek, 2016).

ENGAGING PSYCHICALLY IN THE PSYCHEDELIC MINDMELD

I have described a range of psychic possibilities that can be shared in the mindmeld. But what are the optimum means to engage with your partner in the mindmeld? Telepathy research suggests two critical factors that contribute to psychic engagement and connection: psychic connection is more likely when the potential content is (1) high in originality and (2) personally engaging (i.e., a salient and involved task for both participants) (Kelly, 2011; Ullman et al., 2023). The mindmeld has these attributes—its exploration into new territory is high in originality, with engaging material and a high likelihood of eliciting profound personal interest.* Being open to the possibility of telepathy, being relaxed in the work, sharing trust and emotional rapport between participants, and being open to sharing one's psyche with another also contribute to successful telepathic connections. Personal traits of being adaptable, adventurous, appreciative, curious, enthusiastic, imaginative, sensitive, and suggestible are also helpful (Ullman et al., 2023).

Kelly (2011) also identifies several factors that can undermine psychic engagement and connection: fatigue, cognitive work, disengaging tasks, self-reflective investigation of the experience (while in a telepathic connection), or situational alterations such as a change of focus in the task or interruptions. The meditation techniques discussed in this book are intended to foster a mindset free from excessive cognitive processing, reflective engagement, and analysis in the experience and instead sustain a witnessing focus free from ego-driven bodily movement and interruption. Good preparation of the setting helps ensure minimal disruption during the session to help with focus.

---

*The few research studies trying to elicit telepathic experiences using psychedelics have focused on mundane tasks, such as ganzfeld experiments, where a "sender" attempts to mentally transmit an image/symbol to a "receiver." Multiple researchers have commented that these experiments are likely not engaging enough for test subjects to elicit meaningful telepathic connections in the context of using mind-expanding psychedelics (Luke, 2019, p. 211).

These factors are foundational, but engaging another person psychically in shared consciousness within the mindmeld is a tricky business. In my experience, there is a subtle nuance between surrendering the ego to penetrate the layers of the mind and maintaining enough volition where we can use intent to provide some direction to make a psychic connection to the other. When moving too far in surrendering the ego, it is possible to drop so far into your own "trip" that you lose awareness of the presence of another person. Try to direct your experience too much, and your ego will stay in its executive function and your awareness will not drop into deeper layers of consciousness. I have also found that while the latter is absolutely true, the former has exceptions. As such, it is possible to get completely "lost" in one's trip only to later find the other person in another realm or dimension and make a psychic connection there. A good comparison is a Grateful Dead jam session. When they start jamming all the instruments go off in different directions into chaos but then return instantly to harmonic play in rhythmic synchrony. For the Grateful Dead, this may result from a high interpersonal familiarity and musical performance ability. Or, it may be more a factor of the ego letting go and allowing trust and the higher-self, soul, or grace to be the navigational guide.

Either way, as discussed in chapter 9's section on *surrender*, there is a fundamental *allowing* required in surrender in which all defense mechanisms are relinquished. Engagement intends to allow everything bubbling to the surface from your unconscious, or the other person's, or possibly the collective unconscious, to fully manifest, without judgment, without censoring, and without trying to make sense of it. Everything manifesting is coming to the surface to be experienced and processed, including physical sensations and emotions. All is to move into full expression. As already discussed, this can be both discomforting and blissful.

As the other person's unconscious emotional material surfaces in the mindmeld, it is possible it will overwhelm you, shattering your psychological defenses and causing you to contract. Like Holotropic Breathwork, sensitive material can arise when working with a partner that is normally considered ethically or aesthetically objectionable (e.g., violent outbursts, sexually acting out, or blasphemous material) (Grof & Grof, 2010, p. 48). In these cases, strict physical boundaries are not to be crossed, as discussed in chapter 8 under the heading "Sexuality and Establishing Physical Boundaries." But if these more intense emotional contents arise in the other and you negatively respond or contract from witnessing them, it likely points to corresponding areas in your unconscious that have been triggered and not processed. This reaction indicates there is more material for you to work through, as your response to the other person's material should generally be free of judgment, disgust, or rejection. It is worth noting that when telepathically communicating with discarnate beings, they do not judge your emotions, beliefs, or thoughts, demonstrating complete acceptance of who and what you are (Buhlman, 1996; Monroe, 1994). We can hope to one day reach such levels of loving acceptance and freedom from judgment.

As mentioned further below in chapter 12, under the heading "Being the Bodhisattva," one of the most profound attitudes to hold is *everything is you*: there is no objective separation between you and anything in the universe, despite all appearances to the contrary. With this nondual attitude, everything emerging in the mindmeld is not something to fear or try to run away or hide from. If it is all you, there is nothing to be terrified of. There is nothing against which to defend or protect. All there is to do is befriend and bring forth awareness and curiosity. This attitude can be powerful in a solo journey and the mindmeld.

This approach is similar to the technique used in lucid dreaming to confront the bear, demon, bogeyman or whatever else may be confronting you. The technique is not to flee, resist, or fight but to turn to the antagonist, approach, and ask who they are, what they want, what they have to teach or help you, and what you can offer them. This questioning and probing can help you penetrate deeper into the layers of your mind and your co-melder's mind. The psychedelic psychic space is the same as in a dream, where no physical harm can come to you; you are safe. While you may struggle with the psychic contents, there is an internal story unfolding. You are only confronting yourself. To face the darkness as a manifestation of the Self with awareness and curiosity is to shine light on what has hitherto been distasteful, ugly, rejected, and possibly hated within you or the other, or in the collective unconscious.

When using this technique, what is scary or intimidating can transform into something beautiful and friendly, perhaps an ally, or it may simply dissolve. Either way, an alchemical transformation starts with shifting your thought stream through greater self-awareness and centeredness.

With some work, when using the nondual attitude, you can move beyond words and mentally converse with the darkness, which may be a disowned part of yourself or your co-melder. Try placing your awareness in your heart and opening it to accept any difficulty presenting itself. This process moves away from using the mind's dialogue to resolve problems and toward a more physiological or somatic resonance of resolution by placing the mind's eye or conscious awareness in the body. Somatic sensing is similar to the second meditation technique discussed in chapter 9, under the heading "Opening the Heart." Here, I encourage you to use the heart as the center point or anchor for concentration and awareness, but then slowly expand the awareness outward in a spherical shape through the whole body and beyond its physical boundaries, accepting all that this energetic field of expansion interpenetrates.

With practice, this thoughtform can naturally transform darkness because approaching whatever arises from the heart space is to approach with unconditional love and compassion. However, this doesn't mean this transformation is without energetic movement and force. There may be a need to physically process the underlying energy associated with the challenging contents presenting themselves, which may be uncomfortable and possibly frightening. It could include processing past trauma, egoic patterning, or existential angst, as discussed throughout this and the previous chapter. In rare instances, it may include the release of some form of entity, which will be discussed in chapter 13 under the heading "Possession."

To provide more insight into the technique of using the nondual attitude, I share how I learned it. Years ago, I had an arduous mushroom journey. In brief, I entered a mushroom world with two majestic, massive organic rolling pins studded in radiant gemstones of green emeralds, red rubies, purple sapphires, and aquamarines. The rollers took up my whole field of vision. Between the two rotating, sandwiching rollers was a thin, long event horizon with a beckoning bright golden light shining through it. A voice called to me from the other side, inviting me in. But this was no simple invitation. I was being asked if I was "All in." The invite was to cross the crushing threshold with an eternal commitment to whatever was on the other side. I wanted to go through, but I had doubts about who or what was asking. Nor was it clear what I would be committing to. I didn't want to pledge myself to something I knew nothing about. I flinched in fear and stayed put.

This reluctance resulted in a two-hour nightmare battle with my ego, where I just wanted the trip to end. In the following days, I was flummoxed. I had already worked with psychedelic plants for years and gone through many ego deaths, yet I hesitated and struggled intensely. As I sometimes do when looking for answers, I went to my bookshelves, grabbed a relevant-looking book, and randomly opened it. It was Martin Ball's (2006) *Mushroom Wisdom*. Immediately, I got a provisional answer to my problem: engaging with mushrooms invites hard inner work. I then read the whole book, which I had yet to do. I was so intrigued by Martin's insights that I phoned him. He quickly pointed out that my struggle in the journey was not realizing *I* was beckoning myself in! I had already experienced nondual states of consciousness and read about the concept in various esoteric books, but what Martin did for me was shift my experience into an attitude. His recommendation forever shifted my perspective on how I engaged my inner self while working with psychedelics—and life more generally. This practice requires a lot of effort as the ego is always trying to undermine any efforts attacking its narcissistic penchant for control but pays big dividends on accepting all (or at least more) of life as it continually shifts and manifests around you, for better and worse.

For our purpose in the mindmeld, when something demanding presents itself from the other person, remind yourself it is all you. They are you because you are the macrocosm and the microcosm. You are all light and darkness where all is to be accepted in the polarity of divine perfection playing out in duality. You are one of the infinite shining jewels in Indra's Net, reflecting all others. You have access to the whole network because it is you, and you are the hologram. The more you accept this truth, the farther you can journey in the mindmeld. With this truth, you can summon the courage to avoid flinching in fear, keeping your psychic circuitry open and flowing with the other person, resonating, processing, and releasing. We will dive deeper into learning three specific meditative techniques for maintaining engagement in the mindmeld in the next chapter.

When in the mindmeld, the more calmness you bring to all shared contents, the more the effect of co-regulation can positively influence your partner's experience to similarly navigate choppy waters calmly and dive deeper toward nondual states. The mindmeld, and its nature of dissolving interpersonal boundaries, reflects increments of nondual states of consciousness. In shared consciousness, particularly when penetrating superconsciousness, there is still generally a dualistic sense of subject and object, even if the psychic barriers we are used to in our daily lives dissolve. Each of the tiers of nondual experience can be shared in consonant alignment as a merging and coherence of identities and as a complete dissolution of all identities. We can jointly share in simultaneously feeling polarized emotions in the first tier, and enter heavenly realms and share in harmonious feelings of liberation and bliss in the second tier. We can lose all sense of subject and object in the third tier of the nondual, where there is no felt sense of separation from each other and anything around us: as I look into your eyes, you are me, and I am you. All illusory boundaries experientially dissolve into the unified field of cosmic creative reality, and we jointly share "immanence." In the fourth tier, full absorption is an absolute fusion of minds. Absorption is so complete that the only way to confirm this shared state is after the fact because there is no "other"—namely, a material realm or any person.

All of the nondual experiences I have had in the mindmeld happened spontaneously through grace. There was no intention to create them unless using 5-MeO-DMT. So, know the possibility of nonduality awaits, and allow grace to take you there with your co-melder.

The final consideration for engagement in psychic sharing in the mindmeld is stopping it if one chooses. Normally, the exchange of psychic contents is similar to the exchange of physical energetic contents where there is a limited time arc. But if you want to end the psychic connection prematurely, it normally takes little effort; it is easy because the psychic connection is so tenuous and fragile. Often, just moving the body is enough to terminate a psychic engagement. Sometimes, not unlike a lucid dream, you can also get too excited by this fantastical reality, and you will "wake up" out of the psychic mindmeld.

In my experience, prematurely ending a psychic connection does not have the same consequences as prematurely ending physical energetic work where there is a feeling of energy being left unprocessed. I assume this is because psychic energy is much more subtle than the profoundly denser energy processed through the flesh.

POSSIBLE RESULTS

We have explored diverse possibilities in sharing psychic contents in the Psychedelic Mindmeld, ranging from past traumas to the transpersonal, both at the superconscious level and in nondual states of awareness. But what are the results or impacts of this work? Similar to the results of the physical exchange in the mindmeld, there are short-term and longer-term results from transpersonal psychic work.

Short-Term Results

Immediately following the mindmeld, there usually is a shared and deeper understanding of each other as people and of each other's life experience. When working together through abreaction or catharsis to release challenging unconscious emotional contents, there is usually a shared sense of camaraderie and accomplishment at having made it through the challenges together. Feelings of joy and satisfaction can be present from assisting another human being and intimately witnessing such a personal event. When working through these challenging contents together, feelings of resolution and learning can be shared. There can also be a shared opening of greater inner spaciousness for oneself and the other. Mutual vulnerability promotes intimacy, which can be shared across other relationships. If working with a spouse, partner, family members, or close friend, the relationship can deepen; past transgressions may be transcended and forgiven.

If both people were able to stay present for the psychic contents coming to the surface during the session without judging them, there is usually a shared validation and acceptance of what surfaced, which contributes to healing. When the walls of the ego crumble and the psychic contents of one person interpenetrate another, and the perception of separation dissolves, there is an evocation of a broader shared acceptance and loving compassion for each other as human beings, each working through their trials and tribulations. There can simultaneously be growth in humility, self-trust, and comfort about darker aspects of one's inner life when working through the content so intimately with another. These occasions are nourishing to the psyche.

It is not unusual for people to have epiphanies or realizations during or immediately after a session. Epiphanies can include accelerated psychological change; the desire to connect more closely with loved ones, such as family and friends; living a healthier lifestyle, which could include improving diet, exercising, or stepping away from addictive behaviors or other habits not serving wholeness and homeostasis; or making a change in occupation. People I have worked with have connected more to family and friends, quit drinking alcohol, stopped smoking cigarettes, stopped smoking cannabis (in one case after smoking almost daily for over thirty years), started eating healthier food, and begun taking better care of their physical and mental health overall. Indeed, homeostasis thrives when people feel safe, connected, and relatively satisfied (Hanson, 2013).

Following a mindmeld session you may find your intuitive abilities become stronger, helping you better tune in to other people's energies and realities. Greater intuition can foster increased understanding and empathy for others.

A shorter- to longer-term result can be the gradual accumulation of latent knowledge or gnosis that may not be apparent to the rational mind. As discussed earlier, the contents of psychedelic trips may not necessarily be clearly remembered, including those of the Psychedelic Mindmeld. But inner experiences leave an imprint easily recognized when they recur, allowing for continuous inner development (James, 2009, p. 287). Such is my experience, where over the years I did not see a progression, but there was one. Over time, I have been able to penetrate deeper into consciousness. For example, I worked with psychedelics for years before being able to engage in fractal energetic yoga, which was an unknown phenomenon to me. It spontaneously appeared. As the years pass I also have greater access to past-life regression journeys, lucid dreaming, and out-of-body experiences. There appears to be a developmental path. All of my experiences lend themselves to a profound sense of knowing beyond simpler, faith-based belief systems, bringing with it an increased zest for life.

My path still holds many mysteries. There are experiences I have not fully processed. The process has not been linear, as I have had profound challenges in life and in some psychedelic trips. The ego's play of fantasy also creates traps I have had to be on the lookout for, often causing confusion and struggle. Even so, I have expanded my views of what is possible and developed greater wonder and gratitude for the universe in all its infinite complexity, perfection, and beauty. The potential for personal expansion leads us to the possible longer-term results of the mindmeld.

Long-Term Results

Similar to the difficulties of trying to ascertain the long-term results arising from shared energetic contents of physical consciousness, it is challenging to ascertain the long-term results of shared psychic contents in
the mindmeld. The reasons are the same: working with limited numbers
of people, some only once, without baseline data or follow-up surveys.

I use three different research sources as proxies to triangulate the
longer-term results of the mindmeld. First, based on the feedback I
have received, there is a lot of overlap between psychotherapist John
Welwood's insights (1997) into loving connection and engagement in
the mindmeld. Second, Grof's reports (2008; 2009; 2019a) of LSD
research, and Grof and Grof's reports (2010) from participants in
Holotropic Breathwork share similarities to the longer-term results I
have seen from working with the mindmeld. Third, there is also overlap with the longer-term results of Fadiman's reports (2011) from the
therapeutic use of psychedelics.

When reading Welwood's *Love and Awakening* (1997), it struck me
how much overlap there is between the list of values related to loving
connection that he developed based on responses from clients and the
responses I have received from people I have worked with in the mindmeld using psychedelics:

- A feeling of being part of something larger
- A deep sense of being myself, being who I really am
- A new kind of strength and peace
- A sense of life's magic
- No longer fearing the unknown
- A flowing movement and connectedness
- A fresh acceptance of myself and everything
- More alive in body and senses
- Seeing the world with new eyes
- Feeling blessed
- Coming home

It should not be surprising that the results of making oneself more available through the mindmeld to another are so similar to those described by Welwood. The mindmeld can also foster greater gentleness and openness with others. Because the practice in the mindmeld is focused on surrender and allowing, it can lead us down a more fearless path, one of greater kindness and respect and less concern with manipulating outcomes for personal benefit.

Stanislav Grof (2008; 2009; 2019a) has conducted research with thousands of patients into using LSD for psychological therapy, and Grof and Grof (2010) have worked with thousands of participants in Holotropic Breathwork. Using this work as a proxy, possible long-term benefits arising from the mindmeld can include breaking out of depression, overcoming phobias and anxiety states, freedom from consuming and irrational feelings of guilt, and radical improvement of self-confidence and self-esteem. Grof (2008; 2009; 2019a) has also reported many instances of the disappearance of severe psychosomatic pains, including migraine headaches and improvements or clearing of psychogenic asthma. Grof and Grof (2010) claim the mechanism for this shift toward improvement is the result of bringing forth traumatic memory into full conscious experience, processing it, and integrating it where the energetic signature of the trauma was previously hidden in the body. Now the unconscious ceases to exert a negative impact on the individual's everyday life. Participants thus reach completion and closure with the traumatic material (p. 151).

As mentioned earlier, therapeutic work with psychedelics is showing promise in addressing similar ailments, such as depression, anxiety, trauma, and PTSD. Fadiman's research (2011) into the therapeutic effectiveness of psychedelics also found increased mental flexibility and self-aware adaptability for the vast majority of participants, who then experienced improvements in dreams (e.g., frequency, recall, use, and enjoyment), reading and listening habits, material values (e.g., less emphasis on wealth and status), emotional responsiveness (e.g., greater equanimity), family relations, work, introspection, and interpersonal relations, among others (p. 110).

Epiphanies from the mindmeld that can have a longer-term impact include: a greater awareness of reality and expanded self-concept; connection to one's spiritual self and a decreased fear of death; and a broader view of human potential and evolution.

Another possible long-term result is reconciling with existential angst. The wisdom traditions of East and West tell us the biggest challenge in being human is separation from the Divine. Suppose the Divine created the material realm and consciousness as we know it to experience itself in duality—to see and experience its reflection. In that case, it appears the price we pay as individuals is a longing to return to the perfection and oneness of the Divine. We want completeness, where there is no longing and no suffering and the sense of satisfaction is absolute. As Dante Alighieri so aptly pointed out: "The desire for perfection is that desire which always makes every pleasure appear incomplete, for there is no joy or pleasure so great in this life that it can quench the thirst in our soul" (in Grof & Grof, 2010, p. 131).

This sense of separateness and alienation from the Divine is likely the very drive within us toward spiritual awakening and seeking of (re) connection. This unconscious drive pushes us to find satisfaction and completion outside of ourselves—in all forms of addiction, from alcohol and drugs to gambling, work, money, excessive exercise, hoarding, over-eating, co-dependence, and so on. The yearning does not limit itself to addiction; we want in all forms of *doing*, such as chasing relationships, power, fame, fun activities, possessions, intellectual pursuit, and more. Any sense of satisfaction is fleeting. The ego is always vying for control to steer the human vehicle based on its perception of the past and its illusions of the future, running roughshod over everything in its path. It seems as long as the ego is in the driver's seat, then lasting and abiding peace is not to be found.

All techniques of exploring consciousness give us glimpses of a more connected reality in the totality of cosmic creation through non-dual experiences. The mindmeld is one of many pathways to touch the infinite glory of the Divine. Sharing the path to the nondual through sharing energetic physical and psychic contents is to experience the dissolution of boundaries between one another. And yet even in this deeper connected reality where we find healing and a knowing of divine perfection and the nondual, these moments are fleeting. Even though we can be left in awe when returning to day-to-day reality, we are still left confronting the mundane and our inevitable insatiable existential wanting.

But these experiences broaden our worldview. They are authentic and convincing. They fill in the blanks of religious dogma and spiritual teachings. We morph our understanding by internalizing our experiences of being, stretching from the microcosm to the macrocosm. Our sense of wonder and connection to all creation becomes more profound as we internalize the infinite beauty of all existence, including our suffering. A reverence for ourselves and all around us begins to permeate from our inner consciousness. Our maps of meaning expand. Through transpersonal experience, our worldview can take on a more integral perspective of life and our place in the world and the universe. We open the door of possibilities to the afterlife: perhaps we are souls traveling and reincarnating through space-time.

I have purposely avoided discussing the concept of "enlightenment" because it is a word with many different guises and sundry realizations. The mindmeld is unlikely to gain you enlightenment—whatever your definition of that is. Nor is the mindmeld a silver bullet for the many human struggles, trials, and traumas we are all faced with. Personal change is a long-term process requiring ongoing work and a holistic approach. But with ongoing realization through this work and complementary healthy physical, mental, and spiritual practices, it promises a profound connection to the Divine in each of us and each other. We will return to these themes as we close in chapter 15.

12
Maintaining Flow with Your Partner

The mindmeld can often be wonderful and fantastical but also extremely intense, overwhelming, exhausting, painful, strange, and beyond all known territory. This chapter explores meditative states to create comfort with the bizarreness and enable the continuous flow of energy and connection while in the mindmeld, offering further depth of engagement.

When apprehension and fear arise in one or both participants during the mindmeld, it is easy to fall out of the mindmeld. It is helpful to work with three additional meditative techniques to maintain the flow of physical and psychic energy. One technique is being the witness to one's experience, the second is Holotropic Breathwork, and the third is adopting the mindset of the bodhisattva to all that unfolds. Before discussing these meditative techniques, I will briefly discuss the ebb and flow occurring in the mindmeld between shared work and self-work during the session.

SHARED WORK VERSUS SELF-WORK
DURING THE SESSION

There usually is an ebb and flow in a mindmeld session between doing solo work and sharing consciousness. It is helpful to be aware of this possibility and confirm that it is normal and okay. Nevertheless, if one person is overwhelmed and needs support, they should feel completely comfortable calling out to their fellow co-melder for help, especially if they have left the room. Assistance can be as simple as sitting or lying beside the person and confirming, "I am here for you."

The amount of time spent on solo work versus shared work varies tremendously. In one instance where I worked with Delia, we shared physical and psychic energies for five hours without a break. When the session ended, we reflected on how our athletic histories helped our fortitude through the lengthy exchange.

A few months later, I worked with her again. As my ego began to relax and surrender in this second session, I received an intuitive hit. I was not supposed to work directly with her today and was to only work on myself. The next moment, I found myself pinned, as though by an invisible force, on my back on the bathroom floor, toning at the top of my lungs. The angel Metatron arrived and his energy flowed through me. The primal scream lasted for fifteen to thirty minutes. Soon I found myself in the living room doing fractal energetic yoga, connecting to other angelic beings and Buddhist lamas and engaging in an energetic purging of dark and hateful energies lingering in the collective unconscious. The purging went on for a few exhausting and body-breaking hours. All the while, my fellow co-melder in the bedroom felt connected to what I was going through, relating and finding meaning in any verbalization I made during the unfolding of my experience.

Usually, people do not end up in separate rooms. Most commonly, if the mindmeld connection is reached, you will find yourself staying in the same room, but not necessarily on the bed. Sometimes I have found my body lying perpendicularly over the other person where our torsos are crossed, but my head is over the side of the bed, and my hands are on the floor, bracing my upper body. In other cases where I have engaged in a lot of the other person's energy, I have found myself beside the bed, processing their energy through fractal energetic yoga, sometimes standing and moving through tai chi and dance-like poses and sometimes lying down.

It can be exhausting when two people exchange physical energy. It is not unusual for one or both to stop processing and take a restful break. Each time the body feels more relaxed while taking a break, it's more likely an energetic exchange will begin again. It's best to go with the flow of these cyclical waves.

When an extended break occurs, one sometimes needs to make an effort to reengage with the other person by consciously deciding to lie down side by side and hold hands again. There may be a reluctance to do this as the shared energetic flow can be so overwhelming. The ego can be left questioning whether it is ready to immediately drop back into the intensity of another exchange. There is no right or wrong in a decision to stop or continue the energetic work. However, it is worth trying to take the witness's stance, discussed next, and observe the ego's default toward aversion. To continue the work is to continue processing blocked or stuck energy. In the big picture, the movement of energy is a much larger affair than any one session and it can continue without psychedelics after the session. So there is no need to get hung up with one's decision either way.

Another possibility in exchanging energetic and psychic contents is that a person can become completely wrapped up in the story of their unfolding. I have been in mindmelds where I have let go of the other person as my story branches away from theirs. The momentum of my storyline can become so intense that I am utterly oblivious to the thought of trying to reconnect with the other person. I may enter different dimensions or connect to other beings independently, just as the other person falls into the tunnel of their journey. This divergence can result in my doing fractal energetic yoga, toning, or vocalizing alone.

In any case, there should be an openness to work with what arises. While the mindmeld may be the intended destination for further exploration in a session, it is not something to force. If other things are presented from the unconscious requiring individual processing, there is a need to respect what is presented.

MEDITATION TECHNIQUE: BEING THE WITNESS (AND VOLITION IN THE WITNESSING STATE)

Once the mindmeld is established, the meditation technique of being the "witness" is a means to maintain it. At its simplest, the witnessing approach is to bring the attention of the ego-driven mind to one's internal world and become an impartial observer of one's thoughts and sensations. This meditation style involves broad-ranged, nonjudgmental, and free-floating attention, as opposed to an effortful and sustained concentration on an object of awareness, such as focusing solely on stillness and the breath or actively opening the heart. It points the mind in a direction but in a relaxed manner without being mentally draining. One does not try to affix the mind to anything but instead allows it to wander and brings awareness back to observing what is arising within one's inner experience each time it strays off.

This technique is conducive to psi performance, like telepathy, and maintaining the mindmeld because it fosters the free-floating mindset required to intuitively receive psi information, as opposed to a more effortful ego-driven concentration that can limit it or even shut it off (Kelly, 2011, p. 250). Using this technique, the incessant internal chatter of the ego-mind slows down, and the witness to one's experience creates the opportunity to move closer and closer to the one doing the witnessing and ultimately to nondual states of awareness.

There are several states of witnessing. The first state of witnessing is an awareness of the gross physical body and gross thoughts and feelings. In essence, this state of witnessing involves being aware of thoughts, images, and sensations but not being attached to them. It brings a benign curiosity to one's internal experience. It is a diffuse relationship to the self, broadening the mind to all inputs through the senses, as opposed to concentrating on a focused point, whether the point is a thought as part of an ongoing stream of thoughts or a unique sensation. You know you are in this state of witnessing when the egoic-driven judge in your mind is not judging the thoughts or sensations surfacing as good or bad. Instead, there is a sense of equanimity. There is an acknowledgment of all thoughts but no getting caught in them. This observation is like being a spectator watching a film. When you are so engrossed in the film, you feel like you are part of the story; you are not the witness to your own experience. But when you are aware of watching the film, you are the witness to your experience of being the viewer. It is the same when you are dreaming. Are you lucidly aware you are dreaming, or are you unconsciously lost in the dream as though it is your waking reality?

This stage of witnessing can be overwhelming because you're observing the chaos in your mind that perhaps you were not previously aware of—stray thoughts involuntarily leading to cascades of responses and uncontrolled reactions. But this witnessing technique is penetrating. The more you do it, the more deeply you begin to move toward your center of being. Working with this technique requires one to drop the fear of seeing what is really going on internally within oneself and embrace personal honesty. You begin to see what needs to be seen, including the pain, the suffering, destructive patterns, and what needs to be acknowledged—including the protective part of you that resides in fear. Doing so allows the darkness in one's mind to be embraced and healed. This is a step on the road to more clearly experiencing one's infinite complexity and divinity.

I know I am in the initial phase of witnessing meditation when a particular thought pattern or internal dialogue ends and I become more aware of the sensations in my body. Another thought pattern develops, and it is observed. Another thought pattern develops; it stops—right in the middle of forming. An uncomfortable sensation arises; I am aware of the sensation, perhaps even entering the center of it, but exploring the feeling without judgment and with curiosity and an awareness of the explorer doing the exploring.

A shift to the next level of witnessing is toward the subtle personality. There is a move away from form—physical form and thoughtform—to spaciousness. You increasingly move away from personal judgments, illusions, and projections. There is still a sense of "I," but one is not caught up in the day-to-day personality. From here, it is possible to witness with greater clarity how one is creating their reality, similar to observing the fluidity of a lucid dream where one is consciously aware they are dreaming and can direct and create their reality within the dream.

The next shift is toward the subtlest forms of manifestation in space-time: to the archetypal, the collective unconscious, or superconsciousness, as described in the previous chapter. From this stage, the next shift is to the causal, to transcend space-time to a pure timeless *Now*, focusing on the pure present. At this stage, duality fades into the nondual, where the subtlety of the effort to be the witness becomes effortless. However, the nondual has its own subtleties, as just discussed. The pure witness, often referred to as the true self or real self, has a sense of individuality, but when it is finally transcended, the world is seen as a seamless whole. Here, awareness is one with all gross, subtle, and causal phenomena but exclusively identified with none (Wilber, 2017, p. 110). Sri Nisargadatta Maharaj summarizes the suchness of this state: "In the stillness of the mind I saw myself as I am—unbound" (Maharaj, 1981, p. 173). The final stage in nonduality is where all gross, subtle, and causal phenomena are dropped and one enters a featureless state not connected to the material universe or any object of any kind, and consciousness simply rests in pure awareness as the singularity of all, the God state.

The movement of awareness on this continuum of being the witness creates a dynamic dance of potential in the mindmeld. In this dance, there is no right or wrong, just movement. To drop into this flow altogether is to drop judgment, attachment, prejudice, and resistance and experience peacefulness with whatever surfaces in awareness.

As described in previous chapters, there are two levels of engagement in the mindmeld: the physically energetic and the psychic. Each is briefly discussed here, strictly from the perspective of using the witnessing meditative technique to navigate the mindmeld.

In the sharing of energy at a physical level, there is typically a dominant direction of movement from one body to the other, which occurs beyond the conscious mind. As this movement begins, it is best if both participants invoke the witnessing stance. One person is more likely to physically move and work on the other person as opposed to both doing the work on each other simultaneously. However, this can happen on rare occasions.

Invoking the witness helps maintain the flow and movement of energy. Here the ego has been relegated to a peripheral role, as a witness only. There can still be an internal dialogue of wonderment at what is happening (e.g., "Wow, my body is moving beyond my physical mind"), but for the most part, the mind is simply the witness to the movement itself. If the ego gets too involved, the flow of energy will stop. This is a good safety valve if the receiver of the energetic work is overwhelmed and says to stop, in which case the ego can step forward from its subordinate role and stop the body's movement, even if there may be a delay of several seconds for the message to be received and acted upon.

For the person on the receiving end of the energetic movement, there is also a need to be the witness. Energy work can range from soothing to uncomfortable, to painful. From my experience in moving energy blockages, rarely is the work soothing. So, as the person experiencing discomfort or pain, their job is to step back from reacting to the pain and instead observe the sensations of pain from the witness's perspective as unflinchingly as possible.

When the mindmeld is psychic in flow, bodies may be touching or not touching. I have found half the time I have psychically mindmelded with someone, I am touching them, sometimes similarly to the hand position on someone's head like the Vulcans use in the show *Star Trek*. The other half of the time, I am lying parallel to the person without physical contact. The key, again, is to lie entirely still and only move if the body does so beyond conscious desire or choice.

When the psychic link is established, sometimes it is obvious that you are sharing consciousness with the other person as there is an intuitive and knowing telepathic connection. Other times it is less obvious and is only confirmed after the session ends by each person communicating what they went through.

The psychic mindmeld is much more subtle than the sharing of physical content. As a result, it can be as tenuous as trying to hold a lucid dream. If you get too excited, it ends. If fear or apprehension arises, it ends. If you try to be too controlling of the experience, it ends. For this reason, being the witness to shared consciousness will help maintain the flow; the focus of the witness should be on observing what is coming forward from the unconscious, soul, collective unconsciousness, or higher self without reacting or analyzing.

At the same time, and with repetition, it is possible to gently direct the experience. Most people have yet to train their minds and tame the ego. Most minds run wild with neuroses and futile striving without the awareness of how tamable the mind is. It is ironic that what seeks to tame the ego-governed mind is still the ego. But by taming the ego's monkey mind through witnessing how the ego operates, it is possible to increase one's volition as to how, where, and when to direct awareness via the ego. This effort is an ego-driven process of programming the subconscious mind so that the subconscious brings a particular thought-form into conscious awareness more often. An example is repeatedly bringing your attention to your breath; the more often you practice focusing on your breath, the more often your subconscious will act to remind you to get your awareness back to your breath. Working with mantras evokes the same reinforcement. This volition is never absolute but can contribute to self-activating the song—or state of mind—you want playing more often on your inner radio station.

When you act with a self-limiting degree of volition in the mind-meld while in a state of surrender, you are in an undefended engagement with what is arising. Such engagement is an open curiosity to awe and wonder led by subtle and intentional guidance. To subtly guide your experience in surrender is a creative and constructive act; to force it too strongly is restrictive and imposing and will likely terminate the connection. When walking this tightrope, it is helpful to have experience with meditative approaches requiring a mix of free-flowing witnessing, concentration, and visualization, such as lucid dreaming, tantric meditations, out-of-body experience, shamanic journeying, or past-life regression. This knowledge can lend itself to your acclimatizing to the mindmeld environment and stabilizing your presence within it, reducing fragmentary chaos. Experience in these realms also contributes to shifting the body's energy to higher states, stabilizing access to deeper layers of mind and consciousness.

When working with your volition, you can manifest and gently direct the journey, in a similar way to out-of-body journeys. You can use deliberate thoughtforms (i.e., affirmations) to help improve your navigation (Buhlman, 1996). For example, if visions are blurred you can mentally state to yourself, "Clarity now." This thoughtform can help increase the clarity of vision. If something is confusing, state "Clarification now." Or if you are struggling in negative thought, you can state, "Loving compassionate awareness now." If you are grappling with fear, state "I am safe now," or "I have courage now." If you want to reach a higher healing vibration, state "Higher healing vibration now," "I experience my higher self now," or "I have God's divine loving energy in every single cell in my body." If you want to heal something in particular, name what needs to be healed along with "healed to completion now." To enhance a mindmeld mentally, say "Mindmeld now," "Stronger telepathic connection now," or "I share a deeper energetic dimension now." I encourage you to experiment with manifesting helpful thoughtforms. It is best to start with firm and specific directions. Similar to the sounds of shamanic drumming, the vibration of these intentional thoughtforms can act as carrier waves for deepening the journey. This skill will help you navigate the mindmeld more effectively, stabilize the psychic connection, communicate more clearly with your co-melder, and journey together with purpose. If you want to state your chosen affirmations out loud during the session, I recommend discussing your options with your co-melder so they are not taken by surprise. Also, suggestibility is often high during sessions, so agreement as to what are acceptable affirmations ahead of time reinforces a safe set and setting.

While journeying in the mindmeld, I have discovered a fascinating subtlety: how to approach the persistently unsatisfied ego using the witnessing technique. During a mindmeld with Pat, a seasoned shamanic practitioner, we found ourselves connected in heavenly realms in a blissful state. (I was working with mushrooms; she did not use psychedelics.) We had reached a stable connection to each other and to a heavenly state of consciousness. However, there was a part of me getting bored and wanting to move on to something else. I wondered how this was possible. *I am enraptured in bliss, feeling connected to the Divine in me and my fellow psychonaut, and yet I want to switch gears.* Things were perfect. Why did I want to leave? Of course, it was my ego gnawing at me with its addiction to distraction and penchant for wanting more.

Yet, a resilience of will rose from within me to concentrate, witness, and stay in the "now" moment. As I brought witnessing attention to the part of myself turning away from the heavenly realm and bliss, I observed the tug-of-war in my psyche. At a very subtle level, I could see in this struggle the ongoing creation of my reality. With this epiphany, as my mind strayed away, I would bring it back. At the most subtle level, I was not getting it back to anything but simply creating the heavenly realm anew in each abiding moment in the timeless present. When my mind strayed far enough away from the heavenly bliss that I became aware of bodily sensations, I centered myself back in my breath and could return to where I had cast myself out of. It was not unlike waking from a dream, then consciously returning to sleep with the intent and success of returning to the same dream anew—something achievable with practice. This method worked repeatedly for more than an hour.

What is fascinating about this story is how quickly my ego got bored with being in the blissful paradise of timeless present awareness. Wilber (2017) refers to this looking away from this state as Primordial Avoidance: the force of the separate-self sense that gives birth to the Dualistic World. Avoidance is a contraction of infinite nondual awareness latching on to the relative, finite, conventional, individual self. This evasion places us in a world of choices, discerning between craving and aversion (p. 395). Again, I found the antidote in being the witness to what wanted to contract and using my breath to refocus my mind.

The preceding paragraphs highlight our volition in the journey despite the relegation of the ego. As described earlier, this volition can completely evaporate in the full absorption of nondual states. But short of nondual states, I encourage you to bring awareness to the discretion that exists. By using the witnessing technique, it is even possible to discover the origin of thought and witness its creation and manifestation, like watching a painter paint a canvas. At the most subtle level, you can observe how you create your story and how each thoughtform carries energy. With surrendered volition, you can then playfully create your experience.

To summarize, once in the telepathic connection the trick is to first let experiences surface through effortless witnessing, and then step into the experience where you and the other person may engage with it through subtle guidance. Like lucid dreaming, the more you can master the skill of subtly exerting volition, widening and constricting the parameters of incoming and outgoing data in the psychedelic space generally, and in the mindmeld more specifically, the more rewarding and emotionally positive your experiences will be. Training your subtle volitional abilities to navigate in the sometimes extreme conditions of this space effectively comes with ongoing experience, discipline, persistence, and practice. Attuned navigational skills contribute to a deeper shared psychic exploration and to avoiding premature closure of the psychic connection. You will build enhanced capacity, coherence, and comprehension through practice to assimilate the transmission properties and contents of the mindmeld. With practice, you will better consolidate and remember the information from each session, which is often as fleeting as a dream. With increased capacity for the memory of the experience, a corresponding increase in navigational performance will follow. To master these subtle skills is to master one's psychic cognizance. As Christopher Bache (2021) stresses: "Profound experiences are not simply given to you; you have to train yourself to receive them and hold on to them" (p. 304).

MEDITATION TECHNIQUE: HOLOTROPIC BREATHWORK

As the session reaches the midpoint and the psychedelic begins to wear off, the ego begins to regain its executive function; the mindmelding portion of the session usually wanes and ends. If you have the stamina to continue working, you can try subordinating the ego's function again by using Holotropic Breathwork. I have used this technique successfully but rarely, as I usually feel so spent after the first half of the session that I am not interested in jumping right back into the mindmeld work for the second half.*

Holotropic Breathwork is a technique developed in the 1980s by Stanislav Grof and his wife Christina Grof (2010). The method is straightforward but requires effort. Continue lying down beside your partner. The task is to: "breathe faster and more effectively than usual and with full concentration on the inner process" (p. 32). The Grofs do not emphasize a specific technique of breathing, *per se*. Participants are encouraged to breathe more deeply than normal and to tie inhalation and exhalation into a continuous circle of breath. They are urged to trust the body's intrinsic wisdom. Once in the process, participants usually find their own rhythm and way of breathing.

Breathing is typically accompanied by evocative music. Grof and Grof (2010) recommend music with a steady rhythm and consistent intensity with no lapses between pieces. Selections should not be jarring, dissonant, or anxiety-provoking. Vocals should be kept to a minimum and should not be in languages participants can understand, convey a specific message, or suggest a particular theme (p. 36). Selections typically include trance-inducing music, percussion, classical, instrumentals, chants, world music, and so on. Because you are likely already working with music, it probably can be kept the same.

---

*I have also used Holotropic Breathwork outside of working with psychedelics to induce fractal energetic yoga. However, it usually takes two to three hours of concentrated breathwork to get there, and the fractal energetic yoga only tends to last a few minutes.

While the Holotropic Breathwork technique is simple, it requires significant effort and concentration. Typically, a Holotropic Breathwork session lasts two to four hours, and this exercise can be exhausting. When trying to reengage in the mindmeld, try it for up to an hour. If an hour does not work to reengage the movement of energy precipitated by the psychedelic, consider other plans for the second half of the session.

MEDITATION TECHNIQUE: BEING THE BODHISATTVA

Sharing energetic and psychic content between two people can be very intense, arousing physical and emotional pain. Here I suggest another meditation technique, *being the bodhisattva*, to help work through the difficulty of shared physical and emotional pain. But before describing this approach, I offer three personal examples of how intensely onerous the sharing in the mindmeld can be to illustrate the value of the technique.

Several years ago, Isabel and I were in an extreme accident. She suffered a bad injury on her thigh from a severe impact, resulting in a massive seroma. Several months after the accident, we engaged in a mindmeld. My body was drawn to her thigh at a point, and my fingers began gripping the soft tissue. I was immediately taken by visual fractals and started screaming in horror at the top of my lungs. The fractals turned to blackness, and gradually the room returned to my field of vision. The whole time I continued screaming. Isabel and I then both witnessed dark, black smoke leaving her leg. While I am sure the smoke did not manifest in waking reality, we later joked about how it felt like an exorcism and a demon had left her leg.

The shared experience was reliving the accident. Isabel "knew" I was reliving the accident from her perspective as we jointly discharged the blocked energy in her leg. I had no visuals of the accident, instead more specifically experiencing the raw emotion of her terror leading up to and including the impact of the accident.

During this same session, Isabel's consciousness entered my body. My body had also suffered trauma during the accident. I could feel her presence in particular parts of my body, with her making healing tweaks like a construction road worker rerouting neuronal pathways.

In a later session with Isabel, I was working her lower back, and penetrated the ancestral traumas of the matriarchal line of her family. These were not major traumas, but instead the accumulated trauma of thousands of little cuts by each mother's ego judging and disciplining their daughters. I saw and felt Isabel receiving hurtful judgments from her mother, and the same of her mother from her mother, and so forth through multiple generations. Deep hurt and sadness poured out of her through me. Isabel simultaneously felt this ancestral release. I quickly found myself in fractal energetic yoga for more than an hour, processing this energy, crying nonstop, letting go of the past.

In another session, Winston was lying on his stomach. While I was in fractal energetic yoga, my hands started working his lower back and spine similarly to a massage. Then one hand went to his right upper rib while the other went to his lower left rib. My fingers pointed like an arrow connecting through his rib cage and lungs. I instantly had x-ray vision and saw inside his lungs, polluted with dark black spots from years of smoking. I began screaming. Phlegm started heaving through my mouth, and I coughed and spat onto the floor. I now saw Winston years in the past in a crowd attacked and traumatized by police violence. The release continued until I collapsed from exhaustion.

These experiences were overwhelming. The ego can quickly judge the pain and blame the other person for it. I was doing deep tissue work, resulting in pain for the recipient, and simultaneously I was in pain as I was acting as a vehicle for clearing stored trauma.

Pain is suffering, and in this work, there is no escaping from the pain that inevitably arises. While blissful experiences occur, one has to accept the pain alongside the euphoria. I propose one of the best ways to welcome the emotional and physical challenges as they emerge in connection to your co-melder is to take the meditative stance or attitude of being a bodhisattva.

In Mahāyāna Buddhism the ideal of the bodhisattva is, "the being who takes on the suffering of all sentient beings, who undertakes the journey to liberation not for his or her own good alone but to help all others, and who eventually, after attaining liberation, does not dissolve into the absolute or flee the agony of samsara [the material universe], but chooses to return again and again to devote his or her wisdom and compassion to the service of the whole world" (Rinpoche, 2002, p. 368). The bodhisattva works by the compassionate wish, *bodhichitta*, which translates as "the heart of our enlightened mind." Bodhichitta is a practice of the compassionate heart. The Buddhist practice is to develop a boundless and immeasurable loving-kindness, compassion, joy, and equanimity toward limitless beings. The training teaches the realization that you are the same as all others, leading to the consideration that others are more important than yourself. As such, developing greater generosity, discipline, patience, endurance, diligence, concentration, and wisdom is directed to the benefit of all. The practice includes *tonglen*, taking on the suffering and pain of others while sharing with them your happiness, well-being, unconditional love, and peace of mind (Rinpoche, 2002).

There are several religious or esoteric beliefs compacted into the preceding paragraph, such as the idea of reincarnation, karma, and the possibility of final enlightenment beyond the material universe without a body (*parinirvana*), but what stands out for our purpose is the willingness and commitment to take on the suffering of all beings to help move toward liberation. There is also an underlying belief of oneness or unity consciousness: we are all "energetically" in it together. This nondual perspective is powerful when dealing with demanding things in the mindmeld. If you can see all contents surfacing in the other person, regardless of the light or darkness, ease or difficulty, as an extension of yourself, the work is for you as much as it is for them. This perspective creates profound meaning and a feeling of doing the work for a greater purpose than just you: contributing to the liberation from suffering for all beings. Ironically, adopting this perspective can make the work easier; because it feels like you are working toward something, through the lens of your ego preoccupied with doing, you open yourself to accepting a temporary sense of burden.

A specific example of my invoking the stance of the bodhisattva was in a session with Joan, who was struggling to drop into the mindmeld. She was getting caught in the initial layers of her unconscious mind, struggling with her breathing and restlessly moving her limbs around while we held hands, lying side-by-side in bed. I verbally suggested she try harder not to move and just focus on her breath, not realizing her movements were authentic! (She later described part of her struggle as going through a rebirthing process, including the birth canal and her mother's pubic hair.) Several more minutes passed, and she continued struggling. I felt impatient and agitated by her movements when trying to let go of my ego and go into a deeper experience. But then I stepped back and observed myself. I was agitated and impatient. So what? What is the intent of the session? To mindmeld and be there for each other. I wasn't trying to actively "tune in" and truly listen to her inner experience. With this epiphany, I shifted my awareness to the depth of her experience, not trying to bypass or resist it. I became a compassionate listener to what was happening for her. I quickly found myself in her agitation. The energy was frenetic and felt dirty in an earthy way, like I was in the process of organic composting. I quickly wanted to pull myself out of the uncomfortable experience. But then I invoked the bodhisattva stance: Joan's agitation was my agitation. All of what was manifesting was me, and to face it was to transform the energy for the benefit of all beings. At this moment, I remembered how I, too, had faced similar energetic struggles in a mushroom experience years earlier, as the mushroom contributed to composting blocked energy in me. With this in mind, I continued to sit with the nervous, frantic energy and watch it transform, and we both settled into a profoundly more beautiful experience.

In the mindmeld, we can share our love with the world through the lens of the bodhisattva. A highlight for me working at this level is connecting to people in the mindmeld where we both open our hearts in loving, compassionate kindness and share this energy with the etheric field. It is debatable whether or not it is possible to influence human-wide consciousness through quantum entanglement with this type of work. Still, at a minimum, I have found it contributes to rewriting negative thought streams when they manifest in my mind.

I offer one final suggestion regarding adopting the stance of the bodhisattva: consider dedicating each session to the benefit of all sentient beings, a common Buddhist practice. The act of dedication can be a tool to elicit the seriousness of the session in one's mindset. With this intention, it may also be possible to engage in unforeseen ways to mystically embody the archetype of the bodhisattva, which at a minimum is a powerful collective thoughtform of compassion and self-sacrifice, and at its greatest, within the Buddhist belief system, is to move toward Buddhahood.

13
Navigating Potential Challenges

There are several possible challenges to be aware of during and after the mindmeld, including:

1. Attachment
2. Psychological projection
3. Manifestation of the negative
4. Possession
5. Unprocessed traumatic material
6. Reactivations and overactive intuition
7. Fantasy and delusion

This chapter explores these challenges, but the list is not exhaustive. An individual's unconscious and the collective unconscious offer endless possibilities of content, experience, and realization. Because we are in the early days of mindmelding exploration, we may be unaware of additional unforeseen challenges. In the same way, unforeseen opportunities may abound.

Jung (2011b) provides a suitable warning as we jump into the dangers of what our unconscious can trap us in: "The unconscious is always the fly in the ointment, the skeleton in the cupboard of perfection, the painful lie given to all idealistic pronouncements, the earthliness that clings to our human nature and sadly clouds the crystal clarity we long for" (p. 233). So, as we may get excited about our experiences, our ego is quick to make immediate and proud pronouncements about these experiences. We need to be wary, therefore, of how we move forward and try to make sense of our experiences and the movement of felt energy and emotional sensation bubbling up in the days and weeks after a session.

While chapter 7 listed several ego defense mechanisms, the challenges described below are some of the most obvious and immediate traps and pitfalls the ego can fall into during and following a session.

ATTACHMENT

Attachment can be a trap for any of us at any time. Attachment is associated with wanting and craving. Underlying attachment is our human longing for wholeness. Attachment is the dysfunctional aspect of seeking lasting satisfaction and happiness outside of ourselves in objects, such as another person, wealth, or youthfulness—an ego-constructed image of ourselves that includes stories of beliefs, values, attitudes, or opinions. It is a grasping welded to insecurity, possessiveness, jealousy, and pride. The craving causes suffering, the possessiveness causes suffering, the fleeting interest in an object of ownership causes suffering, and the loss of an object causes suffering: all the trappings of attachment.

A sense of attachment more obviously comes from the desire for what we like or prefer, for what feels good and brings pleasure, for a feeling of security. From a physical point of view of the senses, it is those sensations we find pleasant and want more of—what tastes good, smells good, and sounds good. Similarly, we quickly get attached to emotions that feel good and that avoid or dull uncomfortable emotions. The push and pull of attachment, the grasping and neediness of the ego, easily gives rise to passion and addiction, anger, delusion, and illusion, often resulting in distorted memory and loss of discrimination (Radha, 2013, p. 153).

For our purposes, there are two potential issues with attachment: (1) an excessive attachment to story and (2) attachment to your mind-melding partner.

Attachment to Story

While emotions originating from the unconscious drive us toward attachment, the ego creates its own challenges regarding attachment. As discussed earlier, the ego is the constant mediator of experience and has an agenda of control. Its control agenda includes wanting to know what everything means. The ego is under the illusion that the more it learns, the more power it will have over its destiny. While gaining knowledge can help us to a point, if we really pay attention to our lives we see how little control we truly have. But the ego is caught in the preeminence of knowledge and story and, therefore, attachment to the supremacy and absolute appearance of the constructed small self.

The profundity of this illusion means it is critical to be careful about how one integrates psychedelic experiences. As Ball (2017) points out:

A common mistake that psychedelic users make is to attempt to make sense of their visions by relating the visionary phenomenon to their own personal narrative as filtered through and created by their egos. . . . Based on their visions, people create "missions" for themselves, and give themselves a sense of purpose, or create a narrative of their own victimhood and suffering. Either way, whether victim or spiritual hero, it's all a bolstering of the ego. Egos always want to think that they have a purpose and want to attribute meaning to what they experience and perceive. None of it is in any way fundamentally true. All such views are ego-generated illusions and attachments and are a form of storytelling (p. 78).

From a nondual perspective, I agree with Ball. From this perspective, we all need to be cautious and pay attention to how we create stories from our experiences—whether using psychedelics or not. Definitive explanations or interpretations of personal experiences risk attachment to one's stories and freezing the process of one's unfolding.

Chapter 15 explores how we can use multiple lenses to interpret our experiences. Through these different lenses, we can see all stories hold some truth and, paradoxically, they are all constructs and figments of the Divine Imagination. Giving the ego multiple ways to interpret the same experience helps loosen the grip of the ego's drive to know everything in an absolute and fundamental way, even as it seeks to satisfy its insatiable addiction (attachment) to knowledge. Holding multiple perspectives erodes polarity and the judgment of what is black and white. If the ego can let go of even some of its need for control and judgment, it can open to greater equanimity, empathy, love, compassion, and understanding for the other. Holding our stories loosely also opens our mediating egoic filters wider to experience a broader and fuller range of infinite possible realizations. We open ourselves to seeing in the borderlands that there is no bottom to the rabbit hole, and the tunnel itself is porous and opens to other dimensions, including the multiverse. On the opposite end of the spectrum is the risk of constructing limiting, fantastical, and narcissistic stories. Such stories have the potential to create an exaggerated sense of self-importance and can drive a deep wedge between self and others, as it can become easier to judge others as lesser than. As Campbell (2008) states: "Mythology is defeated when the mind rests solemnly with its favorite or traditional images, defending them as though they themselves were the message that they communicate. These images are to be regarded as no more than shadows from the unfathomable reach beyond . . ." (p. 231). Here we need to make an effort to avoid cognitive rigidity, to avoid attachment— to allow for ambiguity and mystery, opening to infinite realization. "Transformation, fluidity, not stubborn ponderosity, is the characteristic of the living God" (Campbell, 2008, p. 289).

Psychedelics are a double-edged sword. They can help us overcome attachment as the expansive experiences push us toward cognitive and psychological flexibility and greater realization, particularly the truth that we are far more than our perceived and limited physical and egoic self. We can discover our ultimate divine nature. In the psychedelic journey, we can also observe the impermanence of states of consciousness, which can, with practice, contribute to letting go of attachment and riding the waves of endless change. But these truths come through discrimination, and integration, the subject of chapter 15. On the other hand, the ego can easily fall into the trap of attaching itself to stories that falsely inflate its sense of self.

Attachment to Your Mindmelding Partner

There is another risk of attachment: becoming overly attached to your co-melder. The mindmeld is an intimate experience that can create traps of attachment. I was working with Winston when, partway through the session, I found myself seated in a half-lotus position on the bed. Winston was prostrating to me on the floor and chanting a Buddhist Sanskrit yogic mantra. I was the guru or teacher, and he was the devotee. We shared a massive surge of heart-centered loving wonder and beauty. I was struck by the extent of love available to be shared between two human beings, between guru and devotee. This exchange continued for several minutes. He then stood up, and I put my hands on his shoulders. Instantly, the relationship reversed; I was the devotee, and he was the guru. My head fell into his chest, and I felt pure loving devotion toward him and his love emanating to me.

This brief story is one of many such intimate experiences. Someone single, lonely, and longing for a partner may become overly attached to someone following this type of experience. Someone in an unhappy marriage experiencing a profoundly intimate exchange like this one may develop feelings for their mindmeld partner. I point this situation out to highlight the risk of projecting one's love onto someone else and becoming attached to an object outside oneself. Here I recommend mindmelding with numerous people to see how the experiences are similar and different from others. Doing so reduces attachment to any one person or any particular experience. Working with multiple people over the years, I have found my overall experiences to be a beautiful collage of connection where I have not become *attached* to any one participant.

My one exception of attachment is to my wife, Isabel. For me, this relationship is a holy union with a unique intimacy, including sexual union. And I am grateful to her for being open about me doing this work with different people knowing how intimate the mindmeld is.

Closely related to the challenge of attachment is psychological projection.

CONFUSING SELF WITH OTHER: PSYCHOLOGICAL PROJECTION

Psychological projection is the unconscious attribution of internal states and feelings onto others. It is a defensive strategy of the ego to avoid responsibility and maintain its sense of control by casting repressed negative attributes onto others. This phenomenon is to unconsciously misidentify endogenous or internal emotional contents with exogenous or external inputs. The neurotic judgmental tendency of projection is toward distortion: exaggerating or overvaluing external inputs. Both favorable and unfavorable emotional contents can be projected onto one another. An example of a favorable projection would be to feel a loving connection to a guru as the perfect human with all one's desired virtues, not realizing the origin of unconditional, pure love is actually arising within oneself. An unfavorable projection would be to solely blame someone or something for your irritation, like negatively "overreacting" to a person honking their horn at you, not realizing an internal rage has been triggered and is arising from the unconscious. Jung (2011b) remarks how primitive this reflex can be; for example, anything foreign or strange can instantly be judged to be hostile and evil yet have no bearing on reality (p. 57).

At the center of this neurosis is the ego. The ego always wants to be in control. It does not like accepting blame, rejection, or taking responsibility for mistakes. The ego wants to distance itself from the unpleasant, or the threatening. At the same time, its role is to understand the cause of things. Not wanting to take responsibility for what it does not like, it is easy to cast blame for internal discomfort on anything outside the self. A good example is being rejected by someone you like or admire. In the face of rejection, the ego can quickly bring forth all the other person's faults, demonizing them to the point they were never good enough for you anyway. Your pain quickly turns to anger, and the other person is responsible for all of your pain. Projection of the unconscious becomes a psychological defense mechanism of resistance to avoid facing a painful internal problem—the pain of loss and grief, possibly a belief of not being enough, or guilt or shame for the real or perceived failure of a relationship.

In a mindmeld session, projection can manifest in several ways. At its worst, when exteriorizing unconscious material, your co-melder may take on a threatening or demonic form, representing violence, cruelty, or sadism from your unconscious. Or, you may develop paranoid feelings toward your co-melder during the mindmeld. It is possible to concoct delusional diabolical schemes of brainwashing, enslavement, or even the theft of one's soul (Grof, 2008; 2009).* Such projections can lead to a loss of basic trust in your co-melder. Psychologically, this is all complicated to navigate, especially because it is also possible your co-melder may be going through their own very real release of dark energy, as discussed in the following section. In this case, adopting the position of the witness and bodhisattva is best. All energy is in flux, is transformative, and will shift. Fortitude, patience, and acceptance are the answer, then letting it all go with the acknowledgment that we all hold light and darkness.

Given the close physical and psychic proximity of working with another person in the mindmeld, projection is an obvious trap. This trap can be well disguised. One may have fallen into it or be staring

---

*Grof's insights are based on the transference of negative unconscious material by patients onto their therapists during psychedelic sessions.

right at the trap without realizing what it is. For example, one person may crave physical closeness in the session based on severe abandonment and emotional deprivation in infancy and childhood. From here, participants can proceed to displace or project unconscious and inappropriate feelings and wishes onto each other, creating a less threatening problem in the present to distract from more uncomfortable psychic material waiting to be transmuted. On the other hand, a physical connection can satisfy legitimate primal needs of closeness, especially after having been through what often feels like a major ordeal. Because of this complexity, again, it is critical to establish physical boundaries before the session begins, as highlighted in chapter 8, under the heading "Sexuality and Establishing Physical Boundaries."

The bigger risk is when participants have shared physical and psychic content. There is a possibility of psychological transference/countertransference, which may later have unwanted outcomes. Transference is the mistaken projection onto the other person of feeling connected to a primary relationship (e.g., reflecting childhood-parent relationships), which stems from templates of relational engagement created in childhood. Countertransference is the unconscious emotional response we project onto others based on our internal reactions to their presentation of themselves. While these phenomena can play out in many different ways, our concern is the possibility of a desire to be physically intimate with the other person after the session. As such, there is a need to check oneself for the nature of the desire and personal boundaries as time passes after the session(s). Maintaining a respectful ongoing friendship is one thing, but starting a sexual relationship, especially if either person is already in a devoted relationship, can introduce a list of perils.

I have not faced these issues, but I am aware they can occur, especially given the intimate nature of sharing consciousness and physical space. As already mentioned it is not unusual for sexual tension to appear during the mindmeld, regardless of participants' gender and stated sexual preferences. While these feelings are generally fleeting, they may leave one or both participants grasping at wanting something more after the session; this is likely transference. On the other end of the spectrum, I have worked with married women who reported later that their overall intimacy with their partner, including sexual connection, improved.

MANIFESTATION OF THE NEGATIVE

There is debate about whether there is such a thing as a "bad" trip. One argument is that there is no such thing as a bad trip because all that manifests in a psychedelic journey, even the profoundly negative, offers us something to learn from and contributes to our psychological development. From reading this book, it should be clear that all journeys provide us with something to look at and explore, which creates opportunities for learning and making meaning. However, when you or your co-melder is profoundly struggling during a session, one can wonder what the long-term benefit is, even as the months and years pass. Struggling to understand long-term benefits is especially difficult for people who become traumatized by their experiences.

In most cases, negative experiences from psychedelic use occur as a result of poor set and setting. For example, taking high-dose psychedelics and then going to an amusement park is not likely to go well, particularly for the uninitiated. Not feeling safe and secure in the environment can evoke overwhelming fear, panic, or paranoia. But the bad trip can also result from the ego not surrendering to the experience. Ego-based challenges can include feeling trapped with no exit or end, fear of insanity, or absolute annihilation. These challenges can happen with all psychedelics but are probably the most profound with 5-MeO-DMT. If the ego decides to fight, control, or escape the energy of the experience, it can be hellish, filled with the most profound fear and anxiety imaginable. The experience can be pure torture and feel horrendous. These dysphoric responses can have lasting traumatic effects on individuals. In rare but severe cases, they might last for months or even years after the event, potentially leading to post-traumatic stress disorder if not resolved effectively and adequately (Ball, 2017, p. 119).

Challenging journeys occur beyond working with psychedelics. Blackmore (2012) points out that a small percentage of people who have had near-death experiences can also have hellish occurrences. She reports several studies with descriptions of cold grayness, nothingness and frightful vacuums, chattering demons, black pits, naked zombie-like creatures, people chained and tormented and other traditional symbols of hell (p. 401). Although rare, deep meditation can lead to similar experiences for some people. For people who struggle with depression or are overly neurotic and fearful, meditation creates the risk of exacerbating these conditions, potentially increasing anxiety and tension and producing agitation and restlessness (Blackmore, 2012; Compson, 2018; Lindahl, et al., 2017; Sannella, 1987).

Nightmares in sleep can also harm people, particularly if they are repetitive and ongoing (LaBerge, 2009). Past-life regression work or shamanic journeying can similarly lead to tortuous and profoundly traumatic material. My point is the human unconscious can be treacherous, regardless of how mindfully one may approach it, with or without psychedelics. To label these experiences as simply negative or "bad trips" is potentially to deny and avoid responsibility for underlying personal and transpersonal issues hiding under the surface waiting to be addressed.

James Jesso (2013) distinguishes between the "hard" trip and the bad one. He describes the hard trip as presenting the darker, shadowy aspects of the self. The bad trip happens when getting caught in negative mind loops of personal neuroses, creating disorientation and discomfort. Resistance amplifies the potency of uncomfortable emotions, surfacing various thought patterns, memories, or feelings (p. 103). An example from dream research highlights the risks of resistance: to attack a dream character risks the antagonist regressing in form, for instance, from a mother to a witch, then to a beast, which can later elicit feelings of anxiety or guilt (LaBerge, 2009, p. 55). The bad trip only arises, therefore, by *how* a person works with shadowy contents.

Knowing one of the attributes of psychedelics is their capacity to amplify psychological contents, we need to be prepared for repressed and uncomfortable emotions to surface from the unconscious for processing and release. As described earlier, the ability to use witnessing meditative techniques to sit and face the discomfort, both physical and emotional, and let these energies pass through the body through surrender is the antidote capable of leading to resolution. Resolution may lead to the end of problems that may have been plaguing the person in subtle ways for years. By witnessing the discomfort, it is also possible to generate different meaningfulness and resilience to what is emerging.

However, this approach does not encourage absolute passivity resulting in defeat. If the contents become too overwhelming, I recommend more direct, albeit subtle, engagement. For example, try engaging the discomfort by mindfully centering your thoughts on being healed through processing the uncomfortable sensations (e.g., sending loving energy from your heart center); this can potentiate a new relationship to the pain, which can be empowering and build self-confidence. You can also ask yourself what you may be running away from, what you have shut down in yourself, or what unresolved conflicts you are in to help evoke a connection to the presenting difficulty. As mentioned earlier, if you are faced by a demon or other dark archetypal being, you can ask who they are, what they want, what they have to teach or help you, and what you can offer them.* These techniques contribute to accepting the darkness within us, which contributes to transmuting it. This engagement is demanding but necessary for personal growth and development.

The "bad" trip can also arise in the mindmeld. I have only once had a "bad" trip when working with someone else, in this instance Isabel. We wanted to drop into the mindmeld, but on the surface, it wasn't

---

*The one exception, based on dream research, may be that if the dark figure represents a real person, say a sexual or physical abuser, and a real traumatic event, then a more satisfying resolution may result from overcoming, disarming, and transforming the attacker (LaBerge, 2009, p. 55).

happening. The ego was present for both of us; it banged against the inner self's prison walls. We had used the same mushrooms at the same dose with the same set and setting before and never had a problem. Surrendering my ego had historically been easy for me and something I had done for years. And, yet, we both had the same "bad" trip of physiologically feeling we were run over by a truck, draining all our energy. I was so exhausted I had to crawl to the bathroom to pee. I also felt nauseated, although nausea with mushrooms is rare for me. The experience was so negative I did not use mushrooms for the next two years, instead working with other psychedelics. Eventually, I tried mushrooms again and have not had the problem recur. What is interesting from this vignette is both Isabel and I had the same subjective struggles, giving the appearance of something shared in conscious experience. Both of us have since struggled to make meaning from the experience as there were no clear contents beyond the heavy body load and struggle with the ego. Sometimes there is no clear path to integration, but rather an acceptance that the journey was more likely part of an overall arc of physical and psychic cleansing.

According to Grof and Grof (2010), the "negative" can also manifest as dark energy, which some may label "demonic," when working with either psychedelics or Holotropic Breathwork. Given the transitory nature of this state, we can view the movement of dark energy as part of the constant flux of polarity in the competition between dark and light energies. This energy flux is the never-ending flow between positive and negative emotional states. The Grof's suggest that the emergence of dark energy is most likely associated with the need to let go of past severe emotional, physical, or sexual abuse. With this perspective of the manifestation of dark energy, there is less egoic identification with any "demonic thing" and more acceptance of possible shame, guilt, or an exaggerated connection to the darkness. Moving through the dark energy is potentially penetrating a layer deeper into the mind where the essential and ultimate ground of our existence lies: the infinite loving presence of nondual suchness.

When dark energy manifests, there usually is a change of facial expression and vocal expression, where the voice becomes deep and raspy and the eyes assume an indescribably evil expression with the face cramping up into a "mask of evil." The body tenses and spastic contractions can make fingers look like claws. Subjectively, the participants experience within themselves dark alien energy that feels ominous and evil (Grof & Grof, 2010, p. 194).

Dark energy can show up in the mindmeld. The manifestation of this energy may scare participants, but the response is not to judge what is happening negatively. Make all efforts to remain calm and equanimous. If dark energy is being released from your partner, stay neutral and witness the release of what is not serving them. There is nothing to do for them but remain the passive and compassionate onlooker. Allow for the full expression of the energy. A full expression can reach extraordinary intensity, including loud vocalization and aggressive movement. Usually, in a relatively short period (minutes as opposed to hours), this type of energy is processed. A complete discharge of this energy can be truly liberating, as though the person has subjectively exorcized the "demon." Facing the darkness and the fear it induces promotes the resolution of what has manifested. It also builds self-confidence and flexibility in approaching similar challenges in future journeys.

If your partner is profoundly struggling during the session without respite, which at its worst may be some form of psychotic break, there are several proactive steps you can take to support them. First, it is again essential to remain calm, centered, and supportive. To be in the psychedelic state is to be profoundly open to suggestibility. If you panic, regardless of your words, you can infuse greater fear into your partner. Second, it is critical to emphasize the self-limiting nature of psychedelics and that within hours the experience will reach completion. Because there is a time limit, there is no reason to panic or worry. Third, remind them of why they are there: to deeply explore consciousness that includes surfacing and processing traumatic and challenging material. You can encourage redirection to internal self-inquiry into exploring what is surfacing and why. Fourth, encourage them to return to meditating, lying down, and letting the challenges resolve themselves by surrendering to them and feeling the emotional and physical pain, letting it express itself in whatever way it wants to. Finally, you can try holding their hand or asking where they may want physical pressure on their body to help them process energy. If they resist, then back off.

If the person becomes aggressive, a rarity, try to use a calming voice to soothe them and bide your time until the psychedelic wears off. Any form of physical force should only be used in self-defense. Give them space and let them act out.

I have firsthand experience with processing dark energy. I was working in a mindmeld with Isabel. I was intuitively guided to another bedroom, as though to spare her the drama of what was about to unfold. My body entered symmetrical fractal energetic yoga, but I was heaving. I felt like I was throwing up my insides and turning inside out, even though I was not vomiting. The darkness was overwhelming. It was murderously gloomy. What was forcing itself through me was from beyond me, as though processing something from the collective unconscious. As the movement continued, it became a clear manifestation of the heart of darkness: genocide. I felt like I was purging the Holocaust, the death in Cambodia's Killing Fields, and the murderous shadow in all humans. I heaved and screamed. I surrendered to the energy and allowed it to all flow out of me, not in any way trying to fight it.

When the purge ended, all the energy in me shifted. I stood up and walked out into the hallway. I looked down the hallway, and heaven opened up. The opening didn't happen visually. The splendor of heaven more simply arose through my whole consciousness as I experienced pure perfection in the ALL of the UNIVERSE. I suddenly fathomed how heaven could come to earth with a radical shift in human consciousness. The moment was one of the most glorious of my life. In sessions since, the return to heavenly splendor has often come up as a theme, but always fleetingly.

Before moving on, it is valuable to distinguish between the movement of dark energy and the movement of strength in the human body. Fractal energetic yoga and other forms of active discharge discussed earlier can take some bizarre forms. To the onlooker, it may appear as "demonic" energy, with the face contorting, the tongue sticking out, and fluid movements of arms jutting and fingers pointing. But usually, it is energy in the body simply opening itself to healing and moving toward homeostasis. Subjectively, this type of processing does not feel like dark energy but like a flow moving what is stifling or stuck. For clarity, if you suspect possession in your co-melder during a session, do not attempt any interventions. You cannot be sure of your partner's internal experience and may cause harm. Again, just be the witness to their experience.

After researching and observing thousands of psychedelic and Holotropic sessions, Grof (2008; 2009) and Grof and Grof (2010) point out that negative carryover from these sessions is rare and minimal, especially for people who show reasonable emotional stability. Occasionally, people may feel sad, irritable, fatigued, or have headaches after sessions but within "normal" ranges and only for a day to a week after the sessions. For people who did not have serious emotional issues before participating in sessions, prolonged reactions or psychotic breakdowns afterward were generally not observed. The section further below on "Unprocessed Traumatic Material," however, is for people who may struggle with longer-term unprocessed material after a session, which more commonly happens to people struggling with psychiatric disorders, such as severe neuroses or psychosomatic issues.

POSSESSION

In the early drafting of this book, I was reluctant to include anything related to possession by an ontologically independent "demonic" spirit. This reluctance stemmed from my skepticism of demonic possession based on the belief that such experiences were likely limited to one's psyche and its reach into the collective unconscious, similar to the way modern psychology likes to box in such phenomena. I was also still skeptical of the nature of my positive possession experiences, described in chapter 11. Further, possession by a dark, discarnate being is a vast and tricky subject. The concept of pure evil is difficult to come to terms with, even though most cultures around the world, including the world's dominant religions, acknowledge possession by "demonic" forces. But then strange things happened to me in the past year, leading to a shift in my beliefs and approach. Even though it is controversial, I now see the importance of addressing this challenging topic.

My story started when my father left his body a year and a half ago. A friend who knew I had a strained relationship with my father while he was alive recommended talking to a psychopomp, Laurel, who lives in Texas, with the intent of finding greater peace with my father's passing. During our call, Laurel connected to my father's soul and shared things she couldn't have known about him. In short, the dialogue with my father, through her as an intermediary, was rewarding for me.

Several months passed, and I stayed in touch with Laurel. One day, she called me to convey a message from her psychic friend, Jane, who lives in California. Jane regularly interacts with discarnate beings without using psychedelics. Although I knew nothing about Jane, she knew about me because an unfamiliar discarnate being visited her with an important message to pass on to me. The being was a "chief" who had been monitoring my psychedelic work and wasn't pleased. According to the psychic, the chief stayed at her place for two days, insistent that she share his message with me. She imparted the chief's warning to her friend in Texas at the chief's behest, who then shared it with me.

I was not sure what to make of the story. There were no details about what I was doing wrong or what was happening, but I thought it best to take the message seriously. A few days later, I decided to do a high-dose LSD session alone and call in the chief to determine what was going on. At this point, I had only once called in a discarnate being to participate in one of my sessions. I was still generally reluctant and skeptical about proactively working with discarnate beings, preferring to navigate consciousness with my inner intuitive guidance. If discarnate beings showed up, great; if not, also fine.

As I started my LSD session, I respectfully called in the chief. I humbly asked him to show me what I was doing wrong and for his guidance and help to resolve anything untoward. The LSD session proceeded normally with beautiful visuals and a relaxing of my ego. Soon, I was performing fractal energetic yoga in the living room. I was lying face down when suddenly the whole floor opened. I was looking straight into a seething pit of thousands of demons. There was a portal to a hell realm in my living room! The pit of demons had a gravity that was pulling me into it. As I successfully resisted the physical pull with outstretched arms, it felt like dark energies were being sucked out of my body, which strangely felt beneficial. Surprisingly, I was not scared but shocked at what I witnessed.

The portal eventually closed, and I continued doing fractal energetic yoga, although perturbed by what I had just gone through. I sought the chief's help to close the portal, but I was unsure of its status when the session ended. I thanked the chief for revealing what had been opened in the house and wondered what I should do next. My rational mind questioned how "real" the experience was. Was it just a creation of my psyche projected out, or was this a real entry point into a demonic realm?

The next day, I called my psychic friend, Niall, and told him what happened. He confirmed he saw the portal to a hell realm in the house and worked with me to successfully close it by calling in guardian angels and divine light. He also said the chief was a "Chief of Ascension" who was teaching me. I shared what happened with Laurel, and she was glad that I could connect with the chief and work with Niall to close the portal. There was no answer to how the portal was opened. Perhaps it was opened inadvertently or possibly as a synchronicity to teach me a lesson.

Months passed, and I was again on the phone with Laurel. Jane was visiting her from California. I asked Jane if Laurel had told her about the portal in my living room, and she hadn't. I told Jane the story. She said that the chief had told her about the hell portal. I was taken aback that she hadn't initially shared this critical detail. She said she didn't want to overwhelm and scare me. Ultimately, I thanked her for not sharing; if she had shared her knowledge of the portal, my rational mind would have refuted the experience as not "real" because my unconscious could have created the experience, having been prompted by someone's suggestion.

The lesson I learned was that evil spirits are somehow ontologically individual beings and exist outside of our inner worlds, and yet can penetrate our psyche. How else can I explain what other people were seeing from a distance in my home that was later revealed and confirmed by me? The realization that such darkness concretely exists was difficult for me to accept, especially after connecting exclusively to discarnate beings devoid of such evil over the preceding years. Even though I did not become possessed, this experience left enough of an impact that I want to ensure any potential possession event is taken seriously and cautiously.

For our purposes, psychedelics can bring to the surface that which is hidden within us. The emergence of a long-standing possession in someone would be no different from surfacing hidden trauma in the body and would likely look similar. Having said this, I anticipate such an occurrence in the mindmeld to be highly unlikely, given how rare possessions are generally. Possessions by dark entities are known for inducing profoundly self-destructive behavior, like long-standing substance abuse and addiction. As mentioned in chapter 6, if you are discerning in who you choose as a partner, possession issues should not arise.

But dark entities can be good at hiding, possibly within you. The literature on possession indicates that everybody is susceptible to possession, with intense past trauma being the typical gateway for a dark, energetic entity to enter the body. Typically, these beings will not be outright evil. Robert Falconer's extensive work with possessions and research (2023) in this area points to most possessions resulting from lost human souls who did not transition well after death because they were consumed by trauma and addiction before dying. These lost souls are attracted to similar energetic signatures found in the living who have similar histories of trauma. Lost souls take up residence in the person who mirror the same traumatic patterning, often at an early age. Only in rare cases is possession reported as genuinely demonic.

If you work through a session and it feels like a malevolent and unwelcome presence remains in you, beyond what may be your shadow contents (and the distinction between the two may be blurry), I suggest calling in divine light. Feel this light expand from your heart, and respectfully and compassionately ask the dark presence to leave. While the being may act aggressively after being called out, there is a need to bring peace and calm because such entities thrive on fear and confrontation. If the malevolent energy does not leave, start asking it questions. First, confirm it is separate from you by asking, "Are you a part of me?" If the answer is no, ask its name, purpose, what it wants, and the lesson it is trying to teach you. You may have to be persistent. Witnessing and validation are often enough to result in a respectful departure upon further requests to leave (Falconer, 2023).

I recognize these suggestions are brief for such a complex phenomenon and may be difficult while in the throes of psychedelic work. If the menacing presence does not depart, consider finding a practitioner in the healing arts who works with removing malevolent entities or, from a more nondual perspective, can teach you how to embrace, transform, and integrate these energies as virtuous allies within yourself. Such people can be found online and can do the work remotely, but please be discerning in your choice of person and seek recommendations.

I continue to hold a nondual attitude in my journeys with a view that darkness and suffering can teach us and create deeper meaning in our lives, which ultimately might be to show us how bright the divine light truly is. Nonduality also points toward extending loving compassion to the suffering entities caught in the darkness. At the same time, I now exercise more caution. I remind myself that help from more highly evolved and discarnate beings is only a request away, a practice frequently used by shamans, astral travelers, and by people in the world's main religions. As described in chapter 7, I now work with an adapted version of Robert Monroe's intention for journeying, calling in protective guiding forces.*

UNPROCESSED TRAUMATIC MATERIAL

Large amounts of unconscious traumatic material can surface and not be sufficiently released and processed by the end of a session. Reasons for this could be insufficient time to process the energetic contents (potentially of a specific COEX); a lack of egoic surrender to physically release the energy; or the material was too dense to be digestible. It is also possible that later there will be upsurges of additional unconscious material because the removal of certain blockages has made available new contents that were previously repressed. At its worst, trauma arising within a session could result in a longer-term psychotic break. Even though this is very unlikely, it is possible (Aixalà, 2022; Grof, 2008). These are risks when working with psychedelics, much the same as when working with deep meditation or therapeutic techniques like EMDR or somatic therapy. Concurrently, these challenges should not be viewed as failures but as part of a longer, meaningful healing process. Here again, this is another reason for highlighting the importance of having previous experience with psychedelics before trying the mindmeld: with experience, there is more comfort with processing immense energies and less risk of adverse reactions.

If a psychotic break, persistent strange thoughts, deep feelings of fragmentation, excessive anxiety, paranoia, rumination, struggle with

---

*There is a vast amount of literature on the perils of possession. Robert Falconer (2023), an Internal Family Systems Therapy teacher and therapist, does an excellent job of summarizing these challenges and how to effectively and compassionately work with possession.

the emergence of previously unknown traumatic memories, unorthodox visions, or depressive symptoms occur, these challenges should be viewed as an opportunity, even though they may be complicated to work through and may cause initial panic, possibly for both participants. Difficult ongoing symptomologies disruptive to daily life can be viewed as a *spiritual emergency* or *psychospiritual crisis*. Feeling worse after certain sessions can be a signal that important unconscious material was activated but remains unresolved. These episodes sometimes revolve around spiritual themes, including ongoing sequences of psychological death and rebirth, past-life memories, and encounters with mythological beings. Spiritual emergencies can be messy and confusing. Here, the antidote is not resistance or denial but facing the difficulty, facing the unconscious, and moving through and learning from it as a form of metamorphosis (Grof & Grof, 1989). The tension associated with a traumatized psyche may contribute to a striving to resolve the internal struggle that ultimately leads to greater fullness, maturity, personal meaning and purpose, and psycho-spiritual health.

If the person is profoundly struggling when entering the second half of the session, there are four options to help facilitate resolution before the session ends. The first option is to encourage Holotropic Breathwork (intense and deep hyperventilation), discussed in chapter 12; Holotropic Breathwork is an effective way to resolve partially processed energetic material. The second option is trying to tense various muscles in the body where there are feelings of constriction and hold sculpture-like poses for long periods. A third option is an intense dance or yoga. A fourth option is physical massage or applying intense external pressure to tight areas (Grof, 2008).

If confronted with psychological fragmentation and struggle after a psychedelic session, repressed unconscious material may have surfaced, and more work is required. The person should seek appropriate guidance, counseling, and management. While it may sound counterintuitive, this may include further repeated psychedelic sessions to complete the processing of the emerging unconscious material. The purification process of the psyche takes time and effort. Grof's research (2008) questions whether one or two psychedelic sessions can lead to lasting personal change for people struggling with deep-seated issues with lots of unconscious material to process. His discoveries indicate that what contributes to the lasting personal resolution of trauma and transformation is working with psychedelics and expanded states over time, supported by psychological therapy.

Selecting the right therapist is a good start: someone open to the profundity of psychedelics, spiritual awakening, and understanding spiritual emergency.* Mainstream psychiatry and psychology generally make no distinction between mysticism and mental illness. So what may be symptoms of spiritual opening or awakening to someone with a mystical belief system, to the average psychiatrist, would be something to treat medically, usually with pharmaceuticals—keeping in mind that such treatment may be warranted in some circumstances.

Grof (2008) recommends a combination of other possible approaches, depending on the nature of the problems. His list includes: bioenergetic exercises or other neo-Reichian approaches,† Gestalt technique, psychodrama, guided affective imagery, and deep massage, which can help mobilize and work through unfinished matrices of blocked energy (p. 213). Engagement in grounding practices like meditation, prayer, various breathing techniques, yoga, tai chi, and sport-

---

*Christina Grof set up the Spiritual Emergence Network to help people confronted with such crises. Another option is the ICEERS (International Center for Ethnobotanical Education, Research, and Service) Support Center. Both are available online.

†Wilhelm Reich figured out the importance of biology in addressing certain psychological conditions, like neuroses. His theories centered on emotional traumas and sexual feelings being repressed by complex patterns of chronic muscular tensions worn in the body like armor to protect the individual. His techniques focused on hyperventilation, various body manipulations, and direct physical contact to mobilize jammed psychoenergetic blocks in the body and remove them. His work inspired the "neo-Reichian" therapeutic models of the 1960s, including: Alexander Lowen's bioenergetics, John Pierrakos' Core Energetics, Charles Kelly's Radix therapy, Stanley Keleman's Formative Psychology, Arther Janov's primal therapy, and others (Grof, 2019a, p. 218).

ing activities can also be valuable over the longer term. Working with energy healers can be grounding and healing. Connecting to *supportive* family and friends can be invaluable. (Educating nonsupportive family and friends about spiritual emergencies should be considered.) Researching the nature of spiritual emergencies can also be helpful; books and articles on the subject are available online.

At this point, the opportunity is to participate more fully in the disintegration, inviting an amplification of wounds and symptoms to be felt through and processed. Reaching deeper into the recesses of the psyche and higher aspects of ourselves through systematic self-exploration can act as propellants toward integration, radical healing, and personal transformation. In recovery, a person may find personal clarity, expanded maps of making meaning, a more defined sense of the interconnected self, and greater self-responsibility, all leading to greater maturity and individuation. Serial psychological issues may be resolved. If aspects of the suffering do not end but are accepted and embraced with new awareness, it can open a world of new possibilities and become the healing itself. Thus, suffering can be seen as an alchemical opportunity to forge personal growth (Dąbrowski, 2016; Evans & Read, 2020; Grof, 2008; 2009; 2019a; 2019b; Grof & Grof, 1989; Jung, 1969; Metzner, 1998; Peterson, 1999).*

As humans, we are inevitably confronted by suffering. How we approach our suffering can radically influence our path toward growing up and maturing as adults, which is explored further in chapter 15. Suffering can reveal deeper levels of who we are. We can learn to take greater responsibility for our response to the challenges we face in life. We can learn new ways to cope with our difficulties. Experiencing

---

*Polish psychiatrist Kazimierz Dąbrowski (2016) observed this process occurring spontaneously in his patients and labeled it "positive disintegration." Grof (2019a) notes that similar positive disintegration experiences occur in the shamanic initiatory crisis and in rites of passage in some cultures. While shamanic initiations are normally unexpected where the crisis occurs spontaneously, and rites of passage ceremonies are structured and planned, both can lead to psychological disintegration (even dismemberment), where resolution is meant to lead to greater sanity and well-being (p. 13).

suffering and healing from wounds, be they from childhood, accidental injury, acts of physical, sexual, or emotional violence, or even
suffering within the collective unconscious, can increase our empathy
and compassion toward others facing difficulty. On the other hand,
to fail to find meaning in personal suffering is to risk the tragedy of
abandoning redemption, falling into pointless pain and frustration,
and possibly cascading into self-destruction.

We can distinguish between a transpersonal crisis and a pathological condition when discussing trauma. As mentioned in chapter 2, it
is highly recommended that people with a personal or familial history
of psychotic breaks or other similar mental health challenges should
not try the mindmeld and should more generally avoid psychedelics—
at least outside of a managed therapeutic framework. Pathological
conditions of a psychotic nature are usually characterized by a lack
of insight, rigid personality, paranoid delusions, hallucinations, and
extravagant forms of behavior. It is as though the pathological mind
is more open to receiving transpersonal material. Still, the wiring is
crossed, so the messages are confusing and, as such, are often dark
and ominous. With crossed wires, there is limited ability to ground
the psyche in day-to-day reality and responsibilities. Perhaps not surprisingly, there is increasing evidence that psychiatric conditions like
psychosis are often linked to histories of extreme physical, sexual, or
emotional abuse as children (Kolk, 2015). These abuses are certain
to take the human mind and body out of homeostasis and into dysfunction. As the mind tries to make sense of the trauma and simultaneously escape it, both while it is happening and as it resurfaces
from unconscious memory, we cannot be shocked when mental wires
become crossed.

But such psychotic symptoms can even happen to the initiated
without a history of mental health disorder. If psychedelics are tools
to open up the mind and explore consciousness, we should not be surprised if the mind becomes more open after a psychedelic has run its
course through the body. While this is rare (to the disappointment of

some), it can happen. People may be more open to visions of spirits or start having more vivid or lucid dreams. They may have sensations of vibrant currents of energy coursing through their body, accompanied by spasms and violent trembling. Experiencing oneness with the universe may spontaneously happen when walking down the street.

This book does not aim to diagnose spiritual emergencies versus pathological conditions. Nor is its purpose to provide treatment for a complex break from reality. But I want to flag this challenge because participants need to be ready to approach the situation constructively in the unlikely event it materializes.

When seeking to integrate challenging experiences, I again suggest the same advice as earlier: it is helpful to view all that manifests in sessions through the lens of nonduality, as ultimately being all you, where you take responsibility for all of your energy and experience. Owning all of your energy means accepting both what feels "good" and "bad." Ball (2009) states: "The more you own the energy and take responsibility for it, the closer you will get to your energetic center (which is also the center of *all things and the "location" where God resides*). Physically, this is the center of your heart . . ." (p. 83). To have experienced nondual states of consciousness is to know the truth of this statement. While the ego struggles with the bigger truth of unity consciousness in day-to-day life, using the intellect to remind oneself of this truth continually can go a long way to accepting one's struggles in this broader understanding of reality.

REACTIVATIONS AND
OVERACTIVE INTUITION

An overlapping phenomenon with ongoing emotional releases is "reactivations." A reactivation is to enter holotropic states without taking any psychedelics but after a person has earlier been exposed to their use. The theory is psychedelics open the psyche to more expansive awareness even after their effects wear off. If psychedelics are tools to penetrate deeper into the mind and consciousness, we should not be surprised when the doors of perception have been opened wider in our day-to-day lives. Similar reports have been made after multiday silent meditation retreats without the use of psychedelics. In these retreats, new states of consciousness were reached, which then spontaneously presented themselves again after the retreat. Some new states had longer-term persistence and were identified as either challenging/destabilizing or blissful (Blackmore, 2012, p. 439; Compson, 2018; Lindahl et al., 2017; Sannella, 1987).

Reactivations can be surprising and even troubling, at least initially. This is especially so if they happen when engaged in an activity, such as being at work or driving a car, or when they lead to insomnia. But reactivations are usually subtle when you are engaged in activities requiring concentration and more intense if you are relaxing, meditating, or sleeping. I have had reactivations during dreams of fantastical "trips" where I felt like I had ingested a psychedelic or began slipping into nondual awareness. I have had similar dreams of feeling drunk with alcohol, and once had an allergic reaction to a vaccination, leaving me feeling "high." I know people who have taken MDMA and weeks later dream they have taken it with the complete absorption of love and bliss typically associated with its use.

While reactivations can be disturbing and instill fear, especially if the content is discomforting, there is nothing to worry about: they will subside in time. Responding negatively to feeling out of control is a standard response of the ego wanting to remain in control. This reflexive response is similar to rejecting unwanted emotions like anger, anxiety, and sadness. When reactivations occur, the best thing to do is to surf the wave. Trust yourself, bring awareness to what is arising, and relax in your body. Similarly to surfing, the better you get at it, the more you can enjoy it and lengthen the ride of endless self-exploration. Anxiety surrounding the experience can be transformed into feelings of ecstasy, with blissful vibrations running throughout the body. Everything can feel richer, more colorful, and more pleasurable.

If the reactivations continue for weeks and are consistently overwhelming to the point you cannot follow through with your responsibilities, I recommend grounding activities like exercise, which can include sport, yoga, qigong, or tai chi, or eating heavy meals, or taking hot salt baths followed by a cold shower. Getting massages is also an option.

A similar phenomenon to reactivations is you may find your intuitive abilities become overactive, presenting a challenge. This means the brain's filters to all of lived experience are more widely opened and the psyche's capacity to understanding something immediately through instinctive feeling or gnosis rather than conscious reasoning can become hyperaware. While strong intuitive abilities can be advantageous for tuning in to and understanding the environment and other people's energies and realities, it can also be overwhelming.

If you find yourself telepathically opened up to the point of being overwhelmed with a flood of other people's psychic energy, I recommend meditating to turn down the inflow. Visualize a stereo amplifier with a volume control on it. This amplifier represents your intuitive abilities. Very slowly turn the volume control down. Feel deeply into your breath and body, grounding yourself through your feet to the earth, and turn down your telepathic receptors. Do this exercise for fifteen minutes at a time. To see results, you may have to do this exercise repeatedly over several days, or even weeks. Alternatively, visualize and create an energetic bubble of light energy two feet out from all of yourself, emanating from your heart. Expand your awareness and feel into this bubble. This personal energetic bubble can be as porous or as sealed as you want to incoming psychic energy. Meditate on shifting the porosity of your bubble regularly in order to gain more control over what you allow in and out of your psychic field. Working with these tools over time may contribute to greater access to the mindmeld in sessions.

Physical exercise, meditative breathing techniques, and eating whole foods can also contribute to reducing overactive intuition. Avoid using psychedelics until you feel comfortably grounded.

FANTASY AND DELUSION

One way or another, when working with psychedelics, you will enter fantastical states. To explore consciousness is to explore the Divine Imagination. In the Divine Imagination, anything is possible, much like in dreams. Fantasy allows us to consider and deal with the unknown. But fantasy is a double-edged sword: when grounded, it can lead to creativity and understanding; when disembodied, it can lead to delusion.

The Challenges of Fantasy and Delusion

To start with delusion, Judith (2004) states excessive fantasizing can become a buffer for the weak ego trying to increase feelings of importance and power. Here the ego is constantly working to bolster the personality, usually exaggerating grandiosity, whether it is with narcissistic attributes of being the martyr or other archetypal character traits.* Obvious examples are people who have a profound psychedelic experience and conclude they are Jesus or other major historical figures who have been reborn with a new mission. Here I do not want to discount the possibility of people truly experiencing past lives. Yet, people who make grand proclamations of past lives, real or not, often have little awareness of their effect on their family and closest friends and may become quite disconnected from them (p. 372). Grof (2009) argues these fantastical experiences are likely related to the surfacing of unconscious material appearing in the cryptic form of a symbolic disguise, defensive distortions, and metaphorical allusions. He also states fantasy is much more likely to dominate consecutive sessions for someone struggling with profound psychiatric problems (p. 44). Getting stuck in fantasy post-session can obviously make integration difficult for the participant and may warrant psychological help from

---

*Insightful work has been done on exploring archetypal character or personality types and the creation of the ego's self-image and character fixation through the Enneagram. See for example A. H. Almaas's *Facets of Unity: The Enneagram of Holy Ideas* (2000) and Eli Jaxon-Bear's *The Enneagram of Liberation: From Fixation to Freedom* (2001).

a therapist who preferably has a strong grasp of the complexity of the psychedelic journey.

In my own experience, I have been immersed in healing energies throughout a session, giving rise to the impression I am fully healed from my injuries, only to find the next day I am still struggling as though nothing has changed. I have also had delusional experiences of witnessing the end of humans putting toxic substances in their bodies, particularly alcohol and commercial tobacco. Again, the next day I woke up to the world still being the same. The optimistic part of me likes to fantasize I am foreseeing my future healing and that of humanity. We will have to wait and see.

I have also repeatedly connected to one famous ancient character as though I was that person in a past life—fantastically enough, King David of the Jews. This connection has been onerous, as all energetic releases relate to David's murder of one of his elite soldiers, Uriah the Hittite, and a reckoning with *God*. I don't even appreciate this connection because of David's role as a warrior king, responsible for killing many people in a bid to conquer land. I hold five possibilities in this connection but am not attached to any of them. First, I could have been this person in a past life. Second, because it is possible to transcend space-time, and because everything is connected in Indra's Net—the universe's interconnectedness—I could have experienced another person's life as though it were my own. Third, I am being shown something within myself at an archetypal level, such as a psychological shadow element, needing to be processed, healed, and integrated. Fourth, based on my biographical background of attending church during my youth my psyche transposed the character King David onto another discarnate being I am unfamiliar with. Fifth, the experience is a pure hallucination (the apparent perception of something not truly present) and a fantasy (a constructed imagining of the impossible or near impossible). Regardless of the five possibilities, I view my experience as a dream where I am a dream character who does not need to attach to any one view and instead holds all possibilities at once, not acting out with any form of pride or mission.

For an adult to approach fantasy with an infantile mind is to potentially make absurd and harmful life decisions. Here there is a lack of maturity and grounding in discrimination and discretion. And you don't have to take psychedelics to fall into this trap. In the face of epiphany, often when experiencing overwhelming personal suffering, I have seen people join cults and give away all of their wealth, only to be abused, and then leave years later completely lost, disillusioned, and financially broke. Another example is watching some male friends chase different women around the world, continually falling in love with "the one" and creating new fantasies each time of getting married to the perfect partner, only to have everything fail over and over again, sometimes over the course of weeks.

When working with psychedelics, all sorts of mysterious experiences are available. To react and abruptly make big life decisions based on fantastical insights can easily result in bizarre and possibly destructive outcomes. Here, fantasy becomes delusion and can easily cause damage to the individual and possibly others. As one falls further into delusion, one steps closer to psychosis, where there is a disconnection from lived social realities.

It can be hard to return to the routine of day-to-day reality from a tremendous and enlightening journey. The trap of fantasy and delusion lies in wait. Most others will disregard, ignore, or devalue your phenomenal experiences explored in the mindmeld. Such negative reactions from friends, family, or colleagues can trigger a defensive reaction to inflate one's experiences and make internal egoic pronouncements of being special. There is never a need to convince others of anything. Real empowerment is found within—through humility and seeing we are both nothing and everything. We need to recognize we are all human and all capable of having these experiences. In humility, we can find a balance, fostering ease and tenderness in our minds. Thereupon we are closer to accepting the mundane as part of a greater whole, letting go of fantasy and delusion, which themselves can be manifestations of attachment: a craving for something better.

As Fadiman (2011) suggests, do not make major life changes for the first few weeks after a psychedelic session. For example, some people may reevaluate their primary relationship, risking the possibility of making a hasty decision to end it after having only one psychedelic session. If such an epiphany arises, let it settle in. Be careful what information you share. Wait and test insights with additional sessions, lived experience, and, best of all, entering into thoughtful conversations about the nature of your relationship with the other person.

The Opportunity in Fantasy

Fantasy can also be the fountain of creativity. Jung (2017) points out that creative activity springing from imagination and fantasy frees us from our limited self and liberates the spirit of play in us. Fantasy can, accordingly, open people to playing with their nature, moving in the direction of fluidity, change, and growth, where there is no longer anything externally fixed or hopelessly petrified. To dive deep enough is to discover the eternally unknown and what was previously alien—the hidden foundations of psychic life, like wholeness and wellness. Such a deep dive into one's unconscious can shift the personality's center of gravity. In this context, fantasy can serve as a tool to break through neuroses and tap into core insights. And, Jung argues, when fantasy takes people too far away from their core selves, the taproot of human and animal instinct usually serves as course correction. Here too, theoretically, the psyche and its inherent healing intelligence will also try to bring the person into balance and wholeness where there is extreme misalignment.

This latter point of the psyche working to bring a person to wholeness is important because it points us in the direction of putting faith in this unseen guide to help us navigate crises. Psychedelics and other tools for exploring the unconscious, such as sitting meditation, can completely disrupt a person's mental state. I have had a few friends participate in ten-day Vipassana silent retreats who experienced deep holotropic states and then struggled for years afterward before feeling like they regained a solid foothold of grounded stability. If we have the strength to face our suffering and avoid freezing it out, particularly with alcohol or other numbing drugs—like opioids, cannabis, or stimulants—there is the promise of finding greater internal peace. And this is what psychedelics can offer us: a tool to confront the misalignment between our conscious and unconscious.

To navigate fantasy, I like to work in threes, a number the Greeks identified with wisdom and understanding. I pay more attention if something shows up in my field of awareness three times through psychedelic sessions, dreams, visions, or synchronicities in daily life. I am unlikely to make any immediate decisions but allow a slow shifting and broadening of my belief system as more and more data arrives. As I seek to analyze and interpret my own experiences, I use various tools to put things into perspective, contemplate, and make change, which is the subject of chapter 15.

14

Debriefing after
the Session

Debriefing can be a meaningful activity for both participants. The debrief dovetails with the mindmeld, where the practice of loving connection becomes a practice of being the witness to the other person's sharing. Through listening to their story we honor and validate their experience. Debriefing allows for a reciprocal and collaborative partnership in each other's stories. This sharing is the first step in integration, the subject of the next chapter.

Debriefing also provides an opportunity to preserve and consolidate the gains from the session. Debriefing can contribute to regaining composure and centering after the session. It offers the opportunity to discuss and repair anything conflictual at an interpersonal level and confirm personal and emotional safety. Discussion can contribute to making meaning of the experience and appreciating its relevance in the broader spectrum of life. Dialogue can also help us determine what, if any, shifts in life are worth considering during the following weeks and months based on epiphanies and encouraging each other through ongoing difficulties.

PREPARING FOR THE DEBRIEF

Debriefing can be as simple or detailed as you want. Suggestions to consider are given in the following pages.

Journaling is a constructive way to record your experience(s) and compare notes with your co-melder. You may have already written down some bullet points at the beginning of the second half of the session. If not, do so before debriefing your co-melder about what happened during the session. By writing down what was potentially shared psychically, it is easier to determine what was actually telepathically communicated. At a minimum, I suggest the following:

- List in bullet points your session highlights, particularly anything seemingly shared in consciousness. (During the session, create short titles to story episodes to help remember highlights.)
- Describe your most intense sensations/emotions. Describe any stories related to memories (positive or negative) associated with the movement of this energy.
- List and track any points on the body where physical work was done. While the energy needing to be processed from any particular area may be resolved, there may be areas of the body requiring further monitoring and intervention.
- List any spontaneous vocalizations.

When writing your summary, consider adding the following:

- A list of key words and symbols from your experience, including descriptions of personal meaning and associations with each.
- Recent and historical personal events possibly contributing to what arose in the session.
- Initial impressions and interpretations of the experience.
- How any messages or epiphanies may apply to your life.

Another option for summarizing your experience is to create a mind map or concept map. Creating a map of the experience can help integrate the session and improve your memory of what happened, including building memory capacity for future sessions in the same way that dream journals can improve future dream recall. A *mind map* has a central theme or idea listed in the center, with various subthemes, ideas, or experiences branching from it using lines and arrows. A mind map helps visually identify associations and structure among themes, ideas, and experiences. A mind map can include images, symbols, key words or codes and can use different colors. A similar idea is creating a *concept map* with a key concept at the top and branching elements arranged in hierarchical order below it in chart form, using boxes or circles for organizing conceptual insights. A concept map is helpful for making linkages among more specific ideas and concepts in a priority sequence with a focus on a single subject. You can search the internet for examples of mind maps and concept maps for inspiration.

Other options for summarizing your experience include drawing or painting a mandala, music, song, poetry, topiary, or using another art form to capture your experience.

While summarizing your experience it may be beneficial to listen to the same music used during the first half of the session to help evoke memories of your experience. Ensure your co-melder has access to the playlist to do the same during the following days.

WHAT TO DISCUSS DURING THE DEBRIEF

Several things can be discussed during the debriefing: (1) what was potentially shared in consciousness, (2) the details of individual experience, and (3) evaluative ideas on what was learned and what could be improved for future sessions. Below are lists of questions by category to help focus your conversations.

1. What was shared?
   - What was shared through physical energetic flows?
   - What bodywork was done and where? What was the significance of the work?
   - What emotions were shared empathically?

- What was shared psychically in shared consciousness (e.g., biographical content, journeying to other worlds/dimensions, visions, memories, encounters with discarnate beings)?
- What stories arose related to memories (positive or negative) associated with the movement of physical and psychic energies?

2. What was each individual's experience?
   - What were the highlights?
   - What discoveries were made about the relationship between your thoughts, emotions, and behaviors?
   - What connections were made between physical symptoms and thought processes?
   - What intuitive or abstract impressions surfaced?
   - What was surfacing to be processed and released or discharged?
   - What story was behind your emotions (if any), or what did the feelings represent?
   - What was let go?
   - What is the relationship of your experience(s) to your ancestral, biographical, and present-day context?
   - What follow-up, if any, should there be to address (e.g., repair) the underlying history leading to the repression of the emotions surfacing during the session?
   - What epiphanies or insights arose regarding shifting lived patterns and habits to improve your relationship to your body, mind, emotions, spirit, the environment, or other people?
   - What challenged your existing values, beliefs, attitudes, or fears?

3. Evaluative questions
   - What worked well during the session?
   - What were the challenges?
   - How did this session compare to past sessions?
   - What lessons were learned?
   - What could be done better next time?

- Are there unresolved or outstanding personal or interpersonal material or breaches from the session? If so, what are the options to address it?

Discussion in the debriefing should aim to be neutral, safe, and confidential, encouraging full disclosure. The intent is to share what arose without judgment, with each person validating the other. Also, remember you do not have to make immediate decisions based on your insights.

FOLLOWING THE DEBRIEF

Another valuable tool for integrating psychedelic experiences following sessions is tracking dreams using a dream journal. The act of dream journaling stimulates the unconscious to enhance the memory of dreams over time, including overall recollection, which contributes to more meaningful integration. My dream world has expanded since using psychedelics. If you are not familiar with techniques for remembering your dreams, I recommend investigating YouTube presentations and books on lucid dreaming by Stephen LeBerge, Andrew Holecek, Robert Waggoner, and others. For a deeper understanding and analysis of dreams, I recommend books on dreaming by Carl Jung and Swami Sivananda Radha.

In the weeks following a session, add to your notes or artwork any further memories about your session. There is usually an overwhelming amount of material during the hours of a session that is not easily remembered or summarized the same day. By consciously working with the recall of your psychedelic journeys over time, your overall memory of individual sessions should improve.

Stay in touch with your co-melder over the following weeks to continue the debriefing process.

15
Integration of Psychedelic Experience and the Psychedelic Mindmeld

This book has discussed how working with psychedelics and the mindmeld can vastly open up a person's world to their unconscious, shared consciousness, the collective unconscious, connection to mythic and archetypal energies, the nondual, and more. But what do we do with these experiences? What do we do with the profound states and realizations of consciousness experienced with psychedelic use? The current wisdom is to somehow move toward integrating them into daily life. But what does integration even mean? How do we navigate it and accomplish it? And how do we know when we have completed our integration?

After many of my early psychedelic experiences, I became confused when trying to make sense of the strange realities I was entering. I had earlier spent years studying world religions, but nothing prepared me for the profundity of the states I entered. My mystical journeys did not fit into religious dogma, particularly that of the Western religions. Western culture is steeped in a materialist and Newtonian-Cartesian paradigm, which offered nothing. In fact, my culture is openly hostile to what I was experimenting with. I could end up in jail just for using psychedelics. If I were to share my psychedelic experiences with a psychiatrist, I would likely be diagnosed as delusional and put on mind-numbing pharmaceuticals. When I approached shamans in ceremonies, they offered little insight or wisdom, often coming from cultures where it was an accepted norm not to comment on other people's experiences. This practice is understandable for them as their societies have a supportive cultural context to help make meaning of such experiences. But I do not. So, how could I integrate the most bizarre of experiences? How could my ego come to terms with happenings beyond itself and its understanding? What I offer in this book, and this chapter in particular, comes from years of experience and searching cultivated by curiosity and my ego's grasping at wanting answers. I hope some of my insights, many of them gained from others, will contribute to your integration process, assuming integration is of interest to you.

Integration means bringing together into a unified and functioning whole. For Jung (2011b), "everything living strives for wholeness, the inevitable one-sidedness of our conscious life is continually being corrected and compensated by the universal human being in us, whose goal is the ultimate integration of conscious and unconscious, or better, the assimilation of the ego to a wider personality" (p. 78). The move toward wholeness is a move toward *individuation*. Jung (2011b) saw individuation as the ego participating in the integration of previously undeveloped aspects of oneself into a larger, comprehensive Self. This process includes harmoniously integrating our complex and shadowy opposite personalities into a more personally accepted cohesive multiplicity-in-unity. The psyche becomes more effectively organized with higher functional capacity. With greater harmony comes greater personal coherence, presence, and attunement where one can develop an intimate dialectical relationship with the competing components of the self—the taming and acceptance of one's inner monster. We also accept our brokenness. Integration is embodied when our inner experiences then positively shape our worldview, our relationship with ourselves, our behaviors, and by extension, our relationship to the world and those others in it.

To work with undeveloped aspects of oneself is to bring into the light unconscious patterns, such as pathologies or mental disorders (e.g., neuroses such as addictions, obsessive-compulsive or manic-depressive disorders, and excessive perfectionism) and bad habits. Such work creates the opportunity to redirect or overcome dysfunctional behaviors with the possibility of radical personality change. According to Judith (2004), individuation is about the "break away from internalized parents, peers, and culture . . . It is about daring to be unique, risking disapproval for the integrity of your own truth. Individuation is the unfolding of our unique destiny, the unfolding of the soul" (p. 175). The integration process can be healing, transformative, and even evolutionary; new and revolutionary insights can develop concerning the nature of consciousness, the human psyche in health and disease, and some of the most profound philosophical and metaphysical questions. Thus, integration is about working toward a slow shift in personal consciousness where there is an engagement with a process that gains traction over time to continually find increased meaning in one's life. Difficult personal experiences become less destabilizing. There is a movement away from internal and externally projected criticisms toward loving awareness and wholeness.

If integration is to move toward wholeness, broadening our conscious personality, how do psychedelic sessions potentially lead us in this direction? I suggest three parts to the answer: the first is physiological, the second is intellectual, and the third is mindfulness, where the latter two can inform how a person lives their life and therefore impact the first—their physiological well-being. The first part considers the physiological shift arising in the individual from the cathartic discharge of physical and psychic energetic blockages. As discussed already, energetic blockages are likely connected to the unconscious and the energetic signature of a conflicted and entangled ego refusing to accept reality, constantly seeking control where such control is impossible, as well as to physical and psychological trauma. In the days, weeks, and months following psychedelic sessions, integration means to bring awareness to the potential shifts in overall mood or an experience of a broader range of emotions. To notice these shifts is to continually bring awareness and mindfulness to the present of how one is feeling, observing the particular sensations at work in the body. Growing awareness is a journey of consciously engaging in the evolution of our relationship with our inner world. It is also to engage in the alchemy of transmuting, recalibrating, and taking full responsibility for our energy, which includes how we project our energy out into the world.

While high-dose psychedelic sessions can contribute to shifting a person's physiology, in and of themselves they are not enough to cause lasting long-term changes. Individual psychedelic sessions can make minor adjustments to improve one's physiology, and the impact is more substantial over time from multiple sessions. But what one does daily has a more pronounced effect on one's physiology. Obvious examples include diet, exercise, breathing, the quality of one's relationships, work and play, and spiritual practice. Each of these examples can be approached in healthy and dysfunctional ways. The last section of this chapter offers suggestions for a holistic approach to integration and healthy living.

The second consideration for integrating psychedelic sessions is more of an intellectual, cognitive, and educational exercise fueled by curiosity that can lead to greater wisdom and specific actioning in daily life. While one psychedelic session can profoundly impact a person, so can a dream. But it is through multiple sessions—or multiple dreams—that we can begin to look more meaningfully at patterns emerging in experience over time and try to make greater sense of integrated meaning from them. When the ego sees beyond its limited view of reality in psychedelic sessions, it can begin to move beyond its limitations of perspective. It can seek to become more informed about vaster realities, with the potential to influence and broaden its view and the ways that it can more functionally and healthily engage in the world.

In psychedelic sessions or dreams, we experience gnosis, often receiving insight or epiphanies. But what do we do with these insights? This is where the intellect serves. By engaging the mind in learning and using its capacities for imagination and creative thinking, we can begin to make meaning from psychedelic experiences. New maps of meaning can inform how we live our lives, including shaping, balancing, and generating a hierarchy of beliefs, values, attitudes, and motivational demands that, in turn, can impact an individual's goals, behaviors, and habits. There can be movement that takes experiences of profound states of consciousness toward personal development, inner wholeness, and greater embodiment. As old assumptions are undermined and experience reveals old values and beliefs as false pretenses, anxiety and depression can set in and lead to denial, degeneration, and despair. Still, these can be motivational emotions for redemption and personal revolution. This process demands reflection on each experience, and on multiple experiences over time, interpreting the meaning of each and looking for a story arc in all of them through the lenses of day-to-day life, the shadow, symbols, archetypes, and nonduality. Research exploring Eastern and Western wisdom traditions, philosophy, psychology, and other esoteric sources can contribute to making meaning. The resulting analysis and bigger story can then inform a more lasting and expanded personal outlook and transformation to shape daily living. To fail at this task is to risk missing out on personal development and maturation, possibly getting trapped in the unbearable weight of tragic self-consciousness, and struggling with intrapsychic and social pathology.

The last consideration for integration is mindfulness. Mindfulness means to bring attention to the present moment. The meditation techniques in this book all speak to mindfulness: bringing awareness to stillness and to bodily sensations along with the breath, calmly acknowledging and accepting one's thoughts and feelings through the witnessing technique, and similarly accepting those of your partner in the mindmeld. These tools can be used in all moments of life but require diligence and discipline. Many Eastern traditions, in particular, have focused on using mindfulness techniques. They bring with them the potential for greater peace, tranquility, equanimity, and joy. Over time, using these methods makes one feel more grounded and centered in life.

The following sections weave together and discuss the integrative themes of physiological health, integration through using the intellect and making meaning, and bringing mindfulness more consciously into our lives for personal growth and development.

MAKING MEANING: MAPPING THE EXPERIENCE

From the preceding chapters, we have an overview of the ego's functions. One function, in companionship with the intellect and memory, is to make meaning and find purpose. The ego wants to know what everything means. As the ego seeks to mediate our lived experience and protect us, it also wants to understand our experience and make meaning. This is critical for anticipating and projecting our future well-being. Here the ego can be our ally. Peterson (1999) goes further by saying:

> The human purpose, if such a thing can be considered, is to pursue meaning—to extend the domain of light, of consciousness—despite limitation. A meaningful event exists on the boundary between order and chaos. The pursuit of meaning exposes the individual to the unknown in gradual fashion, allowing him to develop strength and adaptive ability in proportion to the seriousness of his pursuit. It is during contact with the unknown that human power grows, individually and then historically. Meaning is the subjective experience associated with that contact, in sufficient proportion. The great religious myths state that continued pursuit of meaning, adopted voluntarily and without self-deception, will lead the individual to discover his identity with God. This "revealed identity" will make him capable of withstanding the tragedy of life. Abandonment of meaning, by contrast, reduces man to his mortal weaknesses (p. 468).

Diving into our underlying stories and narratives is fundamental to making meaning. While they can cause unnecessary suffering because they are often driven by egoic denial, attachments, fantasy, and delusion, they are our way forward. Stories can lead us in creatively thinking about the future and what we want to do with our lives. As Kolk (2015) explains: "Telling the story is important; without stories, memory becomes frozen; and without memory you cannot imagine how things can be different" (p. 219). Storytelling is thus crucial for integrating trauma into one's life and relating to others. Trauma can defragment memory, where sensations, images, and emotions become mixed and confusing. Working toward integration is to have a coherent story with a beginning, middle, and end, fully knowing that the past is the past and there is a transition into a safer present in the now. Integrating one's stories is to see past experiences differently and with more cohesion, possibly resulting in changes in belief and attitude. Finding meaning in our lives also improves measures of mental and physical health (Aftab et al., 2019).

So, what is a constructive way to integrate our experiences by making meaning of them? To start, slowing down and recounting and explaining one's experience helps to avoid reactive or knee-jerk reactions to experiences. There is a need to meditate on the experience—long and thoroughly enough that as it turns over and over in the mind, and sometimes even in dreams, something inevitably comes of it. Eventually, a "right" answer will surface in one's reflection and analysis: whatever makes the most meaning for the experiencer for the developmental stage they are at. The exercises in chapter 14 on debriefing are meant to help with this process.

Nevertheless, explanation alone is not enough. For Carl Jung (2017), it was not enough to have only a description of a cathartic event; to become educated about it to bring about lasting personal transformation was necessary (p. 35). As was suggested at the beginning of the chapter, it is necessary to work through an intellectual and educational exercise to find meaning in one's experiences. By increasing our knowledge, we can better relate to explored and unexplored territory with a more informed understanding of our motivations, fears, and courage. We have the potential to better comprehend the relative significance of the past, present, and future, seeing past our illusions. We can see more clearly that everything in life has something to teach us. We can increasingly draw satisfaction from ordinary things always available in life. Likewise, the absurdity of exaggerated ambitions and the need to prove something to oneself or others becomes more conspicuous. Education and contemplation can help us learn what is serving us and what is not. They show us healthy habits, how to change the habits not serving us, and how we can potentially shift our hierarchy of beliefs and values. Through discipline, new habits can eventually be won, replacing the old (p. 52).

Over time you will know you have found the correct meaning to your experiences because it is the one you integrate most fully, shifting your consciousness and leading to shifts in your worldview, attitude, and habits. Jung (2017) contends that if a mistake is made in the interpretation, the psyche inevitably rejects the error and self-corrects. He warns us to be careful about navigating interpretations with personal expectations based on conscious experience: as a rule, the unconscious is complementary or compensatory to consciousness, as a tool of the psyche to foster homeostasis, and usually, therefore, the underlying meaning is unexpectedly different than expected. In this respect, the looser we hold our stories, the more open we are to possibilities. Campbell (2008) points out that we need to keep the interpretations of our stories and symbols translucent so that they may not block out the very light they are supposed to convey. The essence of luminosity is emphasized in the Kena Upanisad: "To know is not to know; not to know is to know" (in Campbell, 2008, p. 202). In doing so, we accept that the mind is an unreliable narrator: the only truth in life is in the moment lived as now, not as recounted by faulty memory.

Viktor Frankl (2006), a Holocaust survivor who was inspired to find meaning in his life based on the profound suffering he experienced and witnessed in the Nazi death camps, saw three possible sources of meaning: in taking responsible action in work or doing something significant; in love and caring for others; and in courage toward one's choice of attitude in difficult times. He saw suffering as meaningless, but suffering is given meaning by how we respond to it. Often when people discuss meaning in their lives, it relates to these themes, particularly their loving relationship with others. Thomas Merton (2011) writes of the transpersonal nature of love and the meaning to be found in it. When I read the following passage by Merton, I couldn't help but be struck by how much it captured the essence of the mindmeld from its onset to its conclusion:

> Love is, in fact an intensification of life, a completeness, a fullness, a wholeness of life . . . . Life curves upward to a peak of intensity, a high point of value and meaning, at which all its latent creative possibility go into action and the person transcends himself or herself in encounter, response, and communion with another. It is for this that we came into the world—this communion and self-transcendence. We do not become fully human until we give ourselves to each other in love (p. 23).

As we try to make sense of our experiences, we must realize they are fractal by nature and consequently infinite. There is no endpoint. Yet, the ego is addicted to trying to make meaning of what has no limits. We can humor ourselves in the game of making meaning and can use it to improve our ways of being and relating to the world, but there is simultaneously a need to recognize there are limits to human knowledge.

This point was stressed to me during an ayahuasca journey where I ventured to the edge of the expanding universe. There I met two Buddhist figures who I was not familiar with. We debated the meaning of life. For them, life ultimately had no meaning. This realization culminated in overwhelming laughter among all three of us at this cosmic joke, and I found myself laughing in the face of accepting the great mystery.

Indeed, at a certain point, we all reach the human limits of knowledge and are forced to recognize there is no ultimate knowing of the tremendous ineffable mystery. I have had many psychedelic journeys into other dimensions, other worlds, and indescribable places; yet, my mind, used to experiencing a three-dimensional world, cannot fully remember, never mind label and understand, many of these experiences. I have been forced to accept my evolution is about fighting my way forward, floundering my way forward, failing my way forward, and befriending my way through the mystery.

When we fall into pretense and reach the conclusion that, at last, we have understood, life has a way of continually shocking and insulting any assurance. Such is the nature of universal reality: a constantly fluid state of infinite transformation, change, and evolution. The truth of the absolute mystery is lost when we seek to defend our favorite or traditional beliefs, failing to accept our limitations, with our limited senses capable only of experiencing the shadows of the unfathomable, infinite, and ultimate reality. There is nothing to hold on to in the sea of boundless moving energy. To live in the mystery is to embrace ambiguity—being comfortable in uncertainty and not knowing what lies ahead. Here, the knowledge that we cannot always know why things happen is an answer.

THE PSYCHEDELIC EXPERIENCE AS ANOTHER LAYER OF THE DREAMSCAPE

The nature of the psychedelic experience can be compared to the dreamscape. Views of the dreamscape can inform, make meaning, broaden the mystery, and integrate our psychedelic experiences.

Buddhists consider dreaming a vehicle for exploring *reality* by providing insight into the subjective nature of all lived experiences. The premise is that we are always dreaming. When we are awake, we are daydreaming; rarely are we grounded in the present moment, which would require us to be fully embodied and lucid in the present moment.

Instead, we are generally preoccupied with ruminating on the past or projecting our thoughts to the future. By lucidly observing dreams when fully aware of the dream state, it is possible to better understand the malleability of all of one's experience, including the daydream. With more awareness comes the realization that everything in lived experience is a dream: fleeting and impermanent (Holecek, 2016; LaBerge, 2009).

The dreamscape is illusory. This is not to say the dreamscape of lived life and dreamed life does not exist, but it is relative and is made up of appearances skating on the thin ice of a constructed reality, referred to as *samsara* by Hindus and Buddhists. The ego's construct of character is like a dream because it is fluid and has no permanence. The appearance of daily lived reality, filtered through the limitations of the physical senses and the conditioned ego, is in many ways delusional. It is delusional insofar as the ego, in the vanity of believing it is in control, tries to grasp at attachment as though there is something permanent to become attached to. Rigid self-identities and beliefs lose traction with such insight, giving rise to a more flexible mindset where problems begin to lose potency.

To Buddhists, reality is the truth that everything is impermanent and empty of inherent unchanging suchness. Humans, as individual beings, are only an aggregate of physical and psychic energies in a constant flux influenced by the law of cause and effect. We are the mystery in form. We have no permanence—like everything else in the dream of the material universe. The only Big Truth is found in the absoluteness of Big Mind, the fourth tier of nonduality. With this view, we can see our psychedelic journeys and lived experiences as more of an ongoing flow of consciousness through the dreamscape.

The notion of the dreamscape creates an interesting perspective when considering superconsciousness and the various discarnate beings encountered there. Most Buddhists make the distinction that spirits and deities, for example, arise within your field of consciousness but are not ontologically separate beings. They are, in essence, dream characters in a multilayered, multidimensional dream where again, everything is the Big Mind. The living dream is similar to the idea that everything arising in duality is the Divine Imagination of God, or Divine nondual awareness, experiencing itself as flowing through everything. As such, everything manifesting in the universe where there is any sense of subject and object, both externally to us as humans, and internally to us, is but a play of impermanent characters in an impermanent universe of multiple and relative layers or dimensions of reality—part of the absolute all of universal oneness, but not all of universal oneness. Universal oneness is the only ultimately true reality because of its absolute permanence: it is unborn, undying, unchanging, ordinary, actionless, self-revealing, ever-present, everlasting, and limitless. So we, as organic, living, conscious, energetic beings, are but a relative part of reality, just as "real" as a dream we may have and equally illusory because of our impermanence.

On the surface, we can say, "Who cares?" But what lies underneath is the realization that it is the ego's delusional grasping at a sense of permanence, particularly through anything falsely and temporarily creating a sense of completeness or satisfaction, that causes so much human suffering. For Buddhists, the only way to cease suffering is to recognize impermanence and let go of desire and the desiring self. In this way, emotions of sorrow, grief, joy, and happiness can come and go without attachment. Presumably, this avoids the neuroses of getting "stuck" in any particular state of consciousness longer than demanded by the energetic forces causing it in the first place. In this state, the ego is more consciously relegated to a subservient function of acting in equanimity and being more consciously present in each "now" moment. With the ego's function duly regulated and relegated, it does not have the same energy to create energetic blockages in the body, as described earlier. Energy is then allowed to move more freely and naturally in the body, making it easier for the body and mind to be in an ongoing and healthy state of homeostasis—presumably with less suffering. From this place happiness lies in the acceptance of all of life, inclusive of both positively and negatively felt emotions rising and falling away in time.

We can find meaning in dreams and our psychedelic journeys to inform our lives. In the same way, dreams give expression to ineluctable truths, philosophical pronouncements, illusions, wild fantasies, nightmares, memories, plans and guidance, anticipations and warnings, irrational experiences, cycles of birth and death, past lives, and prophetic visions. So too do psychedelic experiences. Both can also offer confirmation and direction. From this perspective, we can interpret the psychedelic experience similarly to dream analysis. My intention here is not to provide details on how to interpret or analyze individual experiences but to offer some general guidelines on how to begin to approach the reflection and interpretation of psychedelic experiences with shared wisdom from those who have studied and worked with dreams.

For starters, Carl Jung (2017), preeminent psychologist and dream analyst, has pointed out it is imperative not to pare down the meaning of a dream to fit some narrow doctrine (p. 13). Every interpretation is hypothetical, as it is rare to interpret dreams with certainty (p. 16). It also helps to work with multiple experiences to begin to put the puzzle together of what is arising from the unconscious, as opposed to just one or two events or stories.

Context matters. As such, experiences need to be mapped onto your overall biography, including what is happening in your daily life (Jung, 2017, p. 22). Triangulating psychedelic experiences with your dreams is an even more powerful way to learn the hidden secrets of the inner self, revealing a fuller understanding of one's unconscious and personality.

Jung (2017) believed that as long as hidden personality factors remained undiscovered, they could disturb a person's waking life and betray themselves in symptoms such as neuroses. Such symptoms can be addressed by thoroughly assimilating the unconscious contents, which may be repressed, neglected, or unknown (p. 18). Assimilation does not simply mean a one-sided valuation and interpretation of the unconscious contents by the conscious mind but ends the dissociation of the personality attending and inspiring the separation of the two realms of the psyche (p. 20).

As discussed earlier, for Jung (2017), the psyche is a self-regulating system seeking to maintain itself in equilibrium as the body does. For our purposes, Jung's reference to the psyche is the equivalent of a force seeking to balance the interests of the ego and the unconscious. The ego is in a proverbial wrestling match with the unconscious for control. And while the unconscious, as a part of the psyche, is perfectly neutral as far as moral sense and intellectual judgment go, it is an active player in the wrestling match for setting the direction of activity (p. 19).

When the ego moves the conscious too far away from the unconscious, there is an inevitable call for compensatory activity. Without such adjustments, a normal metabolism would not exist, nor would the normal psyche (p. 20). When the psyche is in a state of high disequilibrium, the symptoms arising for the person become increasingly pronounced. At its most basic level, emotions may become overly depressive and anxious or, on the opposite end, excessively happy and blissful. Psychedelic journeys may evoke the same emotional states, or they may produce similar extremes with fear where demons may manifest or, on the other end, bliss where angels may arrive, or there may be a direct connection to divine oneness.

Jung's (2017) starting point for interpreting a dream or, in our case, a psychedelic trip, is to ask the question: What conscious attitude is the dream, or psychedelic trip, trying to bring into awareness that is being compensated for to the detriment of the equilibrium of the psyche? (p. 21). The movement toward assimilating the disowned parts of the self, hidden in the unconscious, is toward what he describes as "the whole human being—that is, individuation" (p. 31). This exercise alone moves toward integrating one's psychedelic experiences into one's personality.

Dreams and psychedelic trips can evoke any number of symbols, archetypes, and mythical motifs for interpretation. Symbols and archetypes are human-lived abstractions of primordial patterns, concepts, and governing principles that we cannot adequately define or fully comprehend. Paradoxically they also have a life of their own as living entities functioning as universal templates, residing in the collective unconscious, which continuously give birth to the material universe and all lived conscious experiences. What matters most here is how people connect their experiences to symbols and archetypes. This exercise can bring to the surface realizations and revelations, relating not only to a person's psychedelic experiences but also to their life and others around them. Plumbing the depths of symbols and archetypes can invoke stronger intuition, increasing our ability to feel something with greater resonance and understand it immediately in gnosis without the need for conscious reasoning. Patterns in life events and dreams may take on more meaning.

By working with interpretations of the psychedelic experience, we can begin to play with the contents of the unconscious. By bringing the hidden contents into the light, we can give birth to insight to move in a new direction in life. It is interesting to note that Jung (2017) observed about a third of his patients suffered from no clinically definable neurosis but from the senselessness and emptiness of their lives. By having patients work to remember their dreams and then collaborating with them to analyze them, he found that it was possible for the patient to discover personal insight leading to meaningful shifts. Such shifts are also possible with psychedelic experiences.

Such a shift was true for me. I was in my midthirties when I had my first profound psychedelic trip. I was well educated, had been in senior management roles since I turned thirty, and enjoyed traveling around the world and adventuring, but I was finding life had a dullness. One profound psychedelic experience opened me to another way of experiencing and relating to myself and the universe. I found a spiritual side of me lying dormant. While I was thrown into the proverbial chaos of not understanding what had happened to me in my first psychedelic journeys, they opened up a lifetime of exploration of my inner consciousness: a new frontier.

Radha (2013) offers another consideration for dream analysis. She points out it is vital to look at the condition of one's mind when working with dreams. The mind's state is responsible for how the dream is presented, and refinement of the mind determines how dreams are interpreted. I take refinement to include not only the mind's capacity to think conceptually, identify patterns, and interpret events and its ability to connect to intuition, but also having a broad base of education in symbols, archetypes, motifs, and myth. In this respect, turning to an expert in dream analysis or symbology or studying these fields yourself can be helpful. Radha (2013) also states, "Your mental-emotional state decides what you will do [with the dream] and how you will do it" (p. 151). The same is true for the psychedelic experience.

Campbell (2008) provides additional insight into how we, as finite beings immersed in and tuned to the conditions of space-time, can return and work toward integrating our fleeting absorption into the dream worlds and psychedelic experiences of superconsciousness and the expanse of the infinite. Integration is found in the "Freedom to pass back and forth across the world division, from the perspective of the apparitions of time to that of the causal deep and back—not contaminating the principles of the one with those of the other, yet permitting the mind to know the one by virtue of the other—is the talent of the master" (p. 196). Campbell is telling us living with ambiguity and abiding in the mystery is the talent of the master. There is a need not to construct definitive frames of reference but to consider provisional and relative ones. From this point of view, we can independently see each of the perspectives of the corporeal (e.g., one's physical self, living in the material universe), the psychological, the archetypal (inclusive of symbols, patterns, synchronicity, and myth), the soul, the nondual, the totality of dual and nondual, and the mystery.

How we live our lives depends on which perspective we most often tune in to to make meaning of our experiences and influence our day-to-day decision-making and behaviors. Integration speaks to how well we relate to, honor, and seamlessly move among these different ways of considering our lives. Multiple perspectives give us greater cognitive flexibility to see connections between this *and* that as opposed to this *or* that. In the long run, this can expand our idea or construct of ourselves, broaden our inclusivity of beliefs, rewrite our personal narrative, and tend toward a more flexible and resilient cognitive fluidity in the face of ongoing circumstantial change. The journey itself is truth; there is no final destination in an infinite universe of endless expansive and evolving potential and realization. We are continually transformed by the way we experience and relate to our quest.

To offer further perspective on how one can view psychedelic journeys, and life more generally, I now turn to Ken Wilber's concepts of growing up, waking up, cleaning up, and showing up.

INTEGRAL THEORY: GROWING UP, WAKING UP, CLEANING UP, AND SHOWING UP

Ken Wilber, a metatheorist, is famous for developing integral theory. Integral theory is a useful tool for us because it can help us interpret and integrate our psychedelic experiences into our current state of being. To keep this brief, I provide only a summary of the concepts of Growing Up, Waking Up, Cleaning Up, and Showing Up, which are fundamental aspects of integral theory. Although Wilber (2017) does not discuss psychedelics in his book *The Religion of Tomorrow*, I recommend reading it if my summary resonates with you; it is a tome, but it can serve as the psychonaut's guide to exploring states of consciousness, including detailed descriptions of the stages of Growing Up and Waking Up.

Based on consolidating wisdom from the Eastern and Western traditions and academic inquiry, inclusive of empirical science and the social sciences, Wilber (2017) has identified four key elements in our individual experience, reflecting and demonstrating human growth and development:

- *Growing Up:* all lines of personal development—the stages of moving, growing, and developing through increasingly adequate interpretative frameworks, which determine the different ways we can experience states of consciousness.

- *Waking Up:* all possible conscious states—stages of direct, immediate first-person internal meditative experiences, or states of consciousness that at the highest order are nondual.
- *Cleaning Up:* how a person addresses repressed, unconscious shadow material that, as described earlier, can be projected onto others. Where a person is at in terms of Cleaning Up will affect how they experience daily living (and psychedelics), including how they relate to Growing Up and Waking Up, and directly how they Show Up.
- *Showing Up:* levels of functional behavior, including how a person relates to and interacts with others. Showing Up is related to emotional literacy and social maturity. How a person Shows Up is influenced by the other three elements but also by who they are at a more archetypal level as types (such as masculine and feminine expressions, cultural impressions, and personality types, such as those described by the Enneagram or Myers-Briggs).

Because I have already provided the broad strokes of Waking Up as the various possible states of consciousness described throughout this book, I will not summarize this aspect of Wilber's work here. Instead, I briefly introduce what Growing Up looks like and its relationship to Cleaning Up and Showing Up.

Growing Up occurs in stages. Using insights from Abraham Maslow, Clare Graves, Jane Loevinger, Jean Gebser, Jean Piaget, and others, Wilber (2017) identifies eight main stages in Growing Up:

1. *Archaic Worldview.* The original fusion state. In a child's first year or so, basic sensorimotor drives and physiological needs come online. Survival instincts dominate.
2. *Magic Worldview.* Superstitious beliefs govern this stage. Children ages one to four, for example, will put their heads under a pillow and, because they can't see anybody, think magically that nobody can see them. Or one might magically think one is absolutely not

vulnerable to diseases like COVID-19. It is the world of magical powers, sacrifices (e.g., animal and human), and miracles. At a societal level, people are organized loosely into small groups with little structure and minimal organization.

3. *Power Worldview.* Once the self has fully differentiated itself from its environment, it feels vulnerable. It becomes concerned with its safety and security and, in defense, develops a robust set of power drives. This stage is dominated by egocentricity. It may also be accompanied by beliefs in superpowerful beings who can provide safety and security if approached correctly with prayer, ritual, or other superstitiously enticing actions. This power stage governed humanity's first major agricultural-military empires. Leaders were considered literally to be gods.

4. *Mythic Worldview.* A more conformist, group-oriented stage where people seek belongingness but still believe in supernatural beings. Mythic-religious books are the literal truth of a Supreme Being— the Bible, the Koran, the Pentateuch, and some Pure Land sutras. Myths are taken to be fundamentally true; Moses really did part the Red Sea, for example. The mythic is largely the basis of fundamentalist traditional religious beliefs. Rules dominate, giving life a clear, absolute meaning, direction, and purpose. Everyone has their proper place in society, driven by laws and commandments. Polarized ethnocentric perspectives prevail: believer versus infidel; saint or sinner; you are with us or against us.

5. *Rational Worldview.* Universal systems and principles apply to all humans, such as ideals of equality, liberty, and justice for all. Universality is a worldcentric view. Reason, science, and empiricism are revered as truth. Societal ideals are based on progress, success, independence, achievement, status, and affluence. A competitive marketplace of ideas and opportunities is organized and defended.

6. *Pluralistic Worldview.* Pluralism and egalitarianism predominate. Divinity is seen in all beings; all paths are equal. Diversity is cel-

ebrated, giving voice to the marginalized and underrepresented. Emphasis is on community and consensus decision-making.

7. *Integral Worldview.* This view recognizes that all previous worldviews offer something of truth, identifying how the others tend to de-emphasize or marginalize other views. There is a realization some views are *more* true and less partial than others. Worldviews are seen together as a nested hierarchy of developmental depth and increasing complexity, all of which demand care and respect. *Deficiency* needs are replaced by *being* needs: needs arise from fullness and not from lack.

8. *Superintegral Worldview.* This view is transpersonal, where personal self-awareness extends beyond the individual. The relationship with phenomena is highly intuitive, flexible, and flowing. Existence is seen as a radically interconnected fabric, an ecology of light, life, mind, matter, energy, time, and space. There is a felt sense of oneness. Systemic and transpersonal wholes are self-evident, including ecological, political, and cultural wholes. There is a complete acceptance of the natural flows in the Cosmos of birth, growth, aging, death, joy, and suffering. This view is Cosmocentric.

In the descriptions above, we see the spectrum of the stages of Growing Up. These stages are holarchical in nature, meaning all lower stages are in the higher but not all higher ones are in the lower. As such, the higher the stage a person is at in Growing Up, the greater the breadth and depth in their lived reality of viewing and experiencing the world.

Using a Buddhist notion of enlightenment, which is the union of emptiness (pure unqualifiable ultimate nondual reality) and all form (the actual manifest world in its entirety), Wilber (2017) distinguishes the relationship between Growing Up and Waking Up:

Emptiness is not affected by whatever stage of Growing Up you might be at, but how you experience Form is directly related to the stage of Growing Up that you are at. . . . Emptiness, being beyond manifestation per se, doesn't grow and evolve—it has no moving parts—but remains rather the timeless Thusness, or Suchness, of what is; but the world of Form is exactly what does grow and evolve and change. Therefore, the *union* of Emptiness and Form will likewise change from stage to stage. In other words, the very core of the Enlightenment [Waking Up] experience itself will differ considerably from stage to stage (p. 9).

Another point to distinguish between Growing Up and Waking Up is that it is not enough to believe states of consciousness embodying ultimate truth are possible. Authentic spiritual experiences are a more powerful activator in lived realization than theory or faith in Waking Up. Here the intellect synthesizes insights of the past with the mystical experience. Thus, Waking Up can contribute to Growing Up.

Each stage of Growing Up presents a different way of categorizing, presenting, representing, organizing, and therefore experiencing Waking Up, inclusive of psychedelic experiences. As described earlier, stages of Waking Up are not necessarily linear in the way stages of Growing Up are, but how they are experienced and interpreted is influenced by the stage of one's worldview or where a person is at in Growing Up. Thus, the stage a person is at in Growing Up will influence how they orient themselves and make meaning of their Waking Up experiences.

For our purpose of relating, interpreting, and making meaning of the states of consciousness experienced using psychedelics, inclusive of those arising in the mindmeld, the framework of Growing Up, Waking Up, Cleaning Up, and Showing Up is practical. To illustrate, if a person has a nondual experience (Waking Up) but is at a low stage of development (Growing Up), they may self-identify as a prophet with a special mission. A close encounter with an iconic figure like Jesus Christ may make them believe they are the reincarnation of Christ, who is meant to save all humans from their sins. On the other hand, a high stage of development would lead to the realization that all people can reach nondual states, the Divine flows through all things and all people, and we can all touch the archetypal experience of the Cosmic Christ. In this regard, no one person is uniquely special, yet all people and all creation are integrally essential.

Another example would be a guru with many followers who has had many profound conscious realizations (Waking Up) with a high degree of embodying these states. Yet, he sexually abuses his followers and steals money from the organization for selfish gain, demonstrating a failure to Clean Up or, that is, to fully understand the insights of the Waking Up experience in the context of Growing Up and deal with his shadow material, which impacts how he Shows Up.

Growing Up is then to work with the relative truths, relative realities, and relative solutions of lived experience, all residing within one ultimate truth. Through the processes of Growing Up, Waking Up, and Cleaning Up, the world as we experience it changes: our interpretations, thoughts, feelings, motivations, desires, viewpoints, behavior, capacities, and, ultimately, intentions evolve and expand—affecting indeed our very human identity and all influencing how we Show Up. The integral view is these realizations and changes themselves are part of the evolution and expansion of consciousness itself (Wilber, 2017).

INTEGRATION INTO LIVED LIFE:
A HOLISTIC APPROACH

How do we more specifically approach integrating psychedelic sessions? If integration is meant to lead to wholeness, coherence, attunement, homeostasis, individuation, and awareness of the Self, how do we know we are moving toward this state? What are the signposts? This section describes markers we can look for on the path of integration.

One key signpost for integration is *presence*. Welwood (1997) describes how there needs to be an inner reconciliation to have a conscious relationship with oneself and others. Internal reconciliation comes from the inner presence that grows due to inner inquiry, acknowledgment, allowing, understanding, and opening. It is an exercise in taming the inner critic, stepping away from value judgments, and opening to our trauma. Here we acknowledge and make peace with our own suffering and that in the world. We need to "stop rejecting our experience and make peace with whatever we have made Other inside ourselves" (p. 74). We take responsibility for ourselves and our experience, stepping away from blame and attachment to outcomes. Sollarova and Sollár (2010) describe how integration can be recognized when there is a low discrepancy between the present self and the desired self, which can be seen in higher self-esteem, more proactive coping, less neuroticism, and signs of greater self-love and authenticity.

Derek Scott (n.d.) goes further by saying being connected and integrated to the "Self" in day-to-day life is a connection to a felt sense or energy fostering greater harmony. Embodiment is apparent when there is a noticeable difference in how the body feels: it feels bigger than usual, as though one's energy field has grown, and has a sense of internal flow and fluidity with a gentle vibration. Similar to Schwartz and Sweezy's Internal Family System's list (2020) described earlier, connection to the Self is characterized by certain qualities: authenticity, compassion, clarity, calmness, curiosity, courage, connectedness, motivation and creativity, confidence, harmony, and healing. Judith (2004) has a similar perspective on wholeness and adds qualities like sound health; good social skills (e.g., being a good listener, perceptiveness); being caring, intuitive, imaginative, responsible, reliable, honest and trustworthy, intimate, and empathetic; seeing emotions as allies; and connecting to devotion, self-love, and loving immanence and transcendence (p. 444). Humor is also more easily accessed, even in the face of challenge. Alexander Laszlo (2016, p. 238) provides the following list describing characteristics of attunement, which themselves are signposts of integration:

1. *Passion:* vibrant, intense, and compelling enthusiasm
2. *Integrity:* dignity or elevation of character; worthiness, honor, and respect

3. *Grace:* simple elegance, considerateness, and a composed way of being

4. *Control:* personal mastery in (not of) the situations in which you find yourself

5. *Flow:* tuning your actions and attitudes to harmonize with your surroundings

Profound realizations can surface when working with psychedelics and in the mindmeld where experience interpenetrates insight. Almaas (2014) highlights the following characteristics of abiding in the qualities of realization in daily life connecting to the: "curiosity and the love, the openness and the steadfastness, the enjoyment of reality, the appreciation of authenticity, the delight and the clarity, the happiness in stillness" (p. 19).

The attributes listed above all share a description of psychological maturity and a healthy and functional ego where there is a movement away from negative attitudes, habits, and addictions. Authenticity steps forward where the relationship to self is based on who you actually are versus who you think you *should* be. We find ourselves being more flexible and resilient. There is a fuller, more reverent appreciation for everything arising in the universe. There is recognition that the profane—lived reality and being—is the Divine, the miracle of creation. There is a deeper mindfulness in one's connection to the moment-to-moment of lived *now* experience. Concurrently there is greater interconnectedness leading to healthier and more intimate relationships with oneself and the community. This maturity often leads to enhanced service to the community.

But integration can be challenging. Jung (2017) describes how many of his patients would rationally and intellectually grasp a more profound truth of how they should live their lives but would fail to realize such truths in their lived lives. Here we can find ourselves struggling more, as now we know things can be better, but we are disappointed in how thick the walls of conditioning are and how difficult it is to work through daily challenges and shift persistent bad habits. Jung postulated it is because of the dominant function of the ego at the center of our lives and its bias toward overvaluing its consciousness as the most significant barrier to this shift (p. 81). At the same time, wholeness in the absolute can never be achieved: we cannot be everything at once as we develop certain qualities at the expense of others (p. 106). This dynamic can often leave us struggling in existential angst, constantly searching for wholeness.

When approaching integration in day-to-day living, we can learn from the meditation techniques already outlined for inducing the mindmeld. For example, by stepping into surrender in the experience of daily living, we can unlock a broader sense of emotional depth, expanding a discernment of self and worldview, all of which can lead to greater integration of all aspects of ourselves. From here we see most things in life are beyond our control, and the more we grasp at trying to control outcomes, the more suffering we induce within ourselves. As we stop resisting emotional intensity and simply surrender to it and let it play through us freely, it takes the negative pressure of conditioned resistance off the conscious mind. In reflecting on the flow of these emotional releases, we can gain functional insight to provide us with a greater sense of who we really are and help to generate a consciousness founded on a more dynamic experience of our whole being throughout everyday life, cultivating a more holistic self-awareness (Jesso, 2013).

Integration can lead to stepping outside our conditioned beliefs and the values inherited from parental upbringing, culture, and society. We see more clearly societal constructs and priorities and how they shift over time—there is no permanence in them. Religions, dogmas, ideologies, philosophies, nation-states, money, and the value of excessive material wealth are all social constructs swinging back and forth on the continuum of polarity in duality. We can then step into our own volition, look to our hearts, and actively work toward diminishing the inner critic implanted by external conditioning (Walker, 2013).

When connecting more to the heart, however, we see how wounded it can be. How do we heal our hearts? In his work *Six Pillars of Self-Esteem*, Nathaniel Branden (1994) suggests the wounded heart learns self-love by first overcoming low self-esteem. There are several dimensions of self-esteem to be worked on: the practices of self-acceptance, self-responsibility, self-assertiveness, personal integrity, and living consciously and purposefully. These practices are enhanced by being present. While the ego can be relegated and transcended using psychedelics, when we return to daily life, we can see more clearly that there is a need to be more present, with attention, honesty, and integrity, if we want greater peace and love in our lives. To stay present in the face of life dramas, illusions, and fantasies requires mindfully and lovingly monitoring one's energy in the body, including constantly bringing witnessing attention to sensations of movement, breath, heartbeat, and emotional awareness. As we bring more attention to the flow of the body, feeling, and emotion, we begin to release the grip of the monkey mind. Mindful awareness alchemically creates the solvent to dissolve and metabolize stuck energy and unwanted emotions. As our nervous system relaxes, we are less likely to overreact and instead more mindfully respond to what presents itself from moment to moment. In this state of mindfulness, we connect more deeply to our divine nature.

In daily living, we then find ourselves more often connecting to our fundamental identity as divine. Ball (2022) argues the whole process of integration is about learning to embody one's individual relationship to oneself as the Divine (p. 223). In this context, our bodies are divine temples providing us access to the sanctity of the inner shrine. Here is where we can find the kingdom of heaven. Heaven on earth is a state of mind. From the nondual perspective, we can see everything manifesting around us is also us. We are interconnected to everything and fundamentally we interpenetrate everything. With this perspective, we can seek to act more authentically from the heart center, relaxing the inner critic. The thought of relating to life through the scope of the bodhisattva is no longer such a stretch. And we can cultivate this awareness in stillness and the breath.

As we see our divine nature more clearly, we are compelled to consider new ways of living and acting. Parker Palmer writes in *The Active Life: Wisdom for Work, Creativity, and Caring*:

> To be fully alive is to act. . . . I understand action to be any way that we can co-create reality with other beings and the Spirit. . . . Action, like a sacrament, is the visible form of an invisible spirit, an outward manifestation of an inward power. But as we act, we not only express what is in us and help give shape to the world; we also receive what is outside us, and reshape our inner selves (in hooks, 2018, p. 76).

In Palmer's words, we see the importance of uniting our inner world with our expression of self into the outer world through action. This action requires conscious practice because how we live our lives matters. We then dive deeper into our lifestyle choices of habits, connections, and responsibilities and can actively move ourselves toward greater harmony and homeostasis.

Here we must confront and work through the challenge of existential dissatisfaction. We need to acknowledge we can never be ultimately and long-lastingly satisfied. We must face our neediness and our penchant for addiction. Life is often burdensome, filled with tensions, and we easily succumb to desperation and being overwhelmed. When the inner world feels intolerable, we will do just about anything to feel calmer and more in control. Most people seek to dull or numb their unwanted sensory experiences through drugs (including prescription drugs) or alcohol. The flip side of numbing is seeking sensation: cutting yourself to make the numbing go away, high-risk adventure sports, prostitution, or gambling (Kolk, 2015).

Addiction undermines close human connectedness. Addiction is a narcissistic pursuit, even as it emanates from deep trauma. People in addiction are faced with an insatiable desire: they want release from their pain, from a sense of being abnormal, unworthy, deficient, and dislocated. Substances offer escape from unendurable inner turmoil, self-loathing, doubt, loss of meaning, isolation, hopelessness. Transcendence is sought through false and self-destructive means. In their search people struggling with addiction are not thinking about close connection to others; they are transfixed by their trauma and finding relief from it. As the addicted is consumed by the unquenchable thirst for satisfaction through the "fix" of excessive work, exercise, video games, social media, alcohol, drugs, sex, gambling, shopping, power, and so on, relationships of intimacy and closeness are sacrificed. This occurs not only in relationships with others but also blinds the addicted to the loving intimacy waiting in oneself in meditative forms of activity (Maté, 2008; Maté & Maté, 2022).

Addiction is tricky. We all face addiction at various levels and different points in our lives. The monkey mind in all humans is addicted to distractions—of any kind. The human is caught in an endless search for pleasure and satisfaction, a craving never fulfilled in a lasting way. But strangely, in the unconscious search to connect to the Divine, spurred on by our suffering, we can develop and grow.

We can bring consciousness and awareness to our path of development and growth. Wilber et al. (2008), in their book, *Integral Life Practice*, provide us with a map of developmental lines of growth—lines of intelligence—to explore, chart, and expand into:

- Cognition: What am I aware of?
- Needs: What do I need?
- Self-Identity: Who am I?
- Values: What is important to me?
- Emotional Intelligence: How do I feel about this?
- Aesthetics: What is beautiful or attractive to me?
- Moral Development: What is the right thing to do?
- Interpersonal Development:How should we interact?
- Kinesthetic Ability: How should I physically do this?

- Spirituality: What is of ultimate concern?
- To this list, I add Eco-Intelligence: How should I interact with Nature, the ecosystem?
- and Mystical Intelligence: How should I interact with consciousness and the cosmos?

Each of these developmental lines provides a guide to various aspects of ourselves we can bring into the light of our awareness. With introspection, learning, and active pursuit of finding and exploring different developmental practices, we can grow and expand in new and more conscious ways.

All of the listed lines of development can help us in our quest for integration, balance, coherence, and homeostasis. They can direct us toward optimal physical health, mental health, and emotional stability; social connection and humanitarianism; connection to Nature; spiritual connection; meaningfulness; and our creativity of choice and action. Slowly, we watch as our values, beliefs, and attitudes change and evolve. There can be a concomitant expansion into further spiritual exploration and practice, mysticism, and philosophy. As all of these factors come together, we find ourselves flourishing in living our lives.

There is a comprehensive range of purposeful, healthy, and developmental practices we can engage in beyond the meditative techniques described in this book. The list of possible methods is well beyond the limits of this volume. But Wilber et al.'s book, *Integral Life Practice* (2008), is a practical place to start. The authors researched the best practices for personal growth from around the world and from both Eastern and Western traditions, inclusive of modern scientific insight. They even considered personality types (i.e., through the lens of the Enneagram and Myers-Briggs personality types) and considerations to optimize choices in resonance for each type of individual. In books like these, readers are encouraged to find what resonates and go from there. Using insights from psychedelic sessions and tools found in books like these can contribute to a good jumping-off point for self-correcting and enhancing one's life path to move toward individuation and homeostasis more effectively and efficiently.

As one moves toward individuation and homeostasis, one can find oneself more connected to *synchronicity*—the perfect synchronous flow of the universe. The awareness of synchronicity is another signpost in integration. Synchronicity is the experience of realizing a series of coincidences so deeply meaningful and personally significant they defy simple coincidence (Jesso, 2013). For Jung (2011a), synchronicity is a "simultaneous occurrence of a certain psychic state with one or more external events which appear as meaningful parallels to the momentary subjective state—and, in certain cases, vice versa" (p. 25). Jung observed how many synchronistic events were connected to archetypes in pattern and meaning and, therefore, could be connected to the collective unconscious (p. 65). He also observed how there appeared to be a capability by ESP (extrasensory perception) to tune in to future events by following synchronistic and symbolic psychic images in the present as though the objective event already existed. By monitoring the premonitions of others, time and space appeared to Jung to be reduced to almost zero (p. 29).

Synchronous events can lead us toward personal growth and integration of internal psychic states and experience, provided we are ready to let go of egoic abstractions of what "I" want and instead allow ourselves to float down the river of life more seamlessly. Synchronicity can evoke interest, curiosity, expectation, hope, and fear in connection with archetypes in the collective unconscious beyond the self (Jung, 2011a, p. 65). From this place, transcendental meaning can be made of events.

This chapter has shown us that integration is an evolutionary process caught in space-time, full of bumps and side roads. Personal growth and awakening are not linear but play out in incremental, iterative, and often cyclical ways. These processes are in flux, unpredictable, and influenced by intrinsic and extraneous factors. There is no perfection in it, nor an absolute end point. It is endless realization, healing, and transformation, with an aura of enchantment and mystery. Too much, too fast, can overwhelm you; too little invites stagnation. It is on this path that maps for change, for integration—indeed, for a more thoughtful approach to living—are empowering.

Conclusion

The Psychedelic Mindmeld is a fascinating and revolutionary approach to working with others to explore the cosmos of consciousness. As discussed throughout this book, the mindmeld has potential benefits, risks, and limitations. It can contribute to personal healing, expansion, and growth, even if, in the short term, it may create a crisis point, or spiritual emergency, to work through. The mindmeld can engender an unconditional loving connection, a deeper intimacy, and new ways of relating to a spouse, partner, family members, close friends, or newfound co-melders. It is one of many healing and human potential modalities, with each modality contributing in different ways and often at various times or stages of life.

The mindmeld is also a practice. Like meditation or lucid dreaming, it takes dedication, persistence, and hard work to see meaningful long-term results and become a seasoned explorer, navigator, and cartographer of consciousness.

While there are many peak states possible in the mindmeld and many opportunities for healing and growth through integrating psychedelic experiences, the reality is that being human is difficult. We can face tremendous loss through accident and injury, assault, disease, and death at any moment. We can meet profound states of stress in interpersonal relationships, be it with family, friends, or at work. Human malevolence can unexpectedly strike at us. And there are the traumas we face in utero, in childhood, and as adults that can haunt us throughout life. We can face profound grief, defeat, confusion, and despair in our struggles. Any sense of homeostasis reached can be fleeting. We can get caught in our own pride, selfishness, and greed. Our anger can lash out at others through vindictive and regrettable behavior. But as humans, we endure. No matter who we are, we can face the challenges of life. There is a deep inner strength we can all tap into. As Jung (2017) states, "The human drive to connect to spirit is primordial. To deny this drive is to step into neurotic decay, embitterment, atrophy, and sterility" (p. 142).

As we engage in practices to explore our potential and connect to spirit, we morph and grow—even if not always in a linear direction. Sometimes growth comes as much by grace as it does by effort. As we move forward, we find new courage. We can live with greater ambiguity and in it, wonderment. But personal change is glacial in movement. It is a quest requiring discipline and endurance. It's the hero's journey. Through the mindmeld, we can put in the effort and progress through togetherness. As multidimensional beings, we can all expand our awareness of ourselves, each other, and the cosmos. We can experience richer layers of empathy, understanding, compassion, shared relations, and love. With conscious expansion, an appreciation for the beauty in all things grows. We see beyond gender, race, color, and creed. We experience and see the divine perfection and extreme complexity of the universe. We experience and see that we are all truly connected as one, interpenetrating each other and all of Nature in and around us. And we more clearly see, appreciate, and embody our unique and sovereign expression as the Divine of all that is.

As we connect to spirit, we keep discovering hidden dimensions of ourselves and the cosmos. And the deeper we explore, the bigger the questions we can ask: Where is it all going? What else is the human vehicle capable of? What hidden keys have yet to be found to open doors still unexplored?

Our bodies are an energetic chemical soup. Our bodies and minds are directly affected by our movements and what we eat, drink, and think. Perhaps a molecule or computer chip is waiting to be discovered and placed in our bodies, permanently and positively changing our whole reality and how we relate to each other, and even making it possible to manifest a higher-level reality on our planet with just our minds. Maybe consciousness is moving in the direction of greater complexity and coherence to where, one day, we will all live in a state of embodied nondual realization in form and spirit, engaged in consistently residing in the mental space and awareness of heaven on earth.

In the meantime, we continue, we trudge on, but knowing that holotropic journeys can shift our perspective and engagement in life. As Stanislav Grof (2019b) said, "As we keep discovering and exploring various hidden dimensions of ourselves and reality, our identification with the body-ego becomes progressively looser and less compelling. We continue to identify with the 'skin-encapsulated ego' for pragmatic purposes, but this orientation becomes increasingly more tentative and playful. If we have sufficient experiential knowledge of the transpersonal dimensions of existence, including our own true identity and cosmic status, everyday life becomes much easier and more rewarding" (p. 265).

Indeed, moving beyond our ego during psychedelic experiences, especially in nondual states, allows us to return and better observe the nature of ego in our daily lives and how the ego constructs limited, oft-distorted, individual narratives. In this gnosis, we can be more playful with lived experience, as beautiful and challenging as it can be. Let us play as cosmic citizens in the dream of separateness to learn, create, and grow as the unified consciousness experiences itself in the duality of space-time.

The Flow of a Psychedelic Mindmeld Session

Step 1: Establish the setting
- Transportation logistics
- Start time
- Location
- Type of psychedelic and dosage
- Music
- Safety protocols (e.g., stop when I say stop; exchange emergency back-up phone numbers)
- Personal physical boundaries (e.g., are hugs and cuddling acceptable or not?)
- Plan details for the second half of the session

Step 2: Together, state affirmation to jointly share the intention to energetically mindmeld, to join physically and psychically with your partner.

Step 3: After taking the psychedelic, take three to five minutes and stare into each other's eyes. Then, lie side by side in stillness, preferably holding hands, and begin meditating.

Step 4: Meditate on the breath and let go, allowing yourself to fully drop into the experience. Do not physically move unless something from your unconscious mind drives the movement.

Step 5: As the mind relaxes, shift your awareness to meditating on your heart opening and sharing loving energy with the person you are holding hands with.

Step 6: As the experience becomes increasingly shared, surrender and allow energies to flow unimpeded. Be the witness to the experience. If the work becomes uncomfortable, adopt the Bodhisattva mindset of taking on the other's suffering for the benefit of all sentient beings. If the need to work on yourself surfaces, follow it; return to working with your partner as appropriate and as agreed upon. Avoid conscious conversation until the debriefing at the end of the session.

Step 7: When in the mindmeld, use volition to enhance the experience, such as mentally saying, "Clarity now," "Higher vibration now," or "Stronger telepathic connection now."

Step 8: As the ego regains its executive function, follow through on the intent for the second half of the session, including quickly writing summary notes of the first half of the session for the debriefing.

Step 9: Debrief at the end of the session:
- What was shared?
- Highlights?
- Challenges?
- What worked?
- What was learned?
- What can be improved for the next session?

Step 10: Engage in integration

APPENDIX B

Psychedelic Mindmeld Agreement of Intent

Signing this document confirms my conscious intent to engage in the Psychedelic Mindmeld with my co-melder and fellow psychonaut using psychedelics.

I confirm I am medically fit to consume psychedelics. I am not aware of any contraindications, such as physical or mental illness, or the use of contraindicated medications, as described in the book the *Psychedelic Mindmeld*, to me doing this work.

My intent during the session is to share consciousness with my co-melder. In doing so, I am consensually opening all of myself, including physical and psychic energetic contents, to my co-melder.

In sharing consciousness, I will bring loving awareness to whatever arises. I will accept everything from within me and my co-melder as manifestations of energy meant to be witnessed, processed, and transmuted without judgment.

I recognize the Psychedelic Mindmeld can be a deep engagement of my own and the other person's psychological contents at both a physical and psychic level. I understand that processing and transmuting blocked energies in the body can manifest in many ways. Resolving blocked energies can be strenuous emotionally and physically. I will do my best to work through complex emotional material and any pain during the session without resistance.

If at any time the mindmeld experience is too overwhelming for my co-melder and they say "Stop" or push me away, I will end my engagement in the mindmeld, including any physical contact with my co-melder.

I acknowledge physical movement and engagement during the mindmeld may result in incidental touching of genitals that is not sexual, and I am okay with this. I will in no way sexually engage with my co-melder during the session. If my co-melder sexually engages with themselves, I will provide space for them to release this energy without judgment.

I am comfortable with: _____; _____; _____(examples are hugging or snuggling in an embrace)

I commit to supporting my co-melder throughout the whole of their experience.

If there are any perceived or felt transgressions during the mindmeld session, I will do my best to repair the situation with my co-melder after the session.

I commit to follow up with my co-melder after the session to provide support for the process of integrating our experiences.

Co-melder 1 Signature_____

Printed Name_____

Date_____

Emergency Contact: _____

Emergency Number: _____

Co-melder 2 Signature_____

Printed Name_____

Date_____

Emergency Contact: _____

Emergency Number: _____

Bibliography

Aftab, A., Lee, E. E., Klaus, F., Daly, R., Wu, T.-C., Tu, X., Huege, S., & Jeste, D. V. (2019). Meaning in life and its relationship with physical, mental, and cognitive functioning: A study of 1,042 community-dwelling adults across the lifespan. *The Journal of Clinical Psychiatry, 81*(1).

Aiken, J. W. (2016). *Explorations in awareness: Finding god by meditating with entheogens.* Derivative author: B. A. Potter. (M. Marinacci, Ed.). Ronin Publishing.

Aixalà, M. B. (2022). *Psychedelic integration: Psychotherapy for non-ordinary states of consciousness.* Synergetic Press.

Allegro, J. M. (1970). *The sacred mushroom and the cross: Fertility cults and the origins of Judaism and Christianity.* Doubleday & Company, Inc.

Allione, T. (2008). *Feeding your demons: Ancient wisdom for resolving inner conflict.* Little, Brown.

Almaas, A.H. (2000). *Facets of unity: The Enneagram of holy ideas.* Shambhala.

———. (2014). *Runaway realization: Living a life of ceaseless discovery.* Shambhala.

Arundale, G. S. (1938). *Kundalini: an occult experience.* Theosophical Publishing House.

Atwater, P. M. H. (1994). *Beyond the light: What isn't being said about near-death experience.* Carol Publishing Corporation.

Bache, C. (2019). *LSD and the mind of the universe: Diamonds from heaven.* Park Street Press.

———. (2021). The challenges of integrating an extreme psychedelic journey. In T. Read & M. Papaspyrou (Eds.), *Psychedelics & psychotherapy: The healing potential of expanded states* (pp. 301–314). Park Street Press.

Baker, I. A. (2019). *Tibetan yoga: Principles and practices.* Thames & Hudson Ltd.

Ball, M. W. (2006) *Mushroom wisdom: How shamans cultivate spiritual consciousness.* Ronin Publishing.

———. (2009). *Being human: An entheological guide to GOD, evolution and the fractal energetic nature of reality.* Kyandara Publishing.

———. (2014) *Being infinite: An entheological odyssey into the limitless eternal: A memoir from ayahuasca to Zen.* Kyandara Publishing.

———. (2017). *Entheogenic liberation: Unraveling the enigma of nonduality with 5-MeO-DMT energetic therapy.* Kyandara Publishing.

Ball, M. W. (Ed.). (2022). *Facilitating 5-MeO-DMT: An anthology of approaches to serving the God molecule.* Kyandara Publishing.

Barral, J. (2007). *Understanding the messages of your body: How to interpret physical and emotional signals to achieve optimal health.* North Atlantic Books.

———. (2014) *Understanding the messages of your joints: For the prevention and care of joint pain.* Barral Productions.

Barrett, L. F. (2020). *7½ Lessons about the brain.* Houghton Mifflin Harcourt.

Beyer, S. V. (2010). *Singing to the plants: A guide to mestizo shamanism in the upper Amazon* (2nd ed.). University of New Mexico Press.

Blackmore, S. (2012). *Consciousness: An introduction* (2nd ed.). Oxford University Press.

Branden, N. (1994). *The six pillars of self-esteem.* Bantam Books.

Brennan, B. A. (1988). *Hands of light: A guide to healing through the human energy field* (2nd ed.). Bantam Books.

Brown, D. J. (2016). *Dreaming wide awake: Lucid dreaming, shamanic healing, and psychedelics.* Park Street Press.

Brown, J. P., & Brown, J. M. (2016). *The psychedelic gospels: The secret history of hallucinogens in Christianity.* Park Street Press.

Browne, I. (1990). Psychological trauma, or unexperienced experience. *Re-vision, 12*(4), 21–34.

Bruce, R., & Donaghue, T. (2013). *Evolution: How to succeed with spirituality.* Astraldynamics website.

Buhlman, W. (1996). *Adventures beyond the body: How to experience out-of-body travel.* Harper, San Francisco.

Buhner, S. (2014). *Plant intelligence and the imaginal realm: Beyond the doors of perception into the dreaming of earth.* Bear & Company.

Campbell, J. (2008). *The hero with a thousand faces* (3rd ed.). New World Library.

Carhart-Harris, R. L., Bolstridge, M., Rucker, J., Day, C. M., Erritzoe, D., Kaelen, M., Bloomfield, M. A. P., Rickard, J. A., Forbes, B., Feilding, A., Taylor, D., Pilling, S., Curran, V., & Nutt, D. J. (2016a). Psilocybin with psychological support for treatment-resistant depression: an open-label feasibility study. *The Lancet Psychiatry, 3*(7), 619–627.

Carhart-Harris, R. L., Kaelen, M., Bolstridge, M., Williams, T. N., Williams, L. K., Underwood, R., Feilding, A., & Nutt, D. J. (2016b). The paradoxical psychological effects of lysergic acid diethylamide (LSD). *Psychological Medicine, 46*(7), 1379–1390.

Castaneda, C. (1993). *The art of dreaming.* HarperCollins.

———. (1999). *Magical Passes: The practical wisdom of the shamans of ancient Mexico* (2nd ed.). HarperCollins.

Church, D. (2018). *Mind to matter: The astonishing science of how your brain creates material reality.* Hay House, Inc.

Compson, J. (2018). Adverse meditation experiences: Navigating Buddhist and secular frameworks for addressing them. *Mindfulness, 9*(5), 1358–1369.

Cowan, E. (2014). *Plant spirit medicine: A journey into the healing wisdom of plants* (2nd ed.). Sounds True.

Crowley, M. (2019). *Secret drugs of Buddhism: Psychedelic sacraments and the origins of Vajrayana* (2nd ed.). Synergetic Press.

———. (2023). *Psychedelic Buddhism: A User's guide to traditions, symbols, and ceremonies.* Park Street Press.

Dąbrowski, K. (2016). *Positive disintegration* (2nd ed.). Maurice Bassett.

DeGracia, D. J. (1997). *Do psychedelic drugs mimic awakened Kundalini?* Retrieved September 15, 2022.

Desai, A. (1979). Kundalini yoga through Shaktipat. In J. White (Ed.), *Kundalini, evolution and enlightenment* (pp. 69–75). Anchor Books.

Eliade, M. (2004). *Shamanism: Archaic techniques of ecstasy* (W. Trask, Trans.) (2nd ed.). Princeton University Press.

Evans, J., & Read, T. (Eds.). (2020). *Breaking open: Finding a way through spiritual emergency.* Aeon Books.

Fadiman, J. (2011). *The psychedelic explorer's guide: Safe, therapeutic, and sacred journeys.* Park Street Press.

Falconer, R. (2023). *The others within us: Internal Family Systems, Porous Mind, and Spirit Possession.* Great Mystery Press.

Fisher, T. D., Moore, Z., & Pittenger, M. (2012). Sex on the brain?: An examination of frequency of sexual cognitions as a function of gender, erotophilia, and social desirability. *Journal of Sex Research, 49*(1), 69–77.

Frankl, V. E. (2006). *Man's search for meaning* (5th ed.). Beacon Press.

Freud, A. (2018). *The ego and the mechanisms of defense* (4th ed.). Routledge.

Freud, S. (2019). *The ego and the id* (H. Correll, Trans.) (2nd ed.). Clydesdale Press.

Gilbert, D. (2007). *Stumbling on happiness* (2nd ed.). Vintage Canada.

Grof, S. (1976). *Realms of the human unconscious: Observations from LSD research.* E.P. Dutton.

———. (2008). *LSD psychotherapy* (4th ed.). Multidisciplinary Association for Psychedelic Studies.

———. (2009). *LSD doorway to the numinous: The groundbreaking psychedelic research into realms of the human unconscious* (2nd ed.) Park Street Press.

———. (2019a). *The way of the psychonaut: Encyclopedia for inner journeys* (Vol. 1). Multidisciplinary Association for Psychedelic Studies.

———. (2019b). *The way of the psychonaut: Encyclopedia for inner journeys* (Vol. 2). Multidisciplinary Association for Psychedelic Studies.

Grof, S., & Grof, C. (Eds.). (1989). *Spiritual emergency: When personal transformation becomes a crisis.* Jeremy P. Tarcher.

———. (2010). *Holotropic Breathwork: A new approach to self-exploration and therapy.* State University of New York Press.

Goldsmith, N. M. (2011). *Psychedelic healing: The promise of entheogens for psychotherapy and spiritual development.* Healing Arts Press.

Griffiths, R. R., Richards, W. G., McCann, U. D., & Jesse, R. (2006). Psilocybin can occasion mystical-type experiences having substantial and sustained personal meaning and spiritual significance. *Psychopharmacology, 187*(3), 268–283.

Griffiths, R. R., Johnson, M. P., Carducci, M. A., Umbricht, A., Richards, W. G., Richards, B. K., Cosimano, M. P., & Klinedinst, M. A. (2016). Psilocybin produces substantial and sustained decreases in depression and anxiety in patients with life-threatening cancer: A randomized double-blind trial. *Journal of Psychopharmacology, 30*(12), 1181–1197.

Hancock, G. (2007). *Supernatural: Meetings with the ancient teachers of mankind* (2nd ed.). Disinformation Books.

Hanson, R. (2013). *Hardwiring happiness: The new brain science of contentment, calm, and confidence.* Harmony Books.

Harner, M. (1990). *The way of the shaman* (3rd ed.). HarperSanFrancisco.

———. (2013). *Cave and cosmos: Shamanic encounters with another reality*. North Atlantic Books.

Harris, R. (2021). Ayahuasca and psychotherapy. In T. Read & M. Papaspyrou (Eds.), *Psychedelics & psychotherapy: The healing potential of expanded states* (pp. 18–29). Park Street Press.

Harpur, P. (2003). *Daimonic reality: A field guide to the otherworld* (2nd ed.). Pine Winds Press.

Harvey-Wilson, S. B. (2000). *Shamanism and alien abductions: A comparative study* [Master's thesis]. Edith Cowan University.

Holecek, A. (2016). *Dream yoga: Illuminating your life through lucid dreaming and the Tibetan yogas of sleep*. Sounds True.

hooks, bell. (2018). *All about love: New visions* (2nd ed.). William Morrow.

Ingerman, S. (1991). *Soul retrieval: Mending the fragmented self.* HarperSanFransisco.

James, W. (2009). *The varieties of religious experience: A study in human nature* [eBook edition]. eBooks@Adelaide.

Jaxon-Bear, E. (2001). *The Enneagram of liberation: From fixation to freedom*. Leela Foundation.

Jesso, J. W. (2013). *Decomposing the shadow: Lessons from the psilocybin mushroom*. SoulsLantern Publishing.

Johnstad, P. G. (2020). Psychedelic telepathy: An interview study. *Journal of Scientific Exploration, 34*(3), 493–512.

Jones, L. M. (2021). Underground psychedelic therapy. In T. Read & M. Papaspyrou (Eds.), *Psychedelics & psychotherapy: The healing potential of expanded states* (pp. 101–112). Park Street Press.

Judith, A. (2004). *Eastern body, Western mind: Psychology and the chakra system as a path to the self* (2nd ed.). Celestial Arts.

Jung, C. G, (1969). *The collected works of C.G. Jung, volume 9 (part 1): Archetypes and the collective unconscious* (W. McGuire, H. Read, M. Fordham, & G. Adler, Eds.) (R. F. C. Hull, Trans.) (2nd ed.). Princeton University Press.

———. (2011a). *Synchronicity: An acausal connecting principle* (R. F. C. Hull, Trans.) (4th ed.). Princeton University Press.

———. (2011b). *Dreams: (From volumes 4, 8, 12, and 16 of the collected works of C.G. Jung)* (R. F. C. Hull, Trans.). Princeton University Press.

———. (2017). *Modern man in search of a soul* (W. S. Dell & C. F. Baynes, Trans.). Martino Fine Books.

Katz, R. (1982). *Boiling energy: Community healing among the Kalahari Kung.* Harvard University Press.

Kelly, T. M. (2011). *Telepathy: A quantum approach* [eBook edition]. University of Alternative Studies. Parapsychology | QP.

Kolk, B. (2015). *The body keeps the score: Mind, brain and body in the transformation of trauma.* Penguin Books.

Krippner, S., & Watts, A. (2006, January). *LSD and parapsychological experiences* [Paper presentation]. LSD: Problem child and wonder drug, an international symposium on the occasion of the 100th birthday of Albert Hofmann, 13–15 January, Basel, Switzerland.

Krishna, G. (1967). *Kundalini: The evolutionary energy in man.* Ramadhar and Hopman.

LaBerge, S. (2009). *Lucid dreaming: A concise guide to awakening in your dreams and in your life.* Sounds True.

Laszlo, A. (2016). Seeking syntony with the intelligence of the cosmos. In K. L. Dennis (Ed.), *What is reality? The new map of cosmos and consciousness* (pp. 226–240). SelectBooks.

Laszlo, E. (2003). *The connectivity hypothesis: Foundations of an integral science of quantum, cosmos, life and consciousness.* State University of New York Press.

———. (2004). *Science and the Akashic field: An integral theory of everything.* Inner Traditions.

———. (2016). *What Is reality? The new map of cosmos and consciousness* (K. L. Dennis, Ed.). SelectBooks.

Leary, T., Metzner, R., & Alpert, R. (2007). *The psychedelic experience: A manual based on the Tibetan book of the dead* (2nd ed.). Citadel Press.

Lemercier, C. E., & Terhune, D. B. (2018). Psychedelics and hypnosis: Commonalities and therapeutic implications. *Journal of Psychopharmacology, 32*(7), 732–740.

Levine, J., & Ludwig, A. (1965). Alterations in consciousness produced by combinations of LSD, hypnosis and psychotherapy. *Psychopharmacologia, 7,* 123–137.

Levine, P. A. (2008). *Healing trauma: A pioneering program for restoring the wisdom of your body.* Sounds True.

Lindahl, J. R., Fisher, N., Cooper, D. A., Rosen, R. K., & Britton, W. B. (2017). The varieties of contemplative experience: A mixed-methods study of meditation-related challenges in Western Buddhists. *PLoS ONE, 12*(5), e0176239.

Luke, D. (2019). *Otherworlds: Psychedelics and exceptional human experience* (2nd ed.). Aeon Academic.

Maharaj, N. (1981). *I am that: Dialogues of Sri Nisargadatta Maharaj* (S. S. Dikshit, Ed.) (M. Frydman, Trans.) (2nd ed.). Philosophical Faculty Erasmus Universiteit Rotterdam Holland.

Maté, G. (2008). *In the realm of hungry ghosts: Close encounters with addiction* (2nd ed.). Vintage Canada.

———.(2012). *When the body says no: The cost of hidden stress* (2nd ed.). Vintage Canada.

———.(2021). Psychedelics as a pathway to the self. In T. Read & M. Papaspyrou (Eds.), *Psychedelics & psychotherapy: The healing potential of expanded states* (pp. xi–xvii). Park Street Press.

Maté, G, & Maté, D. (2022). *The myth of normal: Trauma, illness & healing in a toxic culture.* Alfred A. Knopf Canada.

Mayo Clinic. (n.d.). *Yoga: Fight stress and find serenity.* Retrieved September 20, 2022.

McCulloch, D. E., Grzywacz, M. Z., Madsen, M. B., Jensen, P. S., Ozenne, B., Armand, S., Knudsen, G. M., Fisher, P. M., & Stenbæk, D. S. (2022). Psilocybin-induced mystical-type experiences are related to persisting positive effects: A quantitative and qualitative report. *Frontiers in Pharmacology, 13.*

McKenna, T. (1992). *Food of the gods: The search for the original tree of knowledge, a radical history of plants, drugs, and human evolution.* Bantam Books.

———. (1991). *The archaic revival: Speculations on psychedelic mushrooms, the Amazon, virtual reality, UFOs, evolution, shamanism, the rebirth of the goddess, and the end of history.* HarperSanFrancisco.

McKusik, E. (2021). *Electric body, electric health: Using the electromagnetism within (and around) you to recharge, rewire, and raise your voltage.* St. Martin's Essentials.

———. (2014). *Tuning the human biofield: Healing with vibrational sound therapy.* Healing Arts Press.

Merton, T. (2011). *Love and living.* (N. Stone & P. Hart, Eds.) [eBook edition]. Farrar, Straus and Giroux.

Metzinger, T. (2010). *The ego tunnel: The science of the mind and the myth of the self.* Basic Books.

Metzner, R. (1998). *The unfolding self: Varieties of transformative experience* (2nd ed.). Origin Press.

———. (2005). Psychedelic, psychoactive and addictive drugs and states of consciousness. In M. Earlywine (Ed.), *Mind-altering drugs: The science of subjective experience* (pp. 27–48). Oxford University Press.

———. (Ed.) (2006). *Sacred vine of spirits: Ayahuasca* (2nd ed.). Park Street Press.

———. (2015). *Allies for awakening: Guidelines for productive and safe experiences with entheogens.* Regent Press.

Metzner, R., & Darling, D. C. (Eds.). (2005). *Sacred mushroom of visions: Teonanácatl* (2nd ed.). Park Street Press.

Miller, R. L. (Ed.) (2017). *Psychedelic medicine: The healing powers of LSD, MDMA, psilocybin, and ayahuasca.* Inner Traditions International.

Mithoefer, M. C. (2017). *A manual for MDMA-assisted psychotherapy in the treatment of posttraumatic stress disorder.* Multidisciplinary Association for Psychedelic Studies.

Monroe, R. A. (1985). *Far journeys.* Dolphin Books.

———. (2001). *Journeys out of the body* (2nd ed.). Broadway Books.

———. (1994). *Ultimate journey.* Harmony Books.

Moody, R. A. (2015). *Life after life.* HarperOne.

Moody, R. A., & Perry, P. (2010). *Glimpses of eternity: Sharing a loved one's passage from this life to the next* (2nd ed.). SAKKARA Productions Publishing.

Mookerjee, A. (1986). *Kundalini: The arousal of the inner energy* (3rd ed.). Destiny Books.

Muraresku, B. C. (2020). *The immortality key: The secret history of the religions with no name.* St. Martin's Press.

National Center for Complementary and Integrative Health. (n.d.). *Yoga: What you need to know.* Retrieved November 20, 2022.

Newton, M. (2002). *Journey of souls: Case studies of life between lives.* Llewellyn Worldwide.

Newton, M. (Ed.). (2009). *Memories of the afterlife: Life between lives, stories of personal transformation.* Llewellyn Worldwide.

Nuttal, J. (1970). *Bomb culture* (2nd ed.). Paladin.

Ohkado, M, & Ikegawa, A. (2014). Children with life-between-life memories. *Journal of Scientific Exploration, 28*(3), 477–490.

Pert, C. (1997). *Molecules of emotion: Why you feel the way you feel.* Scribner.

Peters, W. J., & Kinsella, M. (2022). *At heaven's door: What shared journeys to the afterlife teach about dying and living better.* Simon & Schuster.

Peterson, J. B. (1999). *Maps of meaning: The architecture of belief.* Routledge.

———. (2022, April 7) *Solving the problem of human perception* [Video]. YouTube.

Puharich, A. (1973). *Beyond Telepathy.* Anchor Press.

Radha, S. (2013). *Realities of the dreaming mind: The practice of dream yoga* (2nd ed.). Timeless Books.

Radin, D. (2006). *Entangled minds: Extrasensory experiences in a quantum reality.* Paraview Pocket Books.

———. (2018). *Real magic: Ancient wisdom, modern science, and a guide to the secret power of the universe.* Harmony Books.

Read, T. & Papaspyrou, M. (Eds.). (2021). *Psychedelics & psychotherapy: The healing potential of expanded states.* Park Street Press.

Renee, L. (n.d.). *What is ascension?* Energetic Synthesis. Retrieved December 10, 2021.

Ring, K. (1980). *Life at death.* Coward, McCann, and Geohegan.

———. (1989) Near-death and UFO encounters as shamanic initiations: Some conceptual and evolutionary implications. *ReVision, 11*(3), 14–22.

———. (1992). *The omega project: Near-death experiences, UFO encounters and mind at large.* William Morrow and Co.

Ring, K., & Valarino, E. (1998). *Lessons from the light: What we can learn from the near-death experience.* Moment Point Press.

Rinpoche, S. (2002) *The Tibetan book of living and dying* (2nd ed.). HarperCollins.

Roth, G. (n.d.). *Gabrielle Roth's 5Rhythms.* 5Rhythms. Retrieved January 27, 2022.

Sannella, L. (1987). *The Kundalini experience: Psychosis or transcendence?* (2nd ed.). Integral Publishing.

SantataGamana. (2018). *Turiya: The God state beyond Kundalini, Kriya & all spirituality* (E. Robins, Ed.). Independently published.

Santos, R. G. D., De Lima Osório, F., De Souza Crippa, J. A., Riba, J., Zuardi, A. W., & Hallak, J. E. C. (2016). Antidepressive, anxiolytic, and antiaddictive effects of ayahuasca, psilocybin and lysergic acid diethylamide (LSD): a systematic review of clinical trials published in the last 25 years. *Therapeutic Advances in Psychopharmacology, 6*(3), 193–213.

Santos, H. C., & Marques, J. G. (2021). What is the clinical evidence on psilocybin for the treatment of psychiatric disorders? A systematic review. *Porto Biomed Journal, 6*(1), e128.

Scaer, R. (2014). *The body bears the burden: Trauma, dissociation, and disease* (3rd ed.). Routledge.

Schultes, R. E., Hofmann, A. & Rätsch, C. (1998). *Plants of the gods: Their sacred, healing, and hallucinogenic powers* (2nd ed.). Healing Arts Press.

Schwartz, R. C., & Sweezy, M. (2020). *Internal family systems therapy* (2nd ed.). Guilford Press.

Scott, D. (n.d.). *IFSCA course manual: Developing skills and competencies in the IFS model*. IFSCA. Retrieved April 26, 2021.

Shannon, B. (2008). Biblical entheogens: A speculative hypothesis. *Time and Mind: The Journal of Archaeology Consciousness and Culture, 1*(1), 51–74.

Shared Crossing Research Initiative. (2021) Shared death experiences: A little-known type of end-of-life phenomena reported by caregivers and loved ones. *American Journal of Hospital Palliative Care, 38*(12), 1479–1487.

Silverstone, P. (2022). *The promise of psychedelics: Science-based hope for better mental health*. Ingenium Books Publishing.

Sivananda, S. (1994). *Kundalini yoga* (10th ed.). Divine Life Trust Society.

———. (2014). *Mind: Its mysteries and control* (18th ed.). Divine Life Trust Society.

Sheldrake, R. (2009). *Morphic resonance: The nature of formative causation*. Park Street Press.

———. (2011). *Dogs that know when their owners are coming home: And other unexplained powers of animals* (2nd ed.). Three Rivers Press.

———. (2012). *The presence of the past: Morphic resonance and the memory of nature* (4th ed.). Park Street Press.

———. (2013). *The sense of being stared at: And other unexplained powers of human minds*. Park Street Press.

Sollarova, E., & Sollár, T. (2010). The psychologically integrated person and the parameters of optimal functioning. *Studia Psychologic, 52*(4), 333–338.

Strassman, R. (2001). *DMT—The spirit molecule: A doctor's revolutionary research into the biology of near-death and mystical experiences*. Park Street Press.

Strassman, R. Wojtowicz, S., Luna, L. E., & Frecska, E. (2008). *Inner paths to outer space: Journeys to alien worlds through psychedelics and other spiritual technologies*. Park Street Press.

Tart, C. T. (1967). Psychedelic experiences associated with a novel hypnotic procedure, mutual hypnosis. *The American Journal of Clinical Hypnosis, X*(2), 65–78.

———. (1993). Marijuana intoxication, psi and spiritual experiences. *Journal of The American Society for Psychical Research, 87,* 149–170.

Thalbourne, M. A. (2001). Measures of the sheep-goat variable, transliminality, and their correlates. *Psychological Reports, 88*(2), 339–350.

Three Initiates. (1912). *The Kybalion: A study of the Hermetic philosophy of ancient Egypt and Greece.* Yogi Publication Society Masonic Temple.

Tirtha, V. (1979). Signs of awakened Kundalini. In J. White (Ed.), *Kundalini, evolution and enlightenment* (pp. 94–97). Anchor Books.

Tolle, E. (2006). *A new Earth: Awakening to your life's purpose.* (2nd ed.). Plume.

Tucker, J. B. (2005). *Life before death: Children's memories of previous lives.* St. Martin's Griffin.

Twitchell, P. (1967). *The tiger's fang.* Illuminated Way Press.

———. (1987). *Eckankar: The key to secret worlds* (2nd ed.). Illuminated Way Publishing.

Ullman, M., Krippner, S., & Vaughan, A. (2003). *Dream telepathy: Experiments in nocturnal extrasensory perception* (2nd ed.). Hampton Roads Publishing Company.

———. (2023). *Dream telepathy: The landmark ESP experiments* (2nd ed.). Afterworlds Press.

Vishnu-devananda, S. (1988). *The complete illustrated book of yoga* (2nd ed.). Three Rivers Press.

Waley, A. (1934). *The way and its power: A study of the Tao tê Ching and its place in Chinese thought.* Allen & Unwin.

Walker, P. (2013). *Complex PTSD: From surviving to thriving.* Azure Coyote.

Waya, A. G. (2004). *Soul recovery and extraction* (4th ed.). Blue Turtle Publishing.

Welwood, J. (1997). *Love and awakening: Discovering the sacred path of intimate relationship* (2nd ed.). HarperPerennial.

Wilber, K. (2017). *The religion of tomorrow: A vision for the future of the great traditions.* Shambhala Publications.

Wilber, K., Patten, T., Leonard, A., & Morelli, M. (2008). *Integral life practice: A 21st-century blueprint for physical health, emotional balance, mental clarity, and spiritual awakening.* Integral Books.

Willson, T. (1987). *How I learned soul travel.* Illuminated Way Publishing.

Wolfe, T. (1968). *The electric Kool-Aid acid test.* Picador.

Yogananda, P. (1998). *Autobiography of a yogi* (13th ed.). Self-Realization Fellowship.

Yü, L. K. (1970). *Taoist yoga: Alchemy and immortality.* Samuel Weiser, Inc.

Ziewe, J. (2015). *Vistas of infinity: How to enjoy life when you are dead* (I. Allen, Ed.). Lulu.

Index

About the Author

Wade Richardson is a psychonaut with more than fifteen years of experience, having participated in and facilitated hundreds of psychedelic and nonpsychedelic meditative sessions. His career has focused on the health and education fields.

Wade encourages you to email your mindmeld experiences to him at psychedelicmindmeld@proton.me. He will post quality stories to his Facebook group, Psychedelic Telepathy. By sharing your stories others can learn more about what works in the mindmeld, new techniques, territories explored, and challenges faced and how to overcome them.

A portion of the author's proceeds is being donated to organizations dedicated to supporting children who are at-risk due to poverty, violence, and sex trafficking.